SWALEDALE & RICHMOND

M000236527

Swaledale & Richmond

the story of a dale

CHRIS PARK

Dedicated to the memory of my parents, Margaret Park (1923–2005) and Alex Park (1926–2009), who, amongst many other things, gave me the great gift of being born in Swaledale (in the house beside The Bar in Richmond, shown on page 168). They travelled far and wide; but for them Richmond always remained 'home'.

First published in 2014
by Palatine Books,
Carnegie House,
Chatsworth Road
Lancaster LA1 4SL
www.palatinebooks.com

Copyright © Chris Park

All rights reserved
Unauthorised duplication contravenes existing laws

The right of the Chris Park to be identified as the author of this work has been asserted in accordance with the Copyright, Designs and Patents act 1988

British Library Cataloguing-in-Publication data
A catalogue record for this book is available from the British Library

ISBN 13: 978-1-874181-95-8

Designed and typeset by Carnegie Book Production

www.carnegiebookproduction.com
Printed and bound by 1010 International

All images copyright Chris Park unless otherwise stated
Images on halftitle and contents pages are copyright Lucie Hinson

CONTENTS

INTRODUCTION

SWALEDALE IS A SMALL VALLEY, little more than 20 miles long and rarely wider than about a mile, with a rich heritage, strong traditions and a strong sense of place. Most of the people who live there are proud of their dale and its achievements, though they rarely shout about them. Those who visit regularly or stumble upon it for the first time often fall under the spell of its scenery, its peace and quiet, and its many opportunities for hill walking, bird watching, and study of industrial archaeology. In many ways Swaledale is an economic and cultural backwater, far removed from the hustle and bustle of city life; but that is a key part of its charm. Over the centuries the dale has endured and survived countless hardships and challenges, and developed its very own character and spirit. It has lent its name to some well-liked enduring products — including the Swaledale sheep, wool and cheese — and provided a setting for some popular books, television programmes and films, most notably the *All Creatures Great and Small* stories about vet James Herriot. More recently it has figured prominently in Adrian Edmondson's television series *The Dales*.

I must declare a personal interest in Swaledale, having been born in Richmond. In 1868 the geologist Adam Sedgwick, after living in Cambridge for 40 years, wrote of Dentdale: 'here is the land of my birth; this was the home of my boyhood, and is still the home of my heart.' I have much the same feeling about Swaledale, and I regard myself as very fortunate to have been born there and to be able to call it 'home'.

This despite having lived and worked for over three decades in exile in Lancaster, some 40 miles away on the 'wrong' side of the Pennines!

In her book *Off to the Dales* (1950), northern travel writer Jessica Lofthouse insists, 'the last thing I intend to do is to lavish praise upon the Yorkshire dalesfolk; so many writers have done so *ad nauseam*, thereby amusing or embarrassing the subjects of their praise. Of course, Yorkshire folk know theirs is the best shire and their folk the best folk; they need no telling.' Who could argue with that?

In *Swaledale: Valley of the Wild River* (2010), archaeologist Andrew Fleming cautions that 'writing about a well-loved place becomes like writing a love-letter, in which it is important to insist that the beloved is unique and special. Yet the reality is otherwise.' Naturally, any writer must take care not to sanitise or idealise the places they write about, or paint too romantic a picture about them. Nowhere is perfect, not even Swaledale. In truth it has always been a remote and inaccessible place. It remains a harsh and challenging environment to cope with and offers limited local employment and few prospects for those seeking fame and fortune. It is a place from which in recent generations the young have often wanted to escape to taste life elsewhere in the wider world. Yet, despite Fleming's caution, I still personally find Swaledale a thoroughly enchanting place, which I hope is clear from what follows.

THIS PAGE: HAY MEADOWS, DRY-STONE WALLS AND STONE FIELD BARNS NEAR MUKER, UPPER SWALEDALE.

OVERPAGE: UPPER SWALEDALE FROM THE BUTTERTUBS PASS.

'I love my mother's country in the heart of Fell-land with a passion that can never die. Its fresh, cool breezes, grey limestone crags, and chattering becks tumbling over mossy boulders, appeal to me with the same instinctive longing that sends a little bird over a thousand miles of seas and land to the beloved old hedgerow in which it first followed its tiny wings and learnt something of the freedom of the air.'

Richard Kearton (1922)

PART I
about the dale

'The dales people are naturally hospitable, and this is the
kind of tea they give their friends: white and brown bread and
butter and tea-cake, jam, Swaledale cheese – which is very
like Wensleydale – biscuits, rock buns, plain cake, currant
cake, apple tart, curd tart, jam tart, all of them home-made.
The people eat a great deal of pastry.'

Ella Pontefract (1934)

SHEEP FOR SHEARING, GRINTON SMELT MILL. COPYRIGHT LUCIE HINSON.

Chapter One
VALLEY OF THE SWALE

'I think Swaledale is the most beautiful part of England.'
James Herriot (1979)

SWALEDALE LIES ON THE EASTERN SIDE of the Pennines, the chain of hills 160 miles long that runs right down through the centre of northern England between the Scottish border in the north and the river Trent in the south. The origin of the name Pennines remains unknown, but it was certainly in use by the early nineteenth century.

The Pennines are often described as the 'backbone of England', because they form the watershed for the main rivers in the north of England – those on the western side flow into the Irish Sea; those on the east flow ultimately into the North Sea. Bill Mitchell (former editor of *The Dalesman*) points out in his biography, *A Dalesman's Diary* (1990), that he was taught how, 'if you thought of a hand – the central plain of Yorkshire was the palm and the Dales the fingers, extending into the high hills, those bleak hills which the Norse settlers of old had called "fells"'. Swaledale, on the eastern side of the Pennines, runs from west to east.

'The backbone [the Pennines] runs north and south, and this is the main range; the vertebrae are the separate hills which compose the range, and from the main vertebrae run the ribs, ridges of high moor extending eastwards. Between the ribs are the arteries, the rivers. A queer skeleton this, with ribs on one side only, for there are none on the west.' Alfred Wainwright (1986)

Valleys (dales) dissect the hills (moors or fells). The word 'dale' is derived from the Old English *dæl* and the Old Norse *dalr*, meaning 'valley'. A dale is simply a valley along which a river flows, and dales are usually named after the river which flows through them (the exception in the Yorkshire Dales is Wensleydale, which is named after the village of Wensleydale but is also known as Yoredale or Uredale after the river Ure which flows through it). Swaledale, the valley of the river Swale, is the most northern of the Yorkshire Dales. As Arthur Raistrick (1986) writes, 'The north Pennines are better known by their numerous "dales" than by their fells.'

Swaledale and the river Swale

Thus the river Swale gives its name to Swaledale, the valley along which it flows. The names of river and dale have evolved through time. Through much of its history the dale has been known as Swadal or Swadale, which is how it appears on some old maps. In around 730 Bede recorded the river Swale as Sualua. Swaledale was recorded in about 1130 as Sualadala, in 1538 John Leland referred to it as Suadale, and in 1607 William Camden called it Swals-dale.

Thomas Dunham Whitaker, whose *History of Richmondshire in the North Riding of the County of York* (1823) has informed all subsequent histories of the area, suggested that the name Swale 'is derived from its mountain character'. Etymologists trace the root of the word to Old Norse/Old English, meaning 'the rushing river'. This is the generally accepted meaning of the name, and is the reason why archaeologist Andrew Fleming gave his book the title *Swaledale: Valley of the Wild River* (2010). But Harry Speight offered an alternative explanation in *Romantic Richmondshire* (1897), suggesting that the name stems from the Viking word *sval* or *svaul*, meaning to cool or refrigerate, because of the cold water or climate of the area. The Swale in Swaledale is not the only river with that name – Speight (1897) points out that 'there is a Svaledal also, Suledal, and a Svalestad (Stavanger) in the province of Christiansand in Norway', and Fleming (2010) notes that 'there are other rivers Swale in Berkshire and Kent, as well as in Angeln, the north German district from which the Anglians came'.

The source of our river Swale lies in the high Pennines to the west of Reeth, around Nine Standards Rigg, High Seat, Lovely Seat and Great Shunner Fell. It is formed by the confluence of two fast-flowing head-water streams, Birkdale Beck and Great Sleddale Beck. The Swale flows eastwards, and around 70 miles downstream from its source it joins the river Ure (which flows down Wensleydale) at Myton-on-Swale. It then becomes the Yorkshire Ouse, which flows through York and eventually drains into the North Sea via the Humber estuary. Of all the rivers in England, Alfred Wainwright (1989) considered the river Swale to rank 'amongst the loveliest, winding through a pleasant countryside and adding charm to the beauty of the surroundings'.

The Swale is a relatively steep river that rises in an upland area with high rainfall and flows over largely impervious rocks. It is noted for its fast flow – reputed to be one of the fastest flowing rivers in England – and after prolonged heavy rain it rises rapidly and has a history of flooding.

The changing character of the Swale, as it flows downstream, has attracted the attention of writers over the years. John Leland (1538) described the Swale as 'a right noble river', and in 1607 William Camden called it a 'violent stream' and wrote that 'the Swale rusheth rather than runneth'. In 1909 Edmund Bogg wrote that the Swale in flood 'does … rave and roar in spate. And the spirit of the mountains seems to be abroad too, overlooking, directing the wild furious waste of the waters with the ban and threat of the master in brute force. It is terrible but inexpressibly grand.' The river Swale, according to the author Ella Pontefract (1934), has an 'impetuous career, dancing down gullies, splashing as a waterfall over rocky ledges, cutting resolutely through gorges, bringing with it as it rushes down in flood great piles of stones, and leaving them on either side as a reminder that it can be a dangerous fellow when roused; until it flows in serener mood past Easby Abbey.'

Swaledale differs from the other dales in several ways, apart from being the most northerly one, situated at the top of the Yorkshire Dales National Park. Compared to the other dales it is relatively narrow and one of the most remote. It also has a different character, particularly displayed in the traditional hay meadows, dry-stone walls and stone field

SOURCE OF THE SWALE, AT THE JUNCTION OF BIRKDALE BECK AND GREAT SLEDDALE BECK.

NEAR THE SOURCE OF THE RIVER.

barns which are most common and best preserved in Swaledale. Its economic and social history, particularly the long history of lead mining, differs from the other dales, too.

boundaries

Whilst the river Swale flows for 70 miles from its source before it joins the Ure, in this book we will concentrate on the first 20 miles, going downstream no farther than Richmond. There are good reasons for concentrating on this upper section of the river.

In terms of topography the upper part of Swaledale – the 'dale' itself, technically – differs from the rest. The western limit to the dale is defined by the hills of the main Pennine watershed. In its upper reaches the river flows along a relatively narrow valley but, as Alfred Wainwright (1989) puts it, 'the high ground of the Dales ends abruptly near Richmond

and a wide plain extends eastwards' – comprising the Vale of Mowbray and Vale of York. The character of the river differs between the two sections; for example, there are numerous waterfalls upstream from Richmond but none below, and above Richmond the river often has bedrock exposed on its bed, whereas downstream it flows across a floodplain composed of fine sediment. The slope of the river also decreases significantly below Richmond. Edmund Bogg (1907) writes how below Catterick the Swale 'is left to make its way somewhat silently through the great Yorkshire plain to the Ouse and [the North] Sea'.

Scenery and land use also differ above and below Richmond. Upstream from Richmond the land use is dominated by open moorland and pastoral farming, with some pockets of woodland, whereas downstream there is much more arable farming and livestock rearing. Alfred Wainwright (1989) comments on this, remarking that in the upper section of Swaledale, 'the countryside is flat … it is strange to see fields fenced by hedges instead of the familiar stone walls, to have manure on the boots instead of honest mud. It is a landscape without contours … '

Place names and dialects are also different above and below Richmond, reflecting different histories of settlement and migration. The relative seclusion of the dale section contrasts with much easier communication on the plain, and this is reflected in the history and character of the dale. The upper section of the river also differs from the rest in terms

SWALEDALE: PART OF THE YORKSHIRE DALES NATIONAL PARK IN RICHMONDSHIRE.

of administration, particularly because Richmond marks the eastern limit of the Yorkshire Dales National Park, and the northern fells of Swaledale mark its northern limit.

administration

Today Swaledale forms part of Richmondshire, a rural area of over 500 square miles that includes Swaledale and Wensleydale, and runs northwards to the river Tees. Much of Richmondshire lies within the Yorkshire Dales National Park. Traditionally, Swaledale was part of the North Riding of Yorkshire, the very name of which gives strong clues to the early history of the area. York is a shortened form of the Viking name *Jorvik*, which evolved from the Anglo-Saxon name *Eoforwic*. When the Vikings settled in the north of England they divided the area (shire) around Jorvik (York) into three parts (ridings), which they called 'thrid-hjungr', meaning literally a 'third part'. By Anglo-Saxon times this had evolved into 'thrithing' or 'triding', and through time it became 'reding'. By 1086, when the *Domesday Book* was compiled by the Normans, the three parts of Yorkshire were called Estreding (East Riding), Nortreding (North Riding) and Westreding (West Riding).

For most of the last millenium the three parts of the shire – the East Riding, West Riding and North Riding – were important administrative units. They were abolished in 1974, and the former North Riding became part of a new county (the largest in England) called North

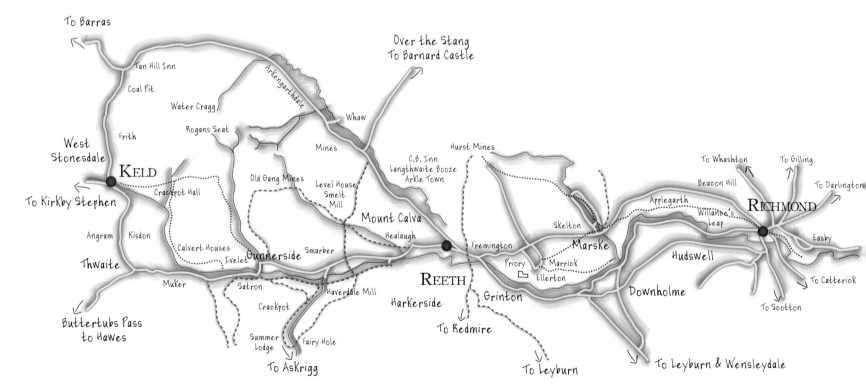

Yorkshire. At the same time, Richmondshire local government district was created from the merger of the municipal borough of Richmond, Aysgarth Rural District, Leyburn Rural District, Reeth Rural District, Richmond Rural District and part of the Croft Rural District.

access

Most drivers enter Swaledale from the east, from the A1, Middlesbrough and Teesside, and they arrive through Richmond, the traditional gateway to the dale, along the main road – the A6108. Those entering the dale from outside have a number of options to choose from.

These days many visitors arrive in Swaledale on foot, usually along either the Pennine Way or the Coast to Coast Walk, but most prefer the comfort, ease and speed of travelling by road. Alfred Wainwright (1989) suggests that walkers doing the Coast to Coast route should walk from west to east, with the weather to their backs. This sensible advice applies equally well to those with wheels, who will then experience the grandeur of the Swaledale scenery as they head down-dale towards Richmond, the jewel in the crown of the dale. Nonetheless, it is difficult to disagree with Ella Pontefract's view (1934) that 'whichever way you enter [Swaledale], and in whatever season, you will feel its spell and be content'.

Cotterby Scar near Keld, outcrop of Main Limestone.

'The most impressive approach to a view of one of the dales is to come upon it from the high moors – what the dalesfolk call, so expressibly, from off the "tops".'
Arthur Raistrick (1968)

The two most widely used roads into Swaledale 'from off the tops' are the road up from Kirkby Stephen in the west, and the Buttertubs Pass which runs north from Hawes in Wensleydale. Both lead into the head of Swaledale, and both offer spectacular views of the dale and the hills that enfold and define it. My personal favourite road into Swaledale is the Buttertubs Pass, which involves a steep climb up from Hawes. It passes through the col between Great Shunner Fell and Lovely Seat, goes past the intriguing Buttertubs, then drops down to the narrow floor of Swaledale near Thwaite. This route offers particularly spectacular views of Kisdon Hill, Rogan's Seat and the high level moors north of the river.

There are alternative roads across the wide moors, on both sides of the dale. On the northern side, a former drovers' road runs from Barras and Kirkby Stephen to the west towards Tan Hill, from where one road heads south along Stonesdale Beck towards Keld, and another runs east over Sleightholme Moor and down Arkengarthdale towards Reeth. There is also a narrow road coming into Arkengarthdale from the north-east, crossing over The Stang from Barnard Castle and dropping down over Eskeleth Bridge. On the southern side of Swaledale, one road heads north from Askrigg in Wensleydale; one branch of it joins the B6270 at Low Oxnop near Ivelet Bridge, and the other runs farther to the east past Summer Lodge and Haverdale. A second road leaves Wensleydale near Castle Bolton and climbs north over Redmire Moor and down into Grinton in Swaledale. A minor road from Leyburn in Wensleydale heads north-west across Bellerby Moor then drops past Grinton Lodge into Grinton. The main road (A6108) from Leyburn to Richmond passes the village of Downholme and joins the B6270 below White Scar.

geology

The landscape and scenery of Swaledale are heavily shaped by the underlying geology, which is dominated by the Yoredale Series of rocks, named after the river Ure (Wensleydale) and sandwiched between Great Scar Limestone and Millstone Grit. The basement rock in Swaledale, which now lies buried beneath the Yoredale rocks, is Great Scar Limestone. Farther south this gives rise to textbook karst (limestone) features such as limestone pavements, caves, potholes and underground passages, but few of these can be found in Swaledale.

STEPPED VALLEY SIDE IN UPPER SWALEDALE, CAUSED BY DIFFERENCES IN ROCK RESISTANCE BETWEEN LAYERS IN THE YOREDALE SERIES.

The Yoredale Series was formed during the Carboniferous period, around 250 million years ago, when what is now northern Britain was submerged under a shallow sea. Limestone formed from the compacted skeletons of corals, shellfish and other organisms which grew in the relatively shallow, warm, tropical sea water. Violent earth movements lifted upwards a large area to the north, creating a new land mass of mountains which today forms the north of Scotland and the Hebrides. Over a long period of time, large rivers eroded valleys in this land mass, and the sediment (mainly mud and sand) they transported southwards was deposited in layers on top of the limestone. As the deposits grew thicker, the layers were compacted to form bands of shale (mud) and sandstone (sand). The deposits built up above sea level in some places, creating low, swampy islands on which luxurious tropical vegetation grew. When the islands later sank below sea level, the dead vegetation was compacted into peat, and eventually into coal, by the weight of overlying layers of mud and sand.

This process – deposition of limestone in shallow seas, followed by river mud and sand – was repeated many times. This gave rise to the alternating layers of hard limestone and gritstone, and relatively softer shales, mudstones and sandstones, with thin layers of coal in some places, 'like layers in a sandwich cake' as Bill Mitchell (1990) graphically describes it. The layers of rock tilt gently towards the east because of earth movements in the geological past after they were deposited. There are seven layers of limestone within the Yoredale Series, mostly less than 60 feet (18 metres) thick. The thicker top layer – the Main Limestone – outcrops along Swaledale in some quite dramatic cliffs, including those at Cotterby Scar (upstream from Keld), Kisdon Scar and Ivelet Scar (upstream from Muker), and Fremington Edge behind Reeth.

Differences in rock hardness, thus resistance to erosion, are clearly displayed in the scenery. In places the valley side has a distinctly stepped or terraced appearance – with harder limestone and gritstone forming the steeper slopes or steps, and relatively softer shales forming the shallower slopes or treads – although the effect is more prominent in Wensleydale than in Swaledale. Along the river Swale and its tributaries, the softer layers have in places been worn away, undercutting and leaving outcrops of harder limestone to form waterfalls, such as those around Keld from Wain Wath Force to Kisdon Force, at Gunnerside and at Swinner Gill.

The Yoredale Series is capped by Millstone Grit, a coarse sandstone deposit that was traditionally used to make grindstones for grain mills (hence the name) and as a building material in the mill towns of Yorkshire. After the Yoredale Series was deposited in the shallow sea, this part of northern England was covered by a huge delta of very coarse sand, deposited by a massive river flowing into it from a granite mountain area now under the sea to the north of Scotland. As the delta grew bigger, the deposit grew thicker and was compacted into a series of coarse sandstone layers, with bands of softer shales between them. There are thin seams of low-quality coal in the lower part of the Millstone Grit in some places, such as near Tan Hill where coal was extracted from the 3-foot thick seam over many centuries for use in nearby lead smelt mills. Local coal was also dug in Swaledale for domestic use, and for lime burning (in which crushed limestone was burned and spread on fields to 'sweeten' the acidic soils).

The Millstone Grit is up to 500 feet thick and is found over much of the Pennines. The gritstone layers are horizontal. Because they are very hard and thus resistant to erosion, they often cap the hilltops, most notably the Three Peaks (Ingleborough, Whernside and Pen-y-ghent) farther south. They also provide the source of many of the rounded pebbles and boulders on the beds of rivers in Swaledale.

The final major geological event that left a strong imprint on the landscape of Swaledale was the tectonic activity (huge earth movements) that occurred after the Millstone Grit was deposited. Sea level fell and the land was pushed up, making northern Britain dry land and creating the Pennines as a chain of rugged mountains. Rivers subsequently started to erode the mountains, reducing their height and creating valleys which

were later dramatically re-fashioned during the much more recent ice age. As well as causing this great uplift, the earth movements caused faults to develop in the rocks of the Yoredale Series, running east to west, into which a series of minerals – particularly ores of lead (galena), zinc and copper – were deposited in some places. The intermittent and small-scale mining of copper in Richmond, and the much larger-scale, more continuous and more extensive mining of lead on the north side of Swaledale between Keld and Arkengarthdale, owe their origins to the process of mineralisation.

glaciation

If geology created the stage on which the Swaledale landscape could develop, glaciation created the scenery on it that we see today. On at least four occasions over the last million years or so, during the Great Ice Age, much of the Northern Hemisphere has been covered in thick ice sheets, creating arctic conditions similar to the North and South Poles today. Glaciers formed in the Highlands of Scotland, the Lake District and the Pennines, which deepened and straightened valleys and spread boulder clay (a glacial deposit of clay and gravel) across a wide area.

The most recent ice age (the Devensian) was shorter, milder, and more localised than earlier ones. It began around 26,000 years ago, lasted around 11,000 years, and covered Britain in thick ice as far south as a line between The Wash and the Bristol Channel. Evidence of earlier glaciation was bulldozed away by great rivers of ice which flowed south, further deepening and straightening valleys and plastering new deposits of boulder clay across low-lying areas. The largest ice stream in the north of England spread out from the Lake District, and one part of it flowed eastwards through the Stainmore Gap to the north of Swaledale; tell-tale signs include the erratic (boulders) of Shap granite that it deposited in the Vale of York. The deep build-up and compaction of snow created glaciers in all of the Yorkshire dales, which moved down-valley, eroded and reshaped the valleys, and left behind sometimes thick deposits of boulder clay. At their maximum,

these valley glaciers were thick enough to reach all but the highest hill-tops, and they extended the full length of each dale and coalesced with other ice streams to form an almost continuous ice sheet across the whole of northern England. In places the ice flowed over lower sections of hills between adjacent dales, creating passes we see today such as the Buttertubs Pass between Swaledale and Wensleydale.

Swaledale developed its own glacier, but towards the end of the last ice age the Stainmore glacier spilled over into Swaledale through what is now Marske Beck. The Swaledale glacier was not deep enough or powerful enough to carve the sort of U-shaped valley that is typical of glaciated upland areas, with steep valley sides and a flat valley floor infilled with sediment, but it did trim the valley sides and created steep cliffs in some places (such as Fremington Edge near Reeth).

The end of the ice age began around 14,000 years ago when the climate warmed: the ice started to melt, causing the ice sheets to thin and the glaciers to retreat. The Great Melt triggered two significant processes which left their mark on the post-glacial landscape – as the ice melted and retreated it deposited vast amounts of glacial sediment, and huge volumes of ice melt caused massive flooding.

In Swaledale, as elsewhere, the glacier shrank progressively upstream and left behind a series of ridges of sediment deposited across the valley floor. These terminal moraines, composed of a mixture of boulders, gravel, sand and clay which had been transported in and on the glacier when it was advancing, were formed at the front end of the retreating glacier during periods of still-stand, between phases of more rapid melt and retreat. When they were deposited the moraines dammed the valley floor, causing freshwater lakes to pond up behind them, into which fine sediment would be deposited by the meltwater. Through time the powerful meltwater river would cut a way through the barrier allowing the lake to drain away, leaving behind a flat former lake bed which survives today as meadows (for example by Gunnerside). Remnants of four breached terminal moraines can be seen in Swaledale – below Gunnerside New Bridge, by How Hill above Low Whita Bridge, below Grinton Bridge, and by Ellerton Priory.

A fifth moraine, near Keld, dammed the original pre-glacial course of the river Swale, but the river – even when greatly enlarged by meltwater – was not able to cut a way through it. Instead, the Swale, which originally flowed to the west of Kisdon Hill, was diverted around the northern side and cut a new channel for itself to the east, between Kisdon and

Beldi Hill, 'thus providing us with the beauty of Catrake and Kisdon falls and its chaotic grandeur of rock and cliff', as Edmund Cooper (1973) so poetically puts it. The new (post-glacial) channel of the river Swale sits within a valley carved by ice. The former course of the river past the villages of Angram and Thwaite is now largely infilled with peat, through which the small Skeb Skeugh Beck flows. The changed course of the river below Keld is the most pronounced example of a meltwater channel in Swaledale, but there is also a much smaller-scale example at Richmond, in the form of Round Howe.

After the ice age a new post-glacial environment existed in Swaledale – a barren-looking world of intense cold, like we might see today in the far north of Scandinavia. It was a bare landscape dominated by rock and boulders, with wet and waterlogged clay, very little vegetation, and a marshy valley floor with some freshwater lakes. Through time, over many centuries, new soil formed and vegetation grew across the hills, initially mosses and lichens but followed by larger plants. In A History of Swaledale, Edmund Cooper (1973) writes: 'On each side [of the river Swale] grew tangled forest trees, alders and ash, providing cover for bears and wolves. Above, on the steep fell slopes and moors, the forest turned into a scrub of birch and hazel, followed by red pine, mountain ash and thorn. Amongst these were areas of rough grass, the feeding grounds of red and fallow deer, wild ox, mountain sheep and goats.'

This was the environment that the first (prehistoric) visitors to and settlers in Swaledale encountered, and that shaped the subsequent history of the dale and its people, as we shall see in Chapter Four.

scenery

It was the attractive scenery and striking landscape that led James Herriot to describe Swaledale as 'the most beautiful part of England', and he is not the only writer to have been captivated by its beauty, although, as Ella Pontefract (1934) points out, 'Swaledale is modest about its beauty spots'.

MARSKE BECK VIEWED FROM NEAR TELFIT FARM; A FORMER PRO-GLACIAL LAKE FLOOR.

Alfred Brown (1952) describes how 'of all the great dales, Swaledale seems to come nearest to one's ideal of a pure, unsullied dale ... The scenery of Upper Swaledale, with its grey limestone crags and great gills, is of the kind that sets the pulses dancing for those who revel in the high solitudes of the Pennines.' More recently, Richard Muir (1989) notes how Swaledale 'embodies all the finest facets of the landscape of the Dales and combines them in vistas which are quite magical. It encapsulates all that is best in the much broader bounds of the region.'

It is appropriate here to make some initial comments about the scenery and landscape of this special dale, but these themes run through the whole book and will re-emerge repeatedly in later chapters. The general character of Swaledale is of unspoiled countryside. Observers through the ages have written positively about it. William Camden noted in 1607 how 'this Swale passeth downe along an open vale of good large-nesse ... having good plenty of grasse, but as great want of wood ...' and Thomas Dunham Whitaker (1823) described the general scenery of the area as 'purely mountainous, though intersected by many pleasing and fertile valleys'.

The earliest, and most complete, description of Swaledale is given by John Leland in 1538.

Few who know Swaledale are not struck by its wild and rugged scenery and would disagree with Edmund Cooper (1948) that in this area 'lies some of the finest fell scenery in England', or Edmund Bogg (1909): 'Those who love wild and desolate scenery will find this remote land a region of strange charm, ever full of new points of interest.' Swaledale is also rich in nature and natural history.

Black's Picturesque Guide to Yorkshire (1874), in describing Swaledale, states that although the dale 'has no spots of special interest on account of their antiquity and historical associations, [it] possesses attractions of no ordinary kind to the tourist who loves to wander in scenes of wild and unfrequented beauty. In common with the other dales, it will

'The tract of country between Ravensworth [to the north] and Richmond is very hilly, with some good arable land but much waste.' ... Arkengarthdale 'produces some big-barley and oats, but little or no wood. Swaledale grows little corn and no woodland, but much grass, as well as heather and some nut trees. The wood they burn for smelting their lead is brought from other parts of Richmondshire and from County Durham ... all the rest of Richmondshire to the east of the hills and dales is well supplied with arable land, on which is grown abundant wheat and rye, and it has reasonably good meadowland and woods. The best woods lie to the east of the Rivers Swale and Ure. In the dales of Richmondshire they use heather, peat and turves for fuel. And in the areas where they clear the heather good grassland springs up, sufficient to feed cattle for a year or two, until the heather infests it again. There are good supplies of building stone in very many places in Richmondshire. The shire has no coal pits, although the eastern parts burn a great deal of sea-coal brought from County Durham.'

JOHN LELAND'S DESCRIPTION OF SWALEDALE IN 1538 (IN MODERN ENGLISH).

reward the diligence of the botanist and geologist who may explore its windings and recesses ... [and] has much to attract the artist and the lover of nature.'

As in other areas of countryside, the scenery of Swaledale reflects the interplay of nature and people. Roly Smith writes in *Swaledale* (2008): 'That harmonious blending of the work of Man and Nature – the lush, alder-lined flood meadows rich in wildflowers; the grey-stone villages clustered around an ancient arched bridge; then one stone barn to every two drystone-walled fields as the slopes rear up to the crags and moorland heights above – is nowhere seen to better effect than in Swaledale.' Bill Mitchell (1990) paints a similar picture: 'The image in my mind when I wrote about the Dales was the windswept upland, with outcropping rock, walls, a few thorn trees, sheep and the indomitable Dales farmer – not forgetting his dog.'

The interplay of people and nature has given rise to the distinctive scenery of Swaledale, created from a mosaic or patchwork of different landscape elements, which we will look at in later chapters. But, whilst scenery is fixed at any point in time, the way it appears to us, the way we view it, and the impact it has on our thoughts and emotions can vary a great deal through time. Even over a matter of hours, a particular scene can change dramatically with the weather, for example, or depending on how crowded or quiet it is.

TYPICAL UPPER SWALEDALE SCENERY, VIEWED FROM SATRON MOOR.

'Each season [in the dales] has its special beauty – summer when the bracken is green and sweet to smell, autumn when it is golden brown and the moors are flooded with purple heather, winter when all is white with snow and an icy wind makes your eyes water. But loveliest of all is spring, when primroses stud the grey stone walls, the lush meadows are sprinkled with cowslips, and pools of bluebells glow luminous in the woods.' Denis Healey (1995)

characteristic elements of the Swaledale landscape

- rounded valleys, crags and hills (fells) left after glaciations
- fast-flowing rivers and impressive waterfalls
- wind-swept open heather moorland and cotton grass bog on the fell tops
- some limestone cliffs
- small patches of woodland
- remnants of juniper scrub
- colourful traditional hay meadows
- pastures and rough grassland
- dry-stone walls
- scattered stone field barns
- isolated farmsteads
- tiny hamlets and small villages
- traditional stone buildings
- the legacy of lead mining

Chapter Two
REMOTENESS

Swaledale is 'a little country in itself... the rest of the world seems unimportant and unreal.' Ella Pontefract (1934)

SWALEDALE IS A VALLEY THAT, through most of its history, has tended to keep itself to itself. It has gone about its business in a quiet, solid, unassuming way, reluctant to draw attention to itself or claim any special status or qualities. It is a rather understated place, a place apart. Yet that is part of its very charm, a key reason why people are drawn to it and cherish it.

isolation

Victorian travellers and writers appreciated the remoteness and isolation of the dale. For example, in 1896, John Leyland described Swaledale as 'a remote and lonely dale, severe in character, impressive in the barrenness of its upper reaches, and flanked by boldly-featured hills, which should attract many by its unfamiliar grandeur'. But, of course, isolation is a mixed blessing, because alongside the peace and quiet sit the challenges of keeping in touch with the realities of

'The upper Swale between Gunnerside and Keld is the most remote and isolated of Yorkshire dales. The hurry, scurry and press of town life is unknown here – and as if it could not be. No railroad drives its iron horse through or up betwixt these hill barriers that protect it from the delights and risks of modern life.'
Edmund Bogg (1909)

the outside world, and engaging with what that world has to offer. It is not hard to think of reasons for the sense of isolation of Swaledale, which has remained more secluded – and for longer – than the other dales in North Yorkshire. Topography works against Swaledale, with its relatively narrow valley aligned from west to east, boxed in by high hills and unwelcoming expanses of bleak moorland at its western end. No major routeway runs through the dale; it is not on the way to anywhere important except itself. Historically, the main route for traffic heading cross country between west and east has been the Stainmore Gap (where the A66 now runs), to the north of Swaledale. There was some movement of people through Swaledale – such as Roman soldiers passing through from Bainbridge in Wensleydale in the south to Teesdale farther north; cattle drovers over the centuries herding stock from the Lake District and Scotland to markets farther south; miners carting lead from mines in the dale down to the market

UPPER SWALEDALE LOOKING NORTH TOWARDS KELD FROM DIRTY PIECE.

in Richmond – but compared to many of the other dales Swaledale preserved much of its remoteness and relative isolation from the world around it. Tourists only started visiting Swaledale in the middle of the nineteenth century, and then only in much smaller numbers than places with greater antiquarian or historic interests. The lack of a railway line farther up the dale than Richmond also made access difficult, constrained visitor numbers and hampered economic development. The traditional economic base for the dale, dominated by pastoral farming and lead mining, was not sufficient to attract large numbers of visitors during the nineteenth century, even from the rapidly-growing industrial towns in Teesside to the east.

Whilst not immune from the tide of history, Swaledale has played relatively little part in the great events of British history, other than being on the receiving end of the Harrying of the North in medieval times, and the unfortunate end of the short-lived Pilgrimage of Grace in the sixteenth century. As Edmund Cooper (1948) explains, the effect of 'the events of the past which happened in this valley … upon the world at large was slight but they were important in the lives of a group of families or clans which lived in a primitive and isolated state, hardly touched by the main streams of civilisation.'

SHEEP MARKING, GRINTON SMELT MILL. COPYRIGHT LUCIE HINSON.

Swaledale people

Given the interplay of these different factors, the relative remoteness and isolation of Swaledale should be no real surprise. What may surprise the outsider, and no doubt greatly annoys locals, is the relish with which some writers over the years have resorted to the anthropologists' now-outmoded notion of the 'noble savage' when describing Swaledale folk.

The present-day dalesmen are partly descended from the Scandinavians who invaded England and Scotland from the West, by way of Ireland and the Isle of Man … Remnants of the Ancient Britons most likely stayed when the Celts and Norse settlers made their homes in Swaledale. Inter-marriage may have taken place and their racial characteristics still seem to re-appear in some features of the present population.
Edmund Cooper (1948)

Today such cultural stereotyping seems extreme and overzealous – patronising even. However, at its root is an undisputed fact: the gene pool of Swaledale people has until recently remained relatively closed, because most families have continued to live there through many generations, with relatively few incomers adding to the diversity. This has allowed traits from the past to survive in a relatively closed community.

One consequence of this demographic stability is the continuity of family names over many generations. For example, the names Alderson, Harker, Coates, Clarkson, and Fawcett appear on graves and memorials through the ages. Another consequence of isolation is the long period over which the character of dales people has been allowed to evolve with minimal disturbance from outside. It is surprising how many writers attribute the character of dales-folk to their relatively isolated existence.

Bogg (1907) even went so far as to suggest that Swaledale men are physically different from those in surrounding valleys. He wrote of how 'in physique the dalesmen of Swale's secluded and sinuous valley are of the big, long-limbed type, loosely knit, not of the short-backed wrestler class which characterises 'the West Country' as the 'Swardal' men call those of the Eden, Lune and Leven valleys'.

Such characterisations might have had some basis in truth in the early part of the twentieth century, but I doubt if most Swaledale folk today – even those with deep roots in the dale – would recognise themselves in them. These sorts of descriptions, firmly rooted in the now

The people of the dales, far removed as they are from towns and cities, are of a sturdy mind, a solid independence, and they possess an intelligence and a sharpness of whit and perception which will often put the mere townsman to shame ... their surroundings breed in them a loftiness of character which soon becomes apparent to the stranger who goes amongst them.
Joseph Fletcher (1908)

discredited environmental determinism paradigm that was strong at the time, reveal more about the preconceptions and prejudices of their writers than they do about their subjects.

A third consequence of remoteness is the persistence of many local traditions, which have survived often long after their equivalents have declined or disappeared in other dales. Oswald Harland explains in *Yorkshire North Riding* (1951) how 'in Swaledale remains a good deal that has perished elsewhere in the Riding – old ways of life, old ways of speech and old customs'. Ella Pontefract reported that, as recently as the 1930s, 'clogs [were] still the chief footwear in Swaledale, for nothing stands the wet so well', and many of the daleswomen occupied themselves during the long, dark winter evenings in hand-making quilts (to traditional patterns) and rugs. Many other examples of traditional dales customs and practices are described in the numerous books written since the 1930s by Ella Pontefract, Marie Hartley and Joan Ingilby.

TRADITIONAL FARMING LANDSCAPE IN UPPER SWALEDALE, HARKERSIDE MOOR, VIEWED FROM REETH.

Given the adversity of life in the Dales ... the toughness of the Dalesfolk is not surprising ... A stubborn nature, which borders on bloody-mindedness, has allowed the people of the Dales to endure centuries of hardship and yet today they stand by with an apparent meekness as strangers price them out of their villages, and as policies formed in the south threaten their livelihoods.
Richard Muir (1998)

landscape names: Scandinavian origin

Beck	stream, from Norwegian *bekk*
Birks	birch wood, from Norwegian *björk*
Ellers	alder wood; Anglo-Saxon *aler*
Foss, force	waterfall; Norwegian *foss*
Garth	enclosure, small field; Old Norse *garthr*
Gill	ravine, narrow valley with a stream; Norwegian *gjel*
Holm, holme	water-meadow; Norwegian *holm*
Howe	mound, small hill; Norwegian *haug*
Ing, ings	wet or marshy meadow; Norwegian *eng*
Keld	spring; Norwegian *kjeld*
Moss	peat bog; Norwegian *mose*
Rigg	ridge, long narrow hill; Norwegian *rygg*
Scar	cliff, crag, escarpment, outcrop; Norwegian *skarv*
Slack	hollow, small shallow valley; Old Norse *slakki*
Thorpe	hamlet; Danish *torp*
Thwaite, wait	farmstead; Norwegian *tveit*
Wath	ford; Norwegian *vasse*

ABANDONED STONE SHEPHERD'S HUT, BIRKDALE, UPPER SWALEDALE.

The persistence of some traditional farming practices in Swaledale – particularly the management of the hay meadows, maintenance of the dry-stone walls, and protection of stone field barns – has turned out to be a blessing, given the importance of such features to the special character of the landscape in and around the dale.

Isolation and long stability of the local population also help to explain the persistence of many words for landscape features which are of Scandinavian origin, many of which have been incorporated into local place names. Some common examples are shown opposite. They also explain why the Swaledale dialect (known as Swardle), most pronounced in the system used for counting sheep and knitting rows (1. Yan. 2. Tan. 3. Tether. 4. Mether. 5. Pip. 6. Azer. 7. Sezar. 8. Akker. 9. Conter. 10. Dick.) – which is derived from Celtic languages – has survived into the twenty-first century, although the number of native speakers continues to decline.

Despite the challenges which it no doubt still offers to those who live in the dale, remoteness also brings peace and quiet away from the hustle and bustle of city life. For those who value tranquility, there are few things more relaxing than sitting outside in a Swaledale village on a sunny summer evening (in the garden or a pub), soaking up the quiet atmosphere, perhaps aware of the nostalgic smell of smoke rising from coal fires through the cottage chimneys, the day-tripper having left for home, the sun setting on the surrounding hills, the quiet broken only by the sound of streams and waterfalls, sheep grazing in the fields or on the fells, birds in the trees, trees rustling in the evening breeze, grouse and pheasants flying overhead, enjoying their own freedoms. A more restful and picturesque scene would be difficult to find in Britain today.

KISDON HILL, VIEWED FROM THWAITE.

opening up Swaledale

Despite its relative remoteness and isolation, Swaledale has a long history of settlement and use by humans, which has been a catalyst for the development of transport systems through the ages. Prehistoric wanderers and settlers needed little more than tracks through the Great Forest after the end of the ice age, and the Roman soldiers who passed through Swaledale on a north–south axis between Wensleydale and Teesdale travelled on foot along tracks through the then open moorland and boggy valley floor, crossing the Swale by ford near Reeth.

In Swaledale, as across the rest of England, the development of the market system in medieval times encouraged much greater movement of people and produce between towns and villages. Most market roads – often little more than unsurfaced trackways, with either fords or stone bridges to cross rivers – developed along existing paths, perhaps with some new sections added to complete a chain. The old road between Richmond and Reeth, which runs east to west, probably started out as a market road.

The market roads were complemented by green lanes and trackways, which often followed prehistoric routes. The green lanes also served as drive-roads for the cattle trade, particularly from the sixteenth century onwards. A major drove road ran from Tan Hill down through

Jagger Ponies by W. Gilbert Foster

Arkengarthdale, reaching Swaledale at Feetham, which allowed cattle to be moved south from the Scottish borders to fairs in Askrigg (Wensleydale), Appletreewick (Swaledale) and Malham Moor.

Packhorse routes were the main form of transport for goods and products up to the 1880s, with single-arched stone bridges (such as the one at Ivelet) across rivers. In Swaledale, there were several coal roads from Tan Hill into the dale. The traditional method for transporting heavy lead ingots was in panniers on the back of packponies, usually Scottish Galloways or German Jaeger ponies, the latter giving rise to the name 'jagger' given to the man in charge of the team of ten or more ponies that travelled together.

Until the mid-1840s, the lead roads were used to transport lead from the main mining areas (Swinner Gill and Arkengarthdale) northwards across the moors into Stainmore and on to Stockton, for loading on to ships. When the railway arrived in Richmond in 1846, shipping ended and new lead roads were built, converging on Richmond.

Stone packhorse bridge over Stonesdale Beck, West Stonesdale.

Some of the roads that today run over the fells between Swaledale and surrounding valleys (such as the road from Tan Hill down Arkengarthdale) have their origins as drove roads and packhorse routes. Many of the green lanes and trackways, drovers' lanes and packhorse routes continue in use as walkers' paths, providing access to the open high moors.

Swaledale also mirrors most of the rest of England in the fact that few new roads were created between Saxon times and the turnpike and enclosure roads of the eighteenth century. Most turnpikes (privately financed toll roads) took over existing routes but improved them with better drainage and a decent surface and bridges, for the use of which travellers paid a fee at the toll houses. Some turnpikes included entirely new stretches of road, particularly in hilly areas where the old roads included steep gradients which were suitable for foot passengers and packhorses, but not for heavy horse traffic or carriage services.

The turnpike roads often crossed open moorlands, and they had surfaces good enough to carry wagons and carts during winter months as well as in summer. There were no turnpike roads in Swaledale above Reeth, but one was constructed from Reeth up to Arkengarthdale (as far as the CB Inn) early in the nineteenth century. The opening of the Richmond–Lancaster Turnpike in 1751, which left Richmond over the Green Bridge and went up Sleegill and continued through Wensleydale, greatly assisted the movement of people and goods in and out of the dale. In 1836, a new, well-surfaced turnpike road was constructed between Richmond and Grinton, along the valley bottom. This new road greatly eased and speeded the movement of people and goods up the dale from Richmond, compared to the sinuous hilly old road via Marske. By 1823, writes Geoffrey Wright (1985), there was 'a regular carriage service from Richmond to most Swaledale villages, and to Darlington, Stockton, Durham, Newcastle, Edinburgh, York, Leeds, Manchester and London. Regular carrier services also operated between Reeth and Hawes, and Muker and Hawes.'

RICHMOND RAILWAY STATION VIEWED FROM THE CASTLE KEEP.

Without doubt the biggest single breakthrough in terms of transport into Swaledale was the arrival of the railway in Richmond in September 1846, when a branch line was opened, connecting Richmond with the York, Newcastle and Berwick Railway (later to become part of the North Eastern Railway Company), providing a link to the main railway network. This effectively opened up Richmond to mainstream traffic around the country. Richmond became the main depot for lead ingots, carried there from the smelt mills in wagons along the newly constructed turnpike road. The wealthy men who owned or leased lead mines in Swaledale were eager to capitalise on the railway, and in 1863 they hatched an unsuccessful plan to extend the line up to Richmond. Cooper (1973) outlines two further plans to extend the railway up Swaledale: one in 1881 to Muker then by tunnel to Hawes in Wensleydale, and one in 1912 to Fremington near Marske. Neither plan came to fruition.

Richmond Castle viewed from Millgate.

Chapter Three
DISCOVERING SWALEDALE

The discovery of the Yorkshire dales as an area to be visited and enjoyed by ordinary folk is a matter of the last hundred years' [since the 1870s]. Arthur Raistrick (1971)

LIKE MANY RELATIVELY REMOTE PARTS of Britain, Swaledale was only discovered by outsiders since about the middle of the nineteenth century. We tend to use the word 'discovery' in the sense of finding something entirely new, something that's never been seen or heard of before, like discovering a new planet, continent or species, something hitherto unknown and unnamed. But I want to use the term 'discovery' here in a slightly different sense – like a child looking into another child's toy box to discover what's inside: they see stuff that's been there for some time and others know about, but it's now been seen afresh by a new pair of eyes. Inevitably, most geographical discovery is personal discovery of this second sort. Even though Christopher Columbus is said to have 'discovered' the New World, it had been there and lived in well before 1642, but had been isolated and inaccessible to people from the Old World; the element of discovery was making it known to outsiders.

early reports

The earliest recorded reports of travellers in Swaledale are probably those compiled for the *Domesday Book*, which was published in 1086 after the Norman Conquest. At that time Richmond did not exist, but there may have been a small settlement called Hindrelac on or near the site of Richmond. Few villages in Swaledale are mentioned by name, and most of the land was described as 'waste' (meaning unproductive in terms of farming). The trail then goes cold for nearly five centuries, when two travellers from the Tudor era passed through Richmond on their grand tours around Britain. In 1538, during the reign of Henry VIII, topographer John Leland published *Travels in Tudor England*, in which he described towns, castles, churches and what he saw in the countryside. In many places he found neglect and decay, and this is true of Richmond, where he found the castle walls and parts of the medieval town wall in ruins. Fifty years later, in 1607, antiquarian and cartographer William Camden published *Britannia*, his survey of the history and topography of the country. He provides more details about Swaledale than Leland, including observations on Richmond, which he described as 'pretty populous'.

From the early eighteenth century onwards, awareness of the dales in general, and Swaledale in particular, was raised thanks to the growth in the number of people who travelled around the country, writing journals of their tours and describing what they saw. One such source is the diary written by Celia Fiennes (1697), an intrepid young woman who toured around much of Britain on horseback between 1697 and 1698, purely for pleasure. She wrote mostly about towns, including Richmond – 'a sad shatter'd town and fallen much to decay and like a disregarded place'.

Daniel Defoe visited the Yorkshire Dales in 1724 as part of his *Tour Through the Whole Island of Great Britain*, although his primary interest was commercial life in the towns. In Richmond, for example, he wrote about the hand-knitting industry. A different perspective is offered in the travel journals published by American Quaker Jabez Maud Fisher based on his tour of England between 1775 and 1779. Fisher (1779) was interested in the character and appearance of Richmond, saying that the town's 'situation [is] full of grandeur, and from the number of churches, towers, and other objects its entrance is very striking'.

Defoe's gaze was fixed more on towns and prosperous areas than on what he called the 'black, ill looking, desolate moors'. Looking towards the Lake District from Settle, he continues: 'we saw nothing but high mountains, which had a terrible aspect … So that having no manner of inclination to encounter them, merely for the sake of seeing a few villages and a parcel of wild people, we turned north-east … ' (1724)

THE GREEN BRIDGE OVER THE RIVER SWALE IN RICHMOND, WITH THE CASTLE IN THE BACKGROUND.

A similar distaste for 'desolate moors' is shown in William Bray's *Sketch of a Tour into Derbyshire and Yorkshire* (1778), which records his tour of Wensleydale, Wharfedale, Malham and Skipton. Defoe and Bray were typical of the travellers to Yorkshire in their day: most were interested mainly in the towns and they stuck to the main roads running north–south to the east of the Pennines; few ventured westwards into the dales. This was true also of English traveller John Byng (later Lord Torrington) who visited Richmond in 1792. Like Celia Fiennes a century earlier, Byng provides details of what he ate and drank and where he stayed, as well as commentary on where he went and what he saw. Richmond, he wrote, stands 'most romantically: the noble castle, the, the River Swale, all catch and charm the eye'. (1792)

This pattern of privileging towns over open countryside very much reflected contemporary ideas about landscape, as well as fashion and taste. Early travellers in upland areas throughout Britain had regarded mountains as wild, inhospitable and dangerous, so they avoided them.

Between the mid-sixteenth and mid-eighteenth centuries there was little interest in natural scenery but great interest in the agricultural potential of different places. From this time we have two valuable reports on the state of agriculture in the dales in general, and Swaledale in particular, by Arthur Young (1771) and John Tuke (1794). In his *General View of the Agriculture of the North Riding of Yorkshire: With Observations on the Means of its Improvement* (1794), Tuke largely agreed with Young, who wrote that on 'the cultivated valleys [between Arkengarthdale and Swaledale which are] too inconsiderable to deserve a mention … [most] are tracts of very improveable land.' (1771)

landscape, art and fashion

From the late eighteenth century onwards, fashion, taste and ideas about landscape began to change, and this helped to promote the growth, at least among the English leisured class, of touring for scenic pleasure. The rise of interest in scenery 'at home' was a direct challenge to the well-established European Grand Tour – the latter orientated around classical themes and refined tastes and sensitivities; the former inspired more by antiquarian interest, a form of poverty tourism, and a new appreciation of how landscape can affect emotions and even give spiritual inspiration and satisfaction.

Particularly influential in shaping this new sensitivity to scenery in general, and especially to wild and rugged mountain scenery, was Hampshire parson William Gilpin, who in 1786 wrote about what he termed 'picturesque beauty', which he defined as 'that kind of beauty which is agreeable in a picture'. Gilpin's ideas of the picturesque, alongside the aesthetic ideals of the beautiful and the sublime, favoured scenes with mountains, lakes and trees, as he emphasised in his influential 1792 book *Observations Relative Chiefly to Picturesque Beauty*.

Gilpin's ideas on the picturesque, which favoured unimproved landscapes and architectural decay, inspired a new form of landscape painting, championed by J. M. W. Turner. Turner made four tours on horseback though Richmondshire in 1797, 1816, 1817 and 1832, some as part of a contract to illustrate Thomas Dunham Whitaker's *History of Richmondshire* (1823). He made quick field sketches, to inform later watercolour paintings, of castles, ruined abbeys, waterfalls and similarly picturesque objects. In Swaledale he sketched Marrick Priory, Richmond, and Easby Abbey.

By the early nineteenth century, inspired by Gilpin's ideas and Turner's paintings, many tourists were out and about hunting for appropriate scenes to sketch and paint. Their task was made easier by improvements in travelling by road towards the close of the eighteenth century, and their minds were more focused on travelling around Britain because of travel restrictions on continental Europe. Perhaps inevitably, the main focus for this new landscape taste was the scenery of the Lake District, but it also encouraged the growth of tourism in the Yorkshire Dales. This, coupled with a healthy local

TRADITIONAL FARMING AND MOORLAND LANDSCAPE IN UPPER SWALEDALE.

interest in antiquities and local history, fuelled a growing interest in the dales at large. Thomas Langdale's *Topographical Dictionary of Yorkshire for the Year 1822* tapped into this newly emerging market, as did Bulmer's *History, Topography and Directory of North Yorkshire* (1890) seven decades later.

The first books specifically about Richmond and Swaledale started to appear in the early nineteenth century. Christopher Clarkson's *History of Richmond* (1814) was the first published history of the town, and although in keeping with the interests of the day, it focused more on stories of prominent people than on the development of the fabric and economy of the town and its surrounding area. It established a pattern that was to be repeated nearly a decade later by Thomas Dunham Whitaker, in his *History of Richmondshire in the North Riding of the County of York* (1823). Both books served local needs but also helped to put Richmond 'on the map', as did local writer and publisher W. R. Robinson's (1833) *Robinson's Guide to Richmond* and William Longstaffe's (1852) *Richmondshire, its Ancient Lords and Edifices*.

GEORGIAN HOUSES AT THE BOTTOM OF BARGATE, BY THE GREEN, RICHMOND.

access and enjoyment

The discovery of Swaledale gathered pace during the second half of the nineteenth century, promoted both by improvements in ease of access and by changes in public interest, taste and behaviour. The opening of the new road between Richmond and Reeth in 1837 opened up the dale significantly, while access to the dale itself was improved with the arrival of the railway in Richmond in 1846. Leyland's *Wensleydale and Swaledale Guide* (1896) was published by the Great North Eastern Railway Company to attract tourists and boost the numbers of train passengers.

As travel to and through the dale became easier and more convenient, more outsiders were encouraged to visit Richmond and Swaledale on day trips and for holidays. But what people did when they got there also changed. Visitors started to appreciate

'The valley of the Swale above Richmond has much to attract the artist and the lover of nature.'
Black's Picturesque Guide to
Yorkshire (1874)

and enjoy the countryside, partly as an antidote to the industrialisation which was dramatically changing many towns and cities, but also because it contained curios (such as unusual natural rock formations), antiquities (such as ruined abbeys and castles) and natural history. Groups were frequently organised by local naturalist and antiquarian societies, which arranged indoor winter meetings with lectures and outdoor 'rambles' on lighter summer evenings and at weekends. The Mechanics' Institutes, like the ones in Richmond (established in 1847) and Reeth (1783), and Literary Institutes like the one in Muker (1867), played a part in encouraging people to take an interest in and learn more about the world around them – the former with its emphasis on natural science and the latter which provided adult education for working-class people.

PURPLE HEATHER MOORLAND, GRINTON MOOR.

LOWER SWALEDALE, LOOKING EAST FROM REETH, WITH MARRICK PRIORY IN THE DISTANCE.

By the turn of the twentieth century there was a growing appetite, from locals and visitors alike, for books which combined both history and scenery, and two historians rose to the challenge. The first was Harry Speight, who between 1891 and 1902 wrote a series of books on different dales, one publication being *Romantic Richmondshire* (1897). This relied heavily on Whitaker for its historic content, and included information on antiquities and local characters, but it also broke new ground in systematically describing each village up the dale. The book was very popular, helped promote wider interest in Swaledale, and still makes very interesting reading today. The second was Edmund Bogg, whose *Regal Richmond and the Land of the Swale* (1907) and *The Wild Borderlands of Richmondshire: Between Tees and Yore* (1909) inevitably covered much the same ground but in a less formal way, including local ballads, legends, anecdotes and memories of the older generation.

Whilst the hills surrounding Swaledale are far too small to think of as mountains, some early nineteenth-century writers drew what today look like rather fanciful comparisons with the Alps of Switzerland. For example, Gordon Home, in *Yorkshire Dales and Fells* (1906), describes 'a Scottish feeling – perhaps Alpine would be more correct – in the steeply-falling sides of the dale', and Bogg (1909) considers upper Swaledale as 'remote, rural, communal, not unlike those other narrow valleys, of the Swiss cantons'. Pontefract (1934) describes a similar view: 'This valley is unlike anywhere else in England. The springy turf, made up of innumerable wild flowers, on its meadows reminds one of the lower slopes of Swiss mountains … The grey houses perched on the very edge of the fells have a suggestion of mountain huts about them.'

Since the 1930s, great areas of countryside have been opened up to walkers across Britain as a whole, and this is true no less of Swaledale. The 'discovery' of Swaledale was also greatly assisted by the establishment of the Yorkshire Dales National Park in 1954, as Arthur Raistrick (1967) described:

Walking was also becoming a popular recreational pursuit in its own right, and a number of books appeared which fed this new desire for 'rambling' on foot, particularly in sedate settings like along rivers rather than in the less hospitable fells and hills. Good examples of the early walking guide books include George Radford's *Rambles by Yorkshire Rivers* (1880), which includes a chapter on the Swale, and Thomas Bradley's *Yorkshire Rivers: No. 4, The Swale* (1891), which is devoted to the river.

The very name National Park has brought an incessant stream of weekend motorists to look at it, and the opening of the Pennine Way along its western ridges, along with a rich sprinkling of youth hostels, has encouraged the younger visitors who are taking more interest in the higher fells and moors than the earlier visitors did. A new period of active discovery has started, and has brought with it problems for the dales folk and for the Park Planning Committee, none of which, however, will be incapable of happy solution.

Much has changed since Raistrick wrote this more than four decades ago, including the closure of many of the youth hostels, the establishment of the Coast to Coast Walk (which passes through Swaledale), continued increases in motor traffic, the rise in popularity of mountain biking and other off-road activities, and the greater freedom to roam offered by the Countryside and Rights of Way Act 2000, which allows the public to walk freely on designated areas of mountain, moor, heath, downland and registered common land without having to stick to paths. Such pressures need to be carefully managed if the character of Swaledale – the very thing that attracts visitors in such large numbers – is not to be damaged and changed forever. Hence the need for appropriate conservation and preservation.

popular culture

Through the twentieth century, particularly the latter part, many people have been introduced to the dales in general through the popular writings of people like Arthur Raistrick, whose love of the area and its history shine through books such as *The Pennine Dales* (1968) and *Old Yorkshire Dales* (1967), and Marie Hartley and Joan Ingilby, who have documented the history and traditions of the dales in books such as *A Dales Heritage* (1982) and *Dales Memories* (1986). Other popular writers who have written about their love of the dales, and of Swaledale in particular, include inveterate fell walker Alfred Wainwright, who first visited the dale in 1938 on his *A Pennine Journey* (1986) and later made sure his *Coast to Coast Walk* (1989) went all

the way along it, and vet James Herriot, many of whose stories are set in the dale, about which he writes affectionately in *James Herriot's Yorkshire* (1979).

Swaledale also provided the setting for the 2011 film version of Emily Brontë's *Wuthering Heights*.

WALKING EAST ALONG THE COAST TO COAST PATH OVER LOWNATHWAITE, TOWARDS GUNNERSIDE BECK.

Woodland along the river Swale near Healaugh.

Chapter Four
HISTORY

*Swaledale is not so much a land that time forgot,
as a land that time has been kind to.*

WHILST SWALEDALE DID NOT PLAY a leading role in any of the great events of British history, it nonetheless was affected both directly and indirectly by many of them, which left their mark on its people and places. Swaledale's history is relatively simple – in many ways it is the story of successive waves of invaders, up to and including the Norman period – but it has provided more than enough challenges for those who lived there and tried to make the best out of what nature and their fellow men threw at them.

prehistory

As the climate grew warmer at the end of the last ice age, around 10,000 years ago, the valley glaciers and ice sheets across northern Britain melted, leaving a bare surface which was colonised by small plants, then shrubs, allowing a soil cover to develop. Through time, trees – initially ash and birch, followed by elm, oak and hazel – migrated northwards into the area, creating the deciduous wild wood which soon covered the whole of Britain, remnants of which would eventually become the Forest of Swaledale. The creation of these new habitats, along with continued improvement in climate, encouraged wild animals – particularly red deer, bears, beavers, and wolves – and, in their wake, human hunters, to migrate into the area and settle there.

The first humans appeared in Europe around 40,000 years ago. They could well have walked northwards into Britain (which was joined to mainland Europe by a land-bridge until sea level rose about 8,000 years ago) during relatively warm inter-glacial periods, but would later have been forced back south during each ice age, leaving few if any traces of their existence.

The earliest evidence of human activity in the dales dates back to the Upper Palaeolithic (Old Stone Age) period about 12,000 years ago, when small groups of hunter-gatherers followed the seasonal migration of herds of grazing animals such as deer, which offered a valuable supply of food. They made hand axes by chipping flakes from chunks of flint, which they used to cut down small trees and make clearings in the wild wood. Their lifestyle was nomadic and they roamed over a wide area in search of food, never settling in one place. Their camps were made of rough shelters of branches and leaves.

No Palaeolithic remains have been found in Swaledale, but a flint point has been found in Wensleydale and a barbed harpoon made from antler (dated to 11,000 years ago) was found in Victoria Cave near Settle, farther south.

Through time, the simple technology of the Palaeolithic people adapted and evolved, leading to the Mesolithic (Middle Stone Age) period, between about 8,000 and 10,000 years ago. The birch woodland had by now been naturally replaced by pine, elm, oak and hazel – species better adapted to the prevailing climate and soils. Mesolithic culture remained a nomadic, subsistence-level, hunter-gatherer one.

Around 5,000 to 7,500 years ago temperatures were 2–3 degrees warmer than today, allowing trees to grow to elevations of up to 2,500 ft (covering all of Swaledale and the surrounding area), and peat to form across the exposed fell tops (which helped to preserve evidence of Mesolithic activity).

The Stone Age hunter-gatherers made arrows, saws and spears using thin flakes of flint (microliths) mounted on wooden shafts. This made it much easier to hunt and butcher wild ox and deer. They also shaped animal bones and deer antlers into harpoons and fish-hooks, used fire to drive large animals over cliffs, and made clearings in the forest to attract browsing animals, making them easier to hunt. Groups of flint microliths have been found on the upper slopes and hilltops in Swaledale, often in eroded areas of peat, suggesting the sites of Mesolithic camps.

The Palaeolithic and Mesolithic hunter-gatherer culture was to change in the Neolithic (New Stone Age) period, roughly 3,800 to 4,500 years ago, with the development of a simple form of pastoral farming, based on keeping animals and growing crops. Population levels remained low.

Neolithic people, who had settled on the light soils of the Vale of Mowbray to the east of Swaledale and lived in farming communities there, probably also hunted in the dales during the summer months, like their ancestors. But they also began to herd some of the wild animals they found there, particularly wild oxen and sheep, to provide meat, milk and skins. They still used flint flakes for arrows and harpoons, but made much larger and more effective ones. They also made axeheads

PEAT COVER IN UPPER BIRKDALE, BELOW HIGH PIKE HILL.

out of stone, which allowed them to chop down bigger trees and create larger clearings for fields, making it possible to farm the land – on a seasonal basis, rather than permanently – in small, scattered patches, particularly on the lighter-wooded higher dale sides.

Neolithic flint arrowheads and scrapers have been found in Swaledale, and two Neolithic axeheads have been found at Healaugh. Part of an axehead found near Muker reveals something particularly interesting about the Neolithic settlers – it was made of volcanic ashstone from Langdale in the Lake District, many miles to the north-west. This suggests one of two things – either Neolithic people migrated eastwards from the Lake District and took their tools with them, or there were trade links between Neolithic people on both sides of the Pennines.

The Stone Age gave way to the Bronze Age around 3,800 years ago, as more sophisticated tribes migrated northwards into Swaledale during a period of cool, wet climate. The first arrivals were the so-called Beaker People, named after the distinctive types of pot they made. Like their predecessors these first metal workers also used flint tools, but they developed them and made them much more efficient.

The Bronze Age peoples were the first permanent settlers in the area. They preferred sites high up on the valley sides, where the forest was thinner (thus easier to clear) and they could keep a look out for attacks from other groups and tribes. Traces of Bronze Age settlements – the oldest settlements in the dale – have been found in Swaledale, for example at Arngill Scar by Kisdon Gorge near Muker, and a small stone circle at Harkerside.

Although the first Bronze Age settlers probably subsisted mainly by hunting and fishing, they gradually introduced a primitive form of agriculture based largely on keeping domesticated animals. Elsewhere they cultivated the land and grew grain crops, and while they were challenged in Swaledale by the marshy valley floor and the forested hillsides, the finding of a grindstone near Healaugh points to the growing of some

corn in the dale. The settlers cleared large areas of forest to create fields and settlements, so that by the end of the Bronze Age much of the valley sides and fell tops were open grazing land. From this time onwards, land use in Swaledale has been dominated by grazing on the tops and sides of the hills and cultivation on the valley floor.

The Bronze Age provides the first tangible signs of human impact on the Swaledale landscape. Finds include a number of arrowheads found in many parts of the dale (including near Keld Springs, near Lodge Green, and on the slopes of Calver Hill), three or four flint-tool-making sites and a bronze axe found near Reeth (now on show in York Castle Museum). The surviving evidence includes a few burnt mounds, round barrows (burial cairns) and hut circles.

The impressive earthworks of Maiden Castle on Harkerside near Grinton, one of the largest and most intact prehistoric monuments in the Yorkshire Dales, is believed to date from the Bronze Age. But until it is properly excavated the mystery of its age and purpose, and who built it, persists.

Extensive forest clearance exposed the upland soils to rapid erosion, during a period when rainfall and storminess were both increasing, which led to silting on the valley floor. As a result, the post-glacial lakes gradually filled in and fine sediment was redistributed on the floodplain of the river Swale. Blanket bog and peat deposits formed on the water-logged fell tops around 2,500 years ago, as climate grew colder than it had been for several thousand years, providing ideal conditions for growth of the moorland vegetation that clothes the tops today.

The Bronze Age gave way to the Iron Age, when the ability to make iron (which is much stronger than bronze) from iron ore was developed and the metal was used to make tools and weapons. The population of northern Britain was much larger during the Iron Age than the Bronze Age, and it was divided between groups which were often quite sizeable, well-structured and socially cohesive. The groups occupied independent kingdoms, the largest of which was Brigantia (the land of the Brigantes) which stretched north from the river Trent to the river Tweed. Swaledale lay within this kingdom, and was subject to its rule.

Although archaeologists have identified the sites of Bronze Age field systems and dwellings, few visible signs of them have survived because the sites were usually re-used by later settlers.

The earliest settlers to leave their mark on the dale were the Iron Age people who built scattered farmsteads, typically consisting of open groups of round houses on levelled platforms dug out of the sloping hillside. These small platforms survive at a few places, such as Low Whita and east of Healaugh. During the Iron Age people lived mostly in single farmsteads or small hamlets and they enclosed fields with dry-stone walls. The archaeological evidence suggests that a large number of people lived in Swaledale at this time.

CALVER HILL VIEWED FROM CUCKOO HILL, NEAR REETH.

Recent research by the Swaledale Ancient Land Boundaries Project, led by archaeologist Andrew Fleming and described in his book *Swaledale: the Valley of the Wild River* (2010), has used air photographs and field surveys to reveal fascinating detail of the prehistoric field systems in mid-Swaledale, particularly on the moorland around Calverside. The evidence shows remains of two overlapping sets of 'co-axial' field systems – with parallel stone walls running up to a cross wall – which enclose large areas and were probably laid out in an open, treeless landscape. The earlier system is believed to date from the Late Bronze Age or Early Iron Age, and appears to have been abandoned before the later system was built, probably around 300 BC.

The most complete surviving Iron Age site in Swaledale is in Whitecliffe Wood just upstream from Richmond. The site, which was discovered at the end of the nineteenth century, lies just north of East Applegarth Farm, down the hill from Willance's Leap. It consists of several large square enclosures, believed to have been for cattle, protected by an earth bank to the south and a natural cliff to the north. Excavation has uncovered the remains of a two-roomed stone hut – which probably originally had a roof made of branches and turf – at the entrance to one of the enclosures. The site is believed to have been occupied until around AD 600, well after the Romans had left Britain, making this a Romano-British enclosed settlement.

SITE OF IRON AGE SETTLEMENT, WHITECLIFFE WOOD, LOWER SWALEDALE.

One hallmark of Iron Age society was the construction of embankments and earthwork structures, particularly hill forts of which there are many across Britain, although relatively few have been excavated. Some appear to have had domestic as well as defensive uses, although many show little (if any) evidence of ever having been occupied. Archaeologists are divided over why they were built; some can be associated with tensions between adjacent tribes or social groups, whilst others may have been used as markets or points of social contact, possibly even conspicuous displays of wealth and power.

Iron Age earthworks survive in Swaledale at How Hill near Low Whita Bridge and at Grinton; both are located on glacial moraines which during the Iron Age would have been islands of dry land on the marshy floodplain. There is also a series of large earth embankments running down Harkerside and across the valley on to Fremington Edge near Reeth. Archaeologists think these are defensive structures built by the Brigantes to stop invasion by the Romans, possibly after they had had to fall back after being over-run by the Romans at the hastily built fort at Stanwick near Gilling, just outside Richmond, in about AD 71.

the Roman period

The Roman period (AD 43 to 450) marks the end of prehistory and the start of 'history' by way of its written records. A Roman army led by Julius Caesar had invaded southern England in 55 and 54 BC with the intention of further expanding the Roman Empire, but it was unable to advance across the country as planned because of fierce local resistance. A second, more aggressive attempt was led by Claudius nearly a century later, in AD 43, and this time the invaders were successful. However, strong and well-organised resistance slowed their advance northwards, and the Romans only managed to take control of what is now Yorkshire, in AD 71. As we have seen, the Brigantes built a series of defensive earthworks – in Swaledale at Stanwick and Harkerside – to try to stop the advancing Roman legions, but to no avail. The invaders, well aware of the prospect of counter-attacks, stamped their authority on their newly won territories by building a series of large forts (for example at York) and the imposing masonry wall (approved by and named after Emperor Hadrian) across the north of England between the Solway and the river Tyne.

Despite the aggressive military campaign to conquer England, once the territory was secured – and after Brigantia was incorporated into the Roman province in the late first century – the local Iron Age population and the occupying army appear to have co-existed peacefully in most places, during a period of relative political stability. Most if not all Iron Age settlements continued to be occupied during the Roman period, and the local Celtic population increased production of food and other products to supply their uninvited but needy guests.

Whilst in other parts of England the Romans built villas, estates and towns, they must have visited and crossed Swaledale but had little interest in settling in it: it offered little that they needed or wanted, other than the lead ore deposits around Hurst which they are believed to have worked, possibly using local Brigantes people for slave labour. The terrain was too hilly, swampy and wild to appeal to Roman farmers.

No Roman buildings or settlements have been found in the dale, and no Roman sites have been identified close to Richmond – the natural gateway to the dale – other than the fort at Catterick.

The Romans left their mark on the landscape around Swaledale, particularly after they built Dere Street (which became the Great North Road, now the A1 motorway) as the main artery for moving people and supplies between the fort at York (Eboracum) and Hadrian's Wall to the north – via Stanwick, Durham and Northumberland – and the road across the bleak moors of Stainmore (now the A66) to ease movement across the northern Pennines. They also built a large fort and supply depot at Cataractonium (Catterick) – where Dere Street crossed the river Swale – along with a fort at Bainbridge farther west in Wensleydale, and a camp farther north at Bowes in Teesdale.

It appears that the main activity by the Romans in Swaledale was the movement of soldiers and lead along a rough track leading north from the fort at Bainbridge, over the moors into Swaledale, which went past Maiden Castle and forded the Swale near Feetham, then continued over the moors to the camp at Bowes. It has been suggested that a small group of Roman soldiers might have been stationed at Maiden Castle to guard the route.

Although no buildings or structures of Roman age have been discovered in Swaledale, a series of smaller archaeological finds testify to the presence of Roman people (probably soldiers) in the dale. These include a hoard of 620 silver Roman coins and spoons found in the bank of the river Swale near Richmond Castle in 1724; the discovery of more coins nearby in 1956; a find of fragments of high-quality Roman pottery near Grinton in 1937; the discovery on Fremington Hagg, during the nineteenth century, of some high-quality bronze harnesses from early Roman cavalry horses; and two heavy pigs (ingots) of lead marked with Roman inscriptions which were found in the dale (and are reportedly since lost).

the Anglo-Saxon period

The Roman army gradually withdrew from Britain and it had largely gone by about AD 70. Life initially went on much the same for the inhabitants of Swaledale, but a long period of instability followed.

Over the next 500 years or so (around 550 to 1066), successive waves of invaders swept into the north of what is now England, importing and imposing sweeping changes. First to arrive, from the early fifth to the early seventh centuries, were the Anglo-Saxons. The Anglo-Saxon invaders comprised members of three Germanic tribes – Angels from the Angeln region in Germany (who gave their name to England), Saxons from Lower Saxony (also in Germany), and Jutes probably from the Jutland Peninsula in Denmark.

The invaders came by boat across the North Sea, initially settling along the east coast of England (for example, along the banks of rivers such as the Ouse, Humber and Tees) and then spreading out and quickly overpowering the Britons they encountered. They reached York and Ripon around AD 600, but their advance west met strong resistance. While they won the Battle of Catraeth (believed to be Catterick) in 598, counter-attacks by the local Celtic inhabitants made it difficult for them to advance far into the dales, although they often managed to drive the locals into the more remote uplands.

At the beginning of the tenth century groups of Norsemen – Vikings, also widely referred to as Danes – sailed westwards across the North Sea from Scandinavia. Many settled in Ireland, the Isle of Man and the Lake District, but some migrated east across the Pennines, probably along the Stainmore Gap.

The Vikings settled in the upper parts of Swaledale and Arkengarthdale, where they found a landscape similar to what they had left behind, and here they lived peacefully. They probably met little serious opposition when they arrived in upper Swaledale, which held few attractions for

MIDDLE SWALEDALE LOOKING WEST FROM FEETHAM PASTURE NEAR LOW ROW.

the Anglo-Saxon people already living farther down the dale. Like most of northern and eastern England at the time, Swaledale was subjected to the laws of the Scandinavian settlers – the so-called Danelaw – until the Norman Conquest in 1066.

The Anglo-Saxons established three powerful kingdoms (Northumbria in the north, Mercia in middle England and Wessex in the south), each governed by a king, across what is today Britain. The three kingdoms were eventually united in 927 to create the English nation. Swaledale initially formed part of the kingdom of Deira, which in the early seventh century was annexed by the adjacent kingdom of Bernicia (to the north, between the rivers Tees and Tweed) and formed part of the large and important kingdom of Northumbria.

Gilling West, a few miles north-east of Richmond, was one of the administrative centres of the rulers of the kingdom of Northumbria, centuries before Richmond was established by the Normans. As Jane Hatcher (2004) points out, 'according to tradition it was one of the main bases of the kingdom of Deira with a 'castle' or, more likely, a defended royal residence, presumably consisting of wooden structures, at Castle Hill on Low Scales Farm. Bede tells of the establishment of a monastery at Gilling in AD 651.'

A linear earthwork known as Scots Dyke runs north–south at the eastern end of Swaledale. It crosses the river Swale from the south, at

GUNNERSIDE; VIKING NAME AND SETTLEMENT.

the eastern edge of what is now Richmond, and runs north for around ten miles, at least as far as the Iron Age site of Stanwick. Archaeologists have found it difficult to date precisely, but it is clearly later than the Iron Age fortifications at Stanwick, and in the 1970s a sixth-century spearhead was found near it. It takes the form of an earth bank with a ditch on its eastern side, apparently designed to defend the area behind it to the west. It is believed to be Anglo-Saxon and is thought to have marked the boundary between the Anglian kingdom of Deira to the east, and the more ancient kingdom of Rheged based at Carlisle and the Eden Valley to the west.

The Danes divided Yorkshire into a hierarchy of administrative units, which had an enduring impact. The largest units were the three thridings (an Old Norse word for 'thirds'), which evolved through time into the well-known and much-missed 'Ridings'. The thridings were sub-divided into shires. Each shire covered a group of adjacent valleys and contained a number of wapentakes (equivalent to the 'hundreds' in the south of England), named after the places where their courts met.

Gilling West was a wapentake in the shire of Richmondshire. The unusual word 'wapentake' comes from the Old Norse term for 'weapon-shaking', which is how people indicated agreement at public assemblies. As local historian Jane Hatcher (2004) points out, the name Richmondshire continued to be used for several centuries; it was used less frequently in the nineteenth century but was adopted for the new district created by local government reorganisation in 1974, although historic Richmondshire was much larger than the modern unit, and had different boundaries.

Place names often reveal interesting things about the history of settlements, and this is particularly true of Swaledale. They tell us, for example, that many villages in the dale date back to the Anglo-Saxon period, and must have been occupied continuously since then. They also give valuable clues about who established particular settlements.

Anglo-Saxon and Norse place names

Place name	Origin	Meaning
Angram	Anglo-Saxon	Grazing land
Appletreewick	Anglo-Saxon	Dairy farm by the apple tree
Arkengarthdale	Old Norse	Arnkell's enclosure
Cowgill	Old Norse	Dam in the ravine
Crackpot	Old Norse	Crevice where crows nest
Downholme	Anglo-Saxon	Hill
Easby	Old Norse	Village
Ellerton	Anglo-Saxon	Enclosure or village
Feetham	Old Norse	River meadow
Grinton	Anglo-Saxon	Enclosure round a house
Gunnerside	Old Norse	Gunnar's hill pasture
Healaugh	Anglo-Saxon	High clearing or wood
Hindrelac	Anglo-Viking	Clearing of the hind
Keld	Old Norse	Spring
Langthwaite	Old Norse	Long meadow or clearing
Marrick	Old Norse	Boundary ridge
Muker	Old Norse	Narrow field
Reeth	Anglo-Saxon	Place by the stream
Richmond	Old French	Strong hill
Thwaite	Old Norse	Clearing, enclosed field

Many of the place names in upper Swaledale – such as Keld, Muker and Thwaite – are Old Norse (Viking) in origin, as they are in neighbouring Teesdale and Wensleydale. The common use of other Old Norse words – such as *sætr* (a hill pasture), for example in Ravenseat (Hrafn's sætr) and Gunnerside (Gunnarr's sætr), both named after people, and even

dalr (a valley) – provides ample testimony to the presence of Norsemen in the area, as indeed does the survival of Old Norse terms in the traditional Swaledale dialect.

It is very noticeable that place names change dramatically in the lower part of Swaledale, from Healaugh, Reeth and Grinton eastwards, when they become Anglo-Saxon in origin. For example, names ending in 'tun' or 'ton' (enclosure or village) start to appear, as in Grinton and Ellerton. These place names, and the settlements they were given to, are much older than the Norse names and settlements farther up the dale.

The place names provide clear evidence of the two main phases of settlement in Swaledale during this formative period, and the types of landscape each group preferred to exploit – the Anglo-Saxons chose flatter valley-floor sites, while the Norsemen felt much more at home on the wilder slopes and fells.

Almost all Anglo-Saxon buildings were made of wood, which was freely available in the surrounding forest. Unlike in some parts of southern England, no Anglo-Saxon or Norse domestic or farm buildings have survived in Swaledale; abandoned ones decayed naturally through time or had the wood re-used elsewhere, and others in continuous use were later rebuilt in more durable stone.

The only buildings constructed of stone by the Anglo-Saxons were monasteries and churches. They built no monasteries in Swaledale, and just a trace of a church building of this age is to be found in the fabric of St Andrew's Church at Grinton, though even that was modified a great deal in subsequent times.

In Swaledale, as in many parts of the north and west of England, the settlers created small hamlets and isolated farmsteads, as well as villages, often in small clearings in the natural forest that still clothed much of the land, particularly on the valley floor and fellsides. As we have seen, the place-name evidence indicates that most settlements in the upper dale

GRINTON BRIDGE OVER THE RIVER SWALE.

WESTFIELD, RICHMOND; FORMERLY PART OF THE MEDIEVAL OPEN FIELD SYSTEM, NOW ALLOTMENTS.

were Norse in origin, while most in the lower dale were Anglo-Saxon. The character and age of the settlements greatly vary between the two areas.

Both groups settled in Swaledale when climate was better than it had been since the end of the ice age (and has been since), during the so-called Medieval Climatic Optimum. The Medieval Warm Period, which lasted from about AD 750 to 1200, saw warm conditions across Europe, reducing the amount of ice in the North Sea as far north as Iceland, and making it possible for the Norse seafarers to sail across a much wider area. Climate was warm enough to allow vines to be grown across much of southern England and crops across most of northern England, even in the valleys and dales of the Pennines.

The Danes had much less of a communal lifestyle than their Anglo-Saxon neighbours, and this is reflected in the types of settlement they built at the end of the tenth century. Almost all of the settlements in upper Swaledale west of Feetham were isolated farmsteads and scattered

hamlets, with buildings on the fellsides running parallel to the contours and facing across the valley, and hamlets strung out along a trackway or road. This is typical of Norse settlements elsewhere. The three exceptions to this general pattern are the villages of Keld, Thwaite, and Muker, each composed of small stone buildings huddled tightly together.

The Anglo-Saxons first settled in the lower part of Swaledale in about the eighth century, preferring to live in communal groups in family farmsteads. As population expanded, three significant changes occurred. First, the family farmsteads usually grew into small hamlets, some of which continued to develop into small villages. Each family would have a small cottage (toft), a few adjoining farm buildings, and a small field (croft) stretching back from the road. Individual homesteads were often grouped around an area where cattle could be kept safely; this would later become the village green (such as the one which has survived in Reeth). Second, increasingly large areas of woodland were cleared to create arable land, along with drainage of marshy floodplain land. Third, the Anglo-Saxon settlers brought with them a co-operative open field system of farming, in which grazing rights for sheep and cows and parcels of arable land were shared between members of the village community. They typically chose sunny south-facing sites on dry slopes above the valley floor (which flooded regularly) – the most striking exception is Grinton, on the colder north-facing side of the valley – often where a tributary joined the main river. Such sites were often at or near pre-existing river-crossing places, usually shallow fords; stone bridges were subsequently built at many such sites.

The Norse men may have started out as warriors, but once settled they laid down their arms and reverted to traditional lifestyles of pastoral farming and hunting. They made clearings among the trees where they could graze their cattle and sheep and build scattered farmsteads and longhouses. In summer they moved their sheep and cattle to summer pastures (shielings) on the fells, establishing the seasonal pattern of stock grazing (transhumance) which survives today.

The Anglo-Saxon settlers continued a tradition of arable farming along the dales, reserving the higher, less productive ground of the valley sides for woodland and grazing. Around a typical village there would be two or three open arable fields with appropriate names, most commonly Eastfield, Westfield and Southfield.

The land associated with each village was held in common, and it was important that the precious land resource was used sustainably, so it was apportioned out amongst eligible villagers (commoners) in a care-fully controlled way. There were typically three zones of land in each village. Low-lying land near the river provided the meadows (ings), which were fenced off, divided between commoners, and mown for hay. Around the village were arable open fields, which were fenced against livestock while crops were growing, but livestock was allowed to graze freely on them after harvest time. On the higher ground of the village, usually above the open fields, were the common pastures, which were 'stinted' (limited to an agreed number of animals) to avoid

over-use. Any commoner found guilty of overstocking and thus using more than their fair share of the common pasture – or any use of the pasture by outsiders, which was strictly forbidden – was punished by the manorial court.

Typically, each family was granted the amount of arable land (as strips in the large open fields) that a man could cultivate in a year with a full team of eight oxen (a unit known as a 'hide'; the precise area depended on the character of the land in question), along with a proportionate

MEDIEVAL LYNCHETS NEAR MARSKE, LOWER SWALEDALE, VIEWED FROM WEST APPLEGARTH.

43

amount of pasture, meadow and common grazing land. An unfree villager, known as a 'gebur', was granted only a quarter of a hide (a 'carucate') and a pair of oxen, one cow and six sheep. A man with only one ox held an eighth of a hide (a 'bovate' or 'oxgang', usually the size of one strip), and the cottar – the lowest of the low – was granted about 5 acres (24,200 square yards) but allowed no oxen, so he had to till his plot manually, using a spade and hoe.

The strips of arable land in the open fields were used to grow crops, rotating over a three-year period between wheat or rye (used to make bread), barley (for brewing ale, more widely drunk than water), and left fallow – spread with animal manure and grazed by stock all winter, to help restore soil fertility. Oats, peas or beans might sometimes be sown in the wheat or barley field, to provide winter fodder.

Over many generations of ploughing with teams of oxen, which had to plough along the strips in the open fields, flat terraces of soil called lynchets developed on sloping sites as the soil was always turned by the plough in the same direction – downhill. Lynchets have survived on south-facing slopes in many parts of the dales; good examples in Swaledale are clearly visible to the north-west of Reeth, and farther down the dale at Marrick, Marske and Downholme.

The upper part of Swaledale, west of Reeth, still had large expanses of forest cover during Anglo-Saxon times, and it is known that wild deer, bears, boars and wolves roamed freely across the area. The chieftains paid game wardens to live in the forest and protect the game from poachers. Anglo-Saxon and Danish chieftains hunted game in this forest and the adjacent moorland in upper Swaledale and Arkengarthdale, which was designated a 'chase' or 'deer forest', even though there were scattered groups of people (descendents of Iron Age settlers and more recent Danish settlers) living there.

the medieval period

The middle of the eleventh century was a turbulent time in English history. By then England had, at least in theory, been a united country for more than a century, although struggles had continued between the Saxons and Danes over that whole period. A greater sense of unity came when Harold Godwinson, Earl of Wessex and the largest land owner in the country, was elected king in 1066, although William, Duke of Normandy, contested his claim to the throne. Months later, after Harold was killed and his army defeated at the Battle of Hastings, William was crowned King of England in Westminster Abbey on Christmas Day 1066.

The Normans were the last group to invade Swaledale and impose their values and practices upon the people of the area. The initial phase of the Norman Conquest was swift and decisive. William quickly seized control of the south of England, but he faced stiff resistance in the north, which he crushed in a heavy and cruel show of strength. Opposition was strongest in the Anglo-Saxon kingdom of Northumbria, where in 1067 the people of York revolted against William. His response was to build a defensive castle at York, but in 1068 that was over-run by local rebels – the freedom fighters of their day. Local resistance was determined and persistent; the following summer (1069) the Norman garrison in York was attacked and slaughtered, and the city plundered, by Danish invaders with local support. William's patience ran out, and between 1069 and 1070 he marched north with his army and launched a brutal scorched earth campaign designed to put an end to the opposition, which was centred on the area between York and Durham.

King William's campaign to subdue the north of his kingdom – generally referred to as the Harrying of the North – was short but devastating.

RICHMOND CASTLE, HIGH ABOVE THE RIVER SWALE, VIEWED FROM EARLS ORCHARD LOOKING NORTH.

RICHMOND OUTDOOR MARKET IN MARKET PLACE.

All houses, crops, grain, cattle and food were burned, thousands of people were killed or starved to death, and famine and pestilence quickly spread across a wide area. After William had brutally put down the northern rebellion, the Norman Conquest was complete. But his campaign left deep and enduring scars on the people and places. The land between York and Durham was almost uninhabited for many years, and Swaledale became an unproductive backwater for at least two decades.

William clearly needed to establish his power over the people, particularly in the north where his authority would be challenged by rebellious native tribes and marauding Scots. His solution was to quickly establish strong defensive bases, and he ordered castles to be built in key places such as Skipton, Richmond and Barnard Castle.

With England and Normandy united in a shared aristocracy, William was able to impose Norman ideas and practices on his new territory, particularly through the introduction of the feudal system which he imported from France. The process of Normanisation spread sweeping social and economic change across England, which the Anglo-Saxons had little option but to adapt to.

The most significant element of the new feudal system was the introduction of a new unified mode of land control, in which King William confiscated and claimed ownership of all land throughout his kingdom. He kept about a quarter of the land as his private property, gave some to the church, and allocated the rest to others in return for loyal support, money (through taxes) and service, which usually meant supplying him with knights for his army in times of war. The clear losers were the existing land owners, who at a stroke had lost all of their rights, property and income – little wonder they resisted the new regime. The greatest beneficiaries were the favoured few – William's most loyal and trusted supporters, typically the 29 noblemen and countrymen who had helped him in subduing the English, during and after the invasion – to whom he granted large estates.

The noblemen granted land in their large estates to their knights (lower lords), who held it as tenants in exchange for serving as vassals (retainers or loyal servants) and providing protection and military service when required. At the bottom of the feudal hierarchy sat the cottars (also known as villeins), the free serfs or peasants who worked the land they were allocated by the knights, to whom they provided food and services when required. The peasant owned no land, had few rights, and lived in tiny hovels.

One of William's staunchest supporters was Count Alan Rufus of Brittany – a second cousin who had fought with him during the conquest – who would be useful in protecting against possible insurrection in the north and invasion from Scotland. In 1086 William made Alan Earl of Richmond and granted him a huge area of land which had been confiscated from the Saxon Earl Edwin of Mercia.

Alan's vast estate – one of the largest land holdings in the country, known as the Honour of Richmond – stretched eastwards from the Pennines, including all of the North Riding of Yorkshire along with land in Suffolk. It comprised 440 manors in various parts of England, including 199 in Yorkshire, 164 of which made up Richmondshire.

Under the feudal system, Alan gave portions of his territory to his Breton Knights (military experts), in return for them supporting him with military service in times of war.

William Longstaffe (1852) explains how the Honour of Richmond consisted of 'fees' (holdings), each of which had to provide Alan with a knight, which created a means of staffing his castle. Each knight had to provide 'castle guard' for 40 days a year, and he would bring his own equipment for the task (horse, armour and weapons, and support staff) in return for the land he held.

In 1071 Alan established his northern base at what is today Richmond, building a stone castle there on an easily defendable hilltop site which gave its name to the new castle and the settlement which grew up around it. Richmond Castle is unusual in two ways. It was one of the first in England to be built of stone: most Norman castles were built of wood and earth, at least initially. In Richmond the defensive curtain walls were built first, and the imposing keep or tower was added a century later. Secondly, most Norman castles were built in existing towns to protect them, but there is no strong evidence of any existing settlement on the Richmond site, which was probably chosen for strategic reasons.

We will look in detail at the birth and development of Richmond in Chapter Eleven, but two particular features of this period are worth noting here. First, during the fourteenth century the Yorkshire Dales were subject to periodic raids by the Scots, and Swaledale was not spared; for example, Marrick Priory was attacked in 1318 and Ellerton Priory lost its charters and historic documents in a raid in 1347. As Richmond developed in front of Alan's castle, it became a target for Scottish raids, and so in 1311 a town wall was built around the outer bailey (courtyard) for added protection. Second, over the following century, Richmond increased in size and status, grew into an important regional centre, and became a chartered borough in 1441 when King Henry IV granted the town a royal charter to hold a Saturday market, which has been held ever since.

At the outset of his reign, William needed reliable information on the size, ownership and resources of each hide (unit) of land, to ensure that he received all of the taxes and revenues he believed he was entitled to, so in 1086 he ordered a survey of all the property in his kingdom. This Domesday (Day of Judgment) survey was effectively the first national census.

The survey was carried out by inspectors working for the king, who visited most parts of England (except for the far north – Northumberland, Cumberland, Westmorland and Durham) on horseback, recording what they found in places as they travelled around. The size of each estate or land holding was measured in carucates – one carucate being the amount of land (roughly 120 acres) that could be tilled in one year using one plough and a team of eight oxen, thus continuing the Anglo-Saxon basis for apportioning land. The results were published in the *Domesday Book*, which provides historians with unprecedented detail of land use and ownership at this important point in time.

Richmundeseire (Richmondshire) appears in the survey as part of the kingdom of Northumbria. We know what route the inspectors took by the order in which they recorded their findings. Arriving in Swaledale from the east, they travelled via Catrice (Catterick) to Tonestalle (Tunstall) and on to Colborne (Colburn); they then rode through Hipleswell (Hipswell), and Hindrelac (unknown, though possibly Richmond), and on to Dune (Downholme). It looks like the intrepid surveyors didn't venture far up Swaledale, because the book mentions no places higher than Reeth and Grinton.

Like many settlements in the north-east of England, both Reeth and Grinton were described in the survey as 'waste'. As Cooper (1948) points out, this 'probably meant that there were no oxen for the plough and little or no livestock, but does not indicate that there were no inhabitants'. Some writers are quick to explain the large amount of 'waste' as the direct result of the Harrying of the North campaign – Harry Speight, for example, explains (1897) how 108 of the manors in the Honour of Richmond were recorded as 'waste', 'showing what fire, slaughter and famine had done in places where only a little time before all had been fruitful and prosperous'. But while 'waste' is generally taken to mean land with little productive value, therefore not capable of returning taxes, there are at least two other plausible explanations for recording the land as 'waste'. Some land was

THWAITE AND KISDON HILL.

probably genuinely unused or unproductive. On the other hand, the landowners may have been trying to hide their assets from the inspectors in order to reduce their tax liability.

Many of the features of land use during the Anglo-Saxon period were continued through the medieval period, so the landscape of Swaledale beyond Richmond (whose origins as a castle, market and town date to this time) remained much the same.

The Normans were great hunters, and they introduced fallow deer into England. But there was also good hunting to be had in the deer forest of upper Swaledale, which their Anglo-Saxon predecessors had established. Under Alan Rufus much of the dale was managed as hunting ground, for the exclusive enjoyment of his wealthy and powerful friends.

Arable farming under the open field system was continued on the south-facing slopes in lower Swaledale, evidenced in the surviving areas of lynchets around Reeth and Marske. A warm period during the thirteenth century allowed the conversion of some areas of moorland to cropland, pushing the frontier of cultivation farther up the valley side, which in turn encouraged an increase in the local population and the expansion of the existing network of small hamlets and villages.

The Church became a major land owner in Swaledale during medieval times, as wealthy families granted land to Rievaulx Abbey and Bridlington Priory for the care of their souls. Much of the monastic land was open moorland best suited for grazing sheep. The two small religious houses established in lower Swaledale – Marrick Priory and Ellerton Priory – had much smaller land holdings.

Lead mining in Swaledale dates back at least as far as Roman times. Although it remained relatively small-scale and localised until the period of major expansion in the eighteenth century, there are records that in the twelfth century, lead from Swaledale was ordered to roof the Tower of London, Dover Castle and Jervaulx Abbey.

The Norman period was also to see the construction and improvement of many roads and bridges, which in a relatively inaccessible place like Swaledale helped to ease the movement of people and goods in and out of (and through) the dale. This helped, and was helped, by the development of Richmond as an important market town and gateway to the dale.

On Alan Rufus's death in 1089, his title Earl of Richmond and his vast land holdings passed to his brother Count Stephen, who lived until 1136. But Stephen granted the whole of Swaledale to his daughter, Maud, on her marriage to Walter de Gant (1092–1139), a Norman knight. This marriage gift created the manor of Healaugh, which included a manor house at Healaugh, meadows, pastures and forest.

The Gant (or Gaunt) family owned the manor of Healaugh for several centuries, during which the land was managed according to the feudal system; most of the hands-on farming work was done by the peasants (cottars) who gave service to the lord of the manor in return for the use of a smallholding of arable land and a cottage (toft). Through time, the de Gant family gave large portions of the manor of Healaugh to the Church. Such actions were common in those days, as families were eager to sponsor prayers for the safe rest of their souls in perpetuity. In Swaledale the process began around 1125 when Walter's wife, Maud, gave the church of St Andrew in Swaledale with Grinton and all its vicinity to the Augustinian priory at Bridlington, which Walter had founded in 1113.

After the Norman Conquest, monks from a variety of religious orders that had established monasteries throughout Europe spread across England, building monasteries using styles and construction techniques they brought with them. Swaledale was affected both directly and indirectly by this monastic revival (which was a hallmark of the Norman period) – directly through the building of religious houses within the dale and indirectly through the ownership of land by monasteries based elsewhere in North Yorkshire.

49

By the middle of the thirteenth century most if not all of upper Swaledale was owned and controlled by two religious orders, Bridlington Priory and Rievaulx Abbey, the land having been donated to them by Alan Rufus and his successors. Both orders had a direct impact on the landscape and economy of the dale, through the exploitation of local mineral resources (including lead in Swaledale) and more importantly through the large sheep-grazing farms (granges) they established on the open moorland, which helped promote early prosperity for Richmond as a centre for the wool trade in north-east England. Records from the early fourteenth century indicate that there were at least 5,000 monastic sheep within easy reach of Richmond. Bridlington Priory held the town and church of Grinton near Reeth. Muker was held by the monks of Rievaulx Abbey near Helmsley on the North York Moors, which was founded in 1132 as the first Cistercian abbey in the north.

Much smaller areas in the lower dale were held by the lesser religious houses built there over the same period. The Benedictines (known as Black Canons after the colour of their habits), the oldest monastic order, built the first monastery in Swaledale in about 1100. Small parts of St Martin's Priory across the river from Richmond Castle survive on private land, most notably the fifteenth-century gateway tower. In 1151 the Premonstratensian White Canons founded the Abbey of St Agatha at Easby – generally known as Easby Abbey – a short distance downstream from St Martin's, on the opposite bank of the river Swale about a mile below Richmond. The extensive ruins of Easby Abbey, which are open to the public, are located in a picturesque site by the river. Next came Marrick Priory, built in about 1154 for black-robed Benedictine nuns and lay sisters, farther up the dale towards Grinton. Last to be established, some time between 1150 and 1227, was Ellerton Priory on the opposite side of the Swale to Marrick, which housed white-robed Cistercian nuns. Over a century later, in 1258, a Franciscan friary was established (for Grey Friars) just outside the town wall of Richmond. The monasteries continued to have a strong impact on the landscape and economy for four centuries, until their dissolution (1536–41) when the Crown confiscated their estates and either sold them or granted them to loyal supporters.

PLAGUE MARKER STONE IN RICHMOND PARISH CHURCHYARD.

The first outbreak of plague – the Black Death – swept across England, starting in the south in the summer of 1248 but quickly spreading and reaching the north the following summer. It was highly contagious and deadly, and at the time there were no known cures or ways of preventing the spread. It is believed to have killed up to a quarter of the population of England, and affected the economy – particularly farming and trade – for generations. The plague did not discriminate amongst its victims; the secluded life of a monastery offered no real protection against it, and it claimed the lives of many monks and nuns, sapping the strength and weakening the stability of many religious institutions. Many people died in villages and towns. Some villages and hamlets lost their entire population, and were effectively wiped out. Crops were left to rot in the fields and livestock had to fend for itself as more and more peasant farmers succumbed to the deadly plague. Details of the losses in Swaledale are scant, but there is no doubt that it claimed the lives of many people.

Whilst the impact of the plague was devastating, widespread and long-lasting, there was one silver lining to the cloud for many of the survivors. With a serious shortage of people left to work the land, the peasants who had previously been compelled to work for free, in exchange for the right to farm their small plots of land, were now able to demand payment for their services. This in turn allowed them to rent their modest cottages and allotments, and through time a system of tenants' rights (of which they had previously had none) evolved. Mobility for peasant workers increased, as they could now move to seek higher wages elsewhere. In some areas the shortage of farm labour also led to changes in land use, as land that had previously been farmed was converted to pasture, which was much less labour-intensive. In an area like Swaledale, which by then already had a well-established wool industry, this would have benefitted the local economy.

the Tudor and Stuart periods

As always, Swaledale was exposed to and affected by the political, social and economic changes which ran through the whole of England at this time, and these left their mark on the landscape. From the sixteenth century onwards, the early enclosure movement saw the consolidation of strips in the open fields, the extension of dry-stone walls to mark new field boundaries, and the construction of the first stone field barns.

By the late sixteenth century, upkeep of the more important bridges along the dale had passed from the village to (the equivalent of) the county, although local districts were responsible for meeting the costs of building and repairing bridges. For example, a new stone bridge over the river Swale was built in about 1575, probably replacing an original wooden one. Districts were also responsible for keeping the highways in a good state. In *A History of Swaledale*, Cooper (1973) reports that in 1609 'all the inhabitants of Grinton were charged for not repairing the highway between Whitaside and Richmond'.

Peace in upper Swaledale continued to be overshadowed by the risk of raids, attack or invasion by marauding groups of Scots – with the border only 50 miles to the north – before the Act of Union between Scotland and England was passed in 1707.

On more than one occasion groups of so-called Moss-troopers (or rievers) – 'clans of robbers who had their lairs in the Northumberland dales and fells', according to Cooper (1948) – rode over Stainmore and into the dale via Tan Hill and West Stonesdale, and attacked the shepherds and peasant farmers, stole their cattle, kidnapped their womenfolk and demanded money with menaces.

The defining feature of Tudor England, certainly as far as Swaledale was concerned, was the dissolution of the monasteries, which had significant and lasting impact on people and places in the dale, as elsewhere across the kingdom. The move, which began in 1529, was driven primarily by Henry VIII's determination to replace the pope as head of the Church in England. His plan was to close the religious houses which were important centres of papal influence and had grown rich and powerful (partly through gifts of property and smart farming and business practices). The prospect of seizing the monastic revenues and estates would also have held great appeal to a king who had lavish taste and great political ambition.

After Henry broke with Rome in 1536–37, he acted quickly to confiscate the monasteries and their lands. A small number of abbey churches located near large towns survived as cathedrals or parish churches, such as Canterbury Cathedral, Durham Cathedral and Westminster Abbey.

But all other abbeys and monasteries throughout the country were closed, often quickly, and typically with great intolerance.

Many of the abandoned monastery buildings were demolished, or robbed of stone by local people as a convenient source of building material. During the dissolution, Ian Dewhirst (1975) describes how in a typical monastery, 'lead from the roofs was melted down on the spot; stained-glass windows were smashed for the sake of even their meagre lead. Woodwork was chopped up for lighting fires, or rotted exposed to the elements. Stone was carted away for rebuilding … Pictures were destroyed, plate [sic] sold, stolen or lost.'

In Swaledale, St Martin's Priory, Easby Abbey, Marrick Priory, Ellerton Priory and Richmond Friary were closed, and, with the exception of Marrick, now lie in ruins. Their residents were pensioned off and forced to live elsewhere and their lay workers were made redundant. Jane Hatcher writes (2004): 'The effects of the dissolution must have been felt both severely and instantly in Richmond. The familiar figures in their black, white and grey habits were now absent from the streets of the town, and with them had gone not only the money spent for them and their guests and corrodians [pensioners], but also the purchasing power of their staff, who had lost their jobs.'

The charitable work that the religious houses undertook and many locals had come to rely on – including helping the sick and the poor, providing hospitality to travellers and education for local people, as well as holding church services and offering spiritual guidance – ceased immediately.

But the losses were not just personal and spiritual, because by this time the great monastic estates – particularly Bridlington and Rievaulx in the case of Swaledale – had a significant impact on the local economy, land use and landscape. When they were closed down, their land was

RUINS OF EASBY ABBEY, TWO MILES SOUTH OF RICHMOND.

given to loyal supporters or sold to speculators and tenants, often relatively very cheaply because so much became available so quickly. Over time, ownership of much of the land in Swaledale passed into private hands, including individual freeholding farmers as well as the great estate owners. What had previously been common land was taken over by individual land owners, and from the early sixteenth century the traditional pattern of communal farming declined. The new land owners built stone farmhouses on their new holdings, creating the mosaic of relatively small farms that we see today spread across the dale.

The break up of the monastic estates also stimulated other economic activities in the dale, particularly the development of the lead-mining industry, as speculators and absentee landlords ploughed money into expanding existing mines, exploring for new veins, and trying different methods of extracting and processing the ores to maximise yields and profits.

Henry's attack on the power of Rome and the Catholic Church had popular support, but not in the North. A rebellion against the dissolution, known as the Pilgrimage of Grace (or the Yorkshire Revolt), was led by Robert Aske, a London lawyer with roots in the north. It began in Lincolnshire on 1 October 1536 and spread quickly to the East Riding and York.

By 11 October the Pilgrimage of Grace had reached Wensleydale, and within days the whole of Richmondshire, particularly the people of Richmond, had got involved and were ready to fight for their cause. Aske and his fellow pilgrims were demanding that the monasteries be re-opened and the pope be restored as head of the Church, and objecting to the high rents and taxes that the poor had to pay. The tipping point came, as Jane Hatcher (2004) explains, after 'the rebels ... reinstated Abbot Robert Bampton and all or some of his canons into the

GABLE END OF BLACKBURN HALL, GRINTON.

53

partially-dismantled [Easby] abbey buildings, and stayed there until early in 1537.' Instructing Thomas Howard, Duke of Norfolk and commander of the royal army, to crush the rebellion, Henry ordered 'such dreadful execution to be done upon a good number of these habitants of every town and village that hath offended in this rebellion as well by the hanging of them upon trees as by the quartering of them and the setting up of their heads and quarters in every town great and small without pity or respect'. (quoted in Ian Dewhirst, 1975) Henry particularly wanted to make examples of the ringleaders, and in late January 1537 216 rebels and sympathisers were executed for treason, including Robert Aske, the Prior of Bridlington and the Abbots of Fountains, Rievaulx and Jervaulx.

Henry's merciless response to the Pilgrimage of Grace, based as it was on swift retribution and the brutal crushing of dissent, sits alongside his predecessor William's Harrying of the North as probably the darkest days in the history of Swaledale.

Despite the problems caused by the dissolution of the monasteries, one positive development in the religious life of Swaledale during this time was the building in 1580 of a parish church and burial ground at Muker, which put an end to the need for funeral processions to walk from the head of the dale across the fells and along the valley bottom to the long-established parish church at Grinton, along the Corpse Way. 'In 1550,' writes W. G. Hoskins (1970), 'most English people were still living in the rather dark, squalid and cramped dwellings of their medieval forefathers. These were generally two-roomed houses – a hall and a bower – built of a timber frame with walls of reinforced mud [wattle and daub], the whole raised upon a rubble foundation. There were no glazed windows, and only one fireplace. The two rooms were not ceiled over, but were open to the rafters and the thatch of the roof.'

The most visible impact on the Swaledale landscape during the Stuart period was what Hoskins called the Great Rebuilding, referring to the replacement or rebuilding (and often the enlargement) in stone of many farmhouses and dwellings in villages and towns which had originally been timber-framed. This movement occurred later in the north than in the south of England, often starting in the late 1600s rather than around the 1620s – dates are preserved carved in stone lintels over front doors; for example, one house in Grinton is dated 1665, and one in Gunnerside is dated 1690 – and stretching into Georgian times. It reflected greater prosperity, confidence and a growing desire to show off; in Swaledale this had come through improvements in agriculture and expansion of the lead industry. Few structures or buildings in the dale pre-date this period.

During this same period, many large medieval houses – originally built in stone, but now often occupied by successful merchants and yeomen (owners of small estates) rather than lords – were also modernised. This was done, for example, by building more rooms for particular purposes – often converting large halls into two stories by adding a staircase – and adding more fireplaces and windows, which could now be glazed. The only surviving Tudor house in Swaledale is Blackburn Hall in Grinton, but Walburn Hall near Downholme is a striking example located right on the southern edge of the dale.

the Georgian and Victorian periods

The growing prosperity that fuelled the early stages of the Great Rebuilding in Swaledale during the late seventeenth century continued into the Georgian period, and it left its mark on the landscape in the form of new or re-fashioned stone buildings. Many of the stone farmhouses in the dale date to this period, as do many of the surviving dry-stone field barns. During the Georgian period many of the houses in and around the centre of Richmond were remodelled in fashionable Georgian styles, leaving a legacy which has helped to create the Richmond we know today.

Of course not everyone in the dale was able to enjoy the fruits of this new prosperity. Indeed, much of the wealth that went to the land owners was won by the hard graft of the working men, both on the farm and in the lead mines which were developing quickly over the eighteenth century. At this end of the socio-economic spectrum things were very different.

Regarding the small, cramped and basic houses of the eighteenth-century lead miners, many of which have survived around Gunnerside, Richard Muir (1998) explains: 'These were mainly of a kind known as 'firehouses', with a fireplace at the gable end of the living room which was served by an external chimney. Originally single-storey thatched dwellings, many were improved by removing the thatch, adding new courses of stonework to the walls to make an upper storey and making a new, shallow-pitched roof of stone slabs.'

The late eighteenth century was also to see a growing interest in agricultural improvement, as part of a nationwide determination to increase yields and output by bringing previously unproductive land into productive use, and applying modern farming techniques to existing farmland. Arthur Young writes in 1771: 'The country [of Swaledale] is mountainous, and full of lead-mines … the vales [sic] are all grass enclosures, rich and let very high … The soil is in general a rich loam and a red gravel … Their stock is chiefly cows, and horses to carry lead … Their flocks of sheep rise as high as 500, by means of turning on the moors … They are all employed either in the lead mines or in knitting.'

Since Norman times the Church, initially through the monastic houses and the parish church in Grinton, had helped to shape both the people and the landscape of Swaledale. Things were to change after the so-called English Reformation during the reign of Henry VIII in the sixteenth century, with the dissolution of the monasteries and the creation of the Church of England.

In Swaledale, as in many parts of England, many families kept their faith and were unwilling to change to the new national church, and this continued over many generations. Roman Catholics who refused to attend the services of the Church of England and pay their tithes or taxes to it, as required by law, were termed recusants. Punishments for recusancy included fines, confiscation of property, and imprisonment.

An important religious trend in seventeenth-century Swaledale was the rise of Nonconformism, membership of a Protestant church which dissents from the established Church of England. Indeed, through a combination of its seclusion and relative remoteness, coupled with the strongly independent character of the dales people, upper Swaledale was to become a Nonconformist stronghold. As Harry Speight (1897) puts it, 'Nonconformity obtained a firm footing', particularly around Low Row. After 1670 the Quakers had many followers in the dale, and they built meeting houses in Healaugh, Smarber and Low Row and a school in Reeth. The Independents or Congregationalists also attracted followers, encouraged by Lord Wharton who in 1691 established a meeting house next to his shooting lodge at Smarber Hall (which was later transferred to Low Row). Chapels were later built at Reeth (1783), Keld (1789), Low Row (1809), and Thwaite (1863).

Methodism also took root in the dale after the first of John Wesley's visits in 1761. A house at Blades, above Low Row, was converted into a chapel, services were held in houses at Low Row and Bible-study classes in cottages and farmhouses, and chapels were later built in Keld (1841) and Muker (1845). Wesley's message appealed to the hard-working miners and farmers of upper Swaledale, who turned to Methodism in large numbers.

As Nonconformity took hold in Swaledale, and with many Catholics refusing to change faith, the number of people regularly attending Anglican church services remained stubbornly low. This reflected class differences as well as theological differences because those who attended church were mostly professional middle class and those who went to (Methodist) chapel were working class.

It also reflected geography, as Cooper (1973) explains: 'Before the dissolution of the monasteries, there was a chapel at Keld, mentioned

CARVED DATE STONE (1687) INCORPORATED INTO A STONE BARN NEAR KELD, ORIGINALLY THE LINTEL OVER THE DOOR OF A HOUSE.

REETH WESLEYAN CHAPEL.

by Leland in 1530. It was closed following a riot by inhabitants, which has never been fully explained ... [and] fell into ruins. The nearest place of worship was at Muker, and people living at the head of Swaledale had no church of their own for many a year.'

Keld Chapel had been derelict since 1706 but in 1791, after preaching in barns, farmhouses and miners' cottages, itinerant preacher Edward Stillman was asked by the people of Keld to settle there, which he did. The villagers rebuilt the chapel and added a small school room and a living room for the minister, much of the work paid for by money collected by Stillman on a walk from Keld to London and back.

The two dominant but inter-related themes of Victorian Swaledale are poverty and depopulation; these were Swaledale's darkest days, and like the other trends outlined above they left marks on the landscape of the dale. Most people living in Swaledale during the early nineteenth century had little to their name; they lived in over-crowded cottages with few facilities, survived on very low incomes, had meagre possessions, and typically had little chance of raising their prospects. The Poor Law Amendment Act of 1834 was designed to make life in a workhouse (where many paupers as well as the elderly, the infirm and children were given food and shelter) less attractive than working in the fields and factories. Life was hard, and expectations were low.

56

Edmund Cooper (1973) underlines the hardships endured by women and children in the parish of Marrick in 1843: about a third of the women chose to work outdoors, pulling turnips (October to February), weeding (March to June) and haymaking (July to September); some worked at washing lead ore; and those who worked indoors knitted stockings and frocks. He notes that 'some families were granted allotments of a quarter to half an acre rent-free. These were dug usually by women and children, and were well cultivated … Benefit or clothing clubs were encouraged and were on the increase.' Children worked from the age of nine, the boys accompanying their fathers to the lead mines or working on farms, and the girls usually knitted.

Life was hard at the best of times for most people living in Swaledale in the nineteenth century, but things were to get much worse with the collapse of the lead-mining industry after about 1850. All of the dales suffered from population decline, but the loss was particularly large and serious in Swaledale.

Census returns show that the population of the dale (excluding Richmond) reached a peak of 8,279 in 1821, then declined gradually but fell by half between 1871 and 1891, and by 1901 it was down to 3,061. The decline was most dramatic in Arkengarthdale (centre of the lead-mining industry), where the population fell from 1,500 in the nineteenth century to around 300 today. Families left the area in search of employment elsewhere, having no regular income and little prospect of being able to buy some land and become self-sufficient. They abandoned their small, simple cottages, most of which remained neglected until the mid-twentieth century, when many were converted and restored as holiday cottages. Many of those who moved away were drawn to the industrial towns along the north-east coast or the cotton towns of east Lancashire across the Pennines, where the women worked in the cotton mills and the men worked in the coal mines. Some fled England altogether, crossing the Atlantic from Liverpool to North America, where many settled in the lead-mining areas of Iowa, Illinois and Wisconsin.

The other major change in Swaledale during the Victorian period was the arrival of the railway at Richmond in 1846, which made it easier for people to get to Richmond from the north-east and beyond, and provided an important means for the transport of freight, particularly lead and cattle. *Black's Picturesque Guide to Yorkshire* (1874) expresses the hope that 'the branch of railway, by which it is connected with the great central line, will perhaps give an impulse to its commerce', but the hope appears not to have been fully realised. Several proposed schemes to extend the railway up the dale during the nineteenth century came to naught.

the Modern period

Through the twentieth century Swaledale survived as a relatively unspoiled rural area, sheltered by its remote location and lack of commercially viable natural resources from the waves of industrialisation and development that have so visibly altered the landscape of much of the rest of the country. The economy of the dale still relies heavily on agriculture, but hill-farming in such a marginal upland environment is a precarious business these days that relies heavily on government grants, paid partly to ensure that hill farmers continue their traditional role of guardians of the landscape. Moorland management is designed to protect the landscape and wildlife, but is directed primarily towards optimising yields and returns for those who own the commercial shooting rights.

The rise of tourism in Swaledale is a hallmark of the twentieth century. Bill Mitchell (1990) looks back to the 1950s and '60s with fond memories, because 'those were the days when the native population [in the dales] was predominant. The 'holiday cottage' was uncommon, and 'off-comers' were simply those who came for holidays in summer.' But nostalgia must be tempered by pragmatism, because there is no doubt that tourism has provided the dales with an important lifeline, as Pontefract (1934) writes:

It is only within the last few years that some of the villages have lost the dilapidated air which the ruined buildings gave them. Holidaymakers have done their part towards this. Tourists have brought money to the dale, either as visitors or by buying and repairing a ruin for a country cottage. Only in a few less fortunately placed villages is the feeling of desolation left.

Perhaps the most controversial element in the development of tourism in Swaledale has been the growth in the number of holiday cottages and second homes. Thanks to the stewardship of the local planning authorities, most are reclaimed and restored structures, made in traditional styles with traditional materials; very few are new builds. Many of the small cottages and farmhouses which were abandoned after the decline of lead mining during the late nineteenth century have been restored (usually very sympathetically) and brought back into use. This has not only brought a much-needed regular income stream for local businesses, especially those associated with the hospitality industry, but it has also helped preserve the visual landscape of the dale and its villages. It also helps break down the sense of isolationism and introversion that typified the dale before mid-century.

The downside is that the growth of holiday cottages comes at a cost: house prices are pushed beyond the means of local people, particularly the young; local facilities such as post offices, small shops and schools suffer from the lack of a full-time resident population; village life and community cohesion are also affected – the conservative hand of Nimbyism can privilege the demands of 'incomers' over the genuine needs of locals.

Swaledale provides a wide variety of excellent opportunities for walking and hiking. Many of the long-established routes which have traditionally been used by packhorses, drovers, or as lead roads now provide accessible and popular walking routes. Walking on the open moors has been promoted since the 1930s, but the Countryside and Rights of Way Act 2000 has given greater freedom to roam by allowing the public to walk freely on designated areas of mountain, moor, heath, downland and registered common land, without having to stick to paths.

The Pennine Way National Trail, which stretches over 268 miles between the Peak District and the Cheviots, crosses the head of Swaledale between Keld and Muker as it passes from Wensleydale north past Tan Hill towards Teesdale. It is well signposted. The Pennine Way enters Swaledale via Great Shunner Fell, drops down into Thwaite, goes past Muker and up the eastern side of Kisdon Hill, crosses the river Swale below Keld, then continues up West Stonesdale to Tan Hill. The other famous walk through Swaledale is Wainwright's popular Coast to Coast Walk, which extends 192 miles from St Bees, Cumbria (west coast), to Robin Hood's Bay, North Yorkshire (east coast). The Coast to Coast Walk passes through Kirkby Stephen in Cumbria, enters the head of Swaledale over Birkdale Common, crosses the moor to Ravenseat, and runs down the dale to Keld. From Keld it crosses the moors north

Pennine Way sign near Keld, upper Swaledale.

NORTH PENNINES SPECIAL PROTECTION AREA, TOP OF ARKENGARTHDALE, LOOKING NORTH TOWARDS STAINMORE.

of the Swale, past Swinner Gill, Melbecks Moor and Reeth, and then continues down the dale to Richmond.

The Yorkshire Dales Cycle Way, a 130–mile circular route through the dales in the Yorkshire Dales National Park which begins and ends in Skipton, also passes through Swaledale, between Fremington and Gunnerside. Cycling along the roads through Swaledale is also popular, although there are few approved routes for off-road mountain biking.

With rising awareness of the special character of Swaledale, and its importance to tourism as well as posterity, came growing commitment to protect it as much as possible in ways that are sustainable and compatible with the need to support the local economy. There are many pressures on the landscape and scenery of the dale, often associated with changing farming practices; examples include the drainage of wetland, more intensive management of meadows and enclosed pastures, dereliction and neglect of stone field barns, decline and lack of management of small broadleaved woodlands, increasing number of farm buildings, conversion of farms and barns for residential and tourism uses, and increased traffic associated with increased tourism.

A major step forward in conserving Swaledale was the National Parks and Access to the Countryside Act 1949, revised in 1995 as the Environment Act. The 1949 Act also established a series of national parks, of which

SHEEP ON HEATHER.
COPYRIGHT COURTESY OF
STEVE BUXTON.

the Yorkshire Dales National Park (1954) was the seventh. It covers an area of 680 square miles, and Swaledale lies at its northern boundary. The purposes of national parks in England and Wales are to 'conserve and enhance the natural beauty, wildlife and cultural heritage; promote opportunities for the understanding and enjoyment of the special qualities of National Parks by the Public; and seek to foster the economic and social well being of local communities within the National Parks.' National Parks and Access to the Countryside Act (1949)

Whilst the Yorkshire Dales National Park Authority owns little land, as custodian it has responsibility for preserving the character of the landscape and wildlife of the dale, which it does as a planning authority through managing access, looking after historic features and buildings, protecting trees and woodlands, and helping others (particularly land owners and farmers) to manage the park. It helps in practical ways, including through implementation of the Dales Woodland Strategy (which seeks to protect, restore, enhance and enlarge the areas of deciduous woodland), the Farm Conservation Scheme (which helps farmers to integrate their day-to-day activities with conservation measures) and the Barns and Walls Conservation Scheme (which provides grants to restore field barns).

Swaledale and Arkengarthdale are home to a diverse range of wildlife, some of it relatively rare in Britain, and its wildlife is an integral part of the character of the dale. The need to carefully conserve wildlife is reflected in a number of initiatives, including the Bolton-on-Swale Lake Nature Reserve just downstream from Richmond, which is run by the Yorkshire Wildlife Trust and contains habitats important for wildfowl and wading birds. Much larger areas covering a wider range of habitat are protected by statutory designations.

There are 22 Sites of Special Scientific Interest (SSSIs) in Swaledale, which are protected by national legislation and are actively managed to maintain their conservation interest. Much of the heather moorland and blanket bog in the dale is covered by three large moorland SSSIs, and a number of the unimproved, species-rich hay meadows in the upper dale are also SSSIs.

A key element in the conservation of wildlife in upper Swaledale and Arkengarthdale is the Pennine Dales Environmentally Sensitive Area (ESA). This was designated in 1986 to provide support for traditional farming practices in the area, whilst at the same time preserving and restoring the traditional hay meadows and maintaining and enhancing the nature conservation interest of pastures, fields, small patches of native woodland and characteristic elements of the dale landscape, such as drystone walls and farm buildings.

Swaledale is also part of the North Pennines Special Protection Area (SPA), a European designation for sites which are internationally important for nature conservation. This includes the three moorland SSSIs, which provide important habitats for breeding upland birds such as the golden plover and the merlin. The European Habitats Directive allows the designation of Special Areas of Conservation (SACs), and the North Pennines Moorlands (including Swaledale) has been submitted to the European Union as a candidate for the SAC scheme because of the international importance of its heathland and blanket bog ecosystems. Some of the unimproved, species-rich hay meadow SSSIs in upper Swaledale and Arkengarthdale have also been submitted as candidates for Special Area of Conservation.

Environmentally Sensitive Area sign, Keld.

Chapter Five
LEAD MINING

*'an industry which in its most prosperous days employed
four thousand men in Swaledale and Arkengarthdale.'*
Edmund Cooper (1973)

THE STORY OF LEAD IN SWALEDALE can be traced right back to the formation of the rocks which have created the distinctive landscape of the Yorkshire Dales. Back in the geological past, around 200 million years ago, the Yoredale Series (beds of limestone and sandstone) and Millstone Grit which had been deposited under water during the Carboniferous period, were tilted, faulted and displaced by powerful earth movements. Some time later, boiling liquids (solutions of minerals), which originated in molten rock from the interior of the earth, were injected into the faults and in places between the layers of rock. As the liquids slowly cooled, minerals were deposited in the form of crystals, creating veins containing ores of lead (galena), copper and zinc. The mineral veins vary greatly in thickness, and are often discontinuous, but some horizontal ones (called 'flats') have been found which contain rich concentrations of minerals.

lead in Swaledale

The richest veins of lead in Swaledale are found towards the upper part of the Yoredale Series, which is why most of the mining sites are on or near the tops of the fells. They are concentrated on the north side of the dale, between Keld and Hurst, and across central Arkengarthdale (see overleaf). The easiest sites to be discovered and worked were where the veins were cut through and exposed by tributaries, as at Swinner Gill, along Gunnerside Beck and in Arkengarthdale, so little wonder these are among the earliest workings in the area.

The mining sites are also scattered across a broad area because of the variability in thickness of the mineral veins. This variability also helps explain why, through much of history, most lead workings were very small, and why many local men invested a great deal of time and effort in prospecting for new finds.

Miners gave some curious names to the sites they worked, sometimes using family names or descriptive names. As Oswald Harland (1951) notes, 'the names of the mines are not enormously impressive or romantic: Old Gang, Beldi Hill, Barbara Level, Cat Shaft, Craw Level, Copperthwaite, Hard Level, Sir Francis Level, Pryes Level, Beezy Mines, Alsop's Shaft, Applegarth Mine, Ashpot Level, Allmaker's Shaft.'

REMAINS OF LEAD MINING, GUNNERSIDE BECK.

the main lead-mining areas

Beldi Hill	Near Keld, with mines above Crackpot Hall and along Swinner Gill. A very productive area with mines, hushes and levels. There are remains of two smelt mills in Swinner Gill. Mining continued between about 1740 and 1860.
Gunnerside Beck	The scene of much lead working, including Lownathwaite Mines and Blakethwaite Mines, as well as hushes and levels. Remains include dressing floors, shafts and levels, and two smelt mills. Mining ceased in about 1880.
Hard Level Gill (near Healaugh)	Very productive mines along Barney Beck, with two well-known smelt mills at Old Gang and Surrrender (near Surrender Bridge). Remains at Old Gang include the peat store, and at Surrender include the long flue stretching from the mill up the adjacent hillside to a chimney. Most mines here had closed by about 1890.
Arkengarthdale	The scene of extensive open-cast surface mining, leaving great areas such as Stoddart Hush and Hungry Hushes deeply scarred and difficult to walk through. The CB Mines and Old Moulds Mine were very productive and other mines along the dale included those at Faggergill and Booze. Remains include the Octagon explosive store at Langthwaite, and the later Langthwaite Smelt Mills. Mining operations in the dale were in decline after about 1880; Faggergill Mine closed in 1910.
Hurst	Mining of lead and copper ores took place here across a wide area. Remains include a small mine near Helwith, and the Marrick Smelt Mills.
Grinton	There were lead mines at Whitaside, Harkerside, Grovebeck and Grinton. Remains include the well-preserved Grinton Smelt Mill, along with extensive remains of workings and hushing.

development of the lead-mining industry

There is no evidence that the mineral veins in Swaledale were worked before Roman times, but it is known that the Romans worked the rich lead veins on the moors around Hurst and above Fremington Edge, probably using slave labour and local natives. The story has often been repeated of a nineteenth-century miner who found a pig (bar) of lead stamped with the name of the Emperor Hadrian (of Hadrian's Wall fame, who lived between AD 117 and 138) on the open moors, but the whereabouts of the pig has long remained a mystery. Swaledale, according to James Herriot (1979), was 'once one of the world centres of lead mining … this green land of silence and solitude was at one time the home of a bustling prosperous mining community.'

The lead-mining industry in the dale grew from the medieval period onwards. Lead was a very useful and valuable metal, being durable and malleable, and it was exported to Europe after the Norman Conquest. Its main use was as a roofing material, for which demand rose sharply with the building of the great monasteries and churches in England, France and further afield. Lead was used to roof the abbeys of Jervaulx

CHIMNEY AT HURST LEAD MINE SITE, MARRICK MOOR.

BUNTON HUSH LEVEL, GUNNERSIDE BECK.

(in Wensleydale) and Easby (in Swaledale, below Richmond), as well as Count Alan's new castle in Richmond and the king's castle at Windsor. There are records of lead merchants in Richmond in the early twelfth century, and it is known that Bridlington Priory (which had been granted the manor of Grinton in 1120) and Rievaulx Abbey (granted the manor of Muker in 1241–42) took an interest in lead mining in the dale.

Lead working continued to develop through the Tudor period. Writing in 1538, Leland commented on the digging of lead ore in the dale (see previous page), and it is known that in the time of Henry VIII two bailiffs were employed by Rievaulx Abbey to look after its woods and lead mines in Swaledale. By this time, mining involved much more than the toil of individual miners, and was growing into a prosperous business. Cooper (1973) writes that after the Wharton family acquired the manor of Healaugh as a result of the dissolution of the monasteries in 1538–39, 'they and their successors lived outside the dale, but derived a considerable income from the rich deposits of lead. They not only leased small areas to local men, but engaged in mining themselves, employing agents and business managers.'

The lead-mining industry in Swaledale expanded and developed further during the eighteenth and nineteenth centuries, enabled by changes in lead-mining practices and fuelled by rising demand. Trade flourished and new mines were opened up. Whilst originally the lead workings were largely confined to the open moorland tops, it now became profitable to work the veins lower down on the valley sides. Digging vertical shafts to reach the veins was appropriate on the tops but created difficulties with drainage, but on the valley sides it became possible to dig horizontal shafts (called 'levels'), which allowed water to drain out at the entrance.

As demand continued to rise and lead prices remained profitable, the scale of operations increased. Independent mine operators who traditionally leased small areas of moorland were gradually replaced by well-funded mining companies. They could afford to bring in new technology, including water wheels, pumping machinery and steam engines to dig and process the ores on an industrial scale. Local gentry as well as outsiders invested money in these companies and fortunes were made, though little was re-invested back in the dale. Mining companies such as the Old Gang Company, the AD Mining Company, the London Lead Company and the South Swaledale Lead Mining Company were formed to work the richer veins.

mining operations

The three key stages in turning galena (lead ore) into lead are extraction, dressing and smelting. Extensive evidence of each stage has survived in Swaledale. The miners had particular terms for the various processes and the tools they used in them; indeed, the colourful language of the former miners sits alongside the traditional Swaledale dialect as testimony to the tightness of the Swaledale community through much of its long history.

1. Extraction: First, the material had to be extracted from the ground. Unlike coal mining, for example, where coal can be mined from thick seams, lead mining involves extracting a mixture of lead ore and waste rock, which the miners called 'bouse'. The mixture then had to be processed (dressed) to separate the waste from the ore; large quantities of bouse typically yielded small quantities of ore.

Through most of history, and certainly up to the late seventeenth century, bouse was extracted from surface pits (locally called 'bell pits') in which a vertical shaft was dug until a lead vein was encountered. The men then mostly used picks and hard hammers (but they sometimes used explosives) to dig out the bouse, which was then carried up to the surface in wooden buckets (called 'kibbles') using ladders or pulled up using hand winches. Shafts were rarely deeper than about 100 feet, though depths could be increased after the introduction of winding machines driven by horses above the shaft. In suitable areas, a series of

SIR FRANCIS DRESSING FLOOR, GUNNERSIDE BECK.

pits would be dug along the line of the vein, with underground passages to join them. Working conditions for the miners were cramped and dangerous, drainage was often a problem, and quantities extracted were typically relatively small. Workings would have to be abandoned when the vein ran out, or if serious flooding persisted.

As the lead-mining industry developed and vast fortunes were available to successful mining companies, new techniques were introduced to increase production and efficiency, and thus increase profits. One such innovation was the digging of horizontal tunnels ('levels') into hillsides, designed initially to decrease flooding in the mine by allowing water to drain out. With advances in blasting technologies from the late eighteenth century onwards, larger levels were dug and often fitted with metal rails to allow much greater quantities of bouse to be pulled out in wooden wagons with metal wheels, which were pulled by ponies or sometimes by men. This raised efficiency because larger

Bunton Hush lead workings, Gunnerside Beck.

quantities could be extracted from fewer shafts, so the material was brought out in a small number of places and could be processed in fewer but larger dressing floors. Remains of many of these levels are today clearly visible in the main lead-mining areas of Swaledale.

An alternative approach – indeed, a traditional approach, believed to date back to the Romans – to extracting the bouse material was by a form of open-cast mining known as 'hushing'. A hillslope was selected where lead ore was known or believed to exist below the surface covering of the ground, usually by following veins which had already been worked. In *Wainwright's Coast to Coast Walk* (1989), Wainwright explains:

> A hush, in mining terms, is a shallow ravine contrived by prospectors on a steep slope and caused by the sudden release of water from streams dammed above in such force that the surface vegetation is stripped and the subsoil scoured with the object of revealing any mineral content that might indicate the presence of a vein. Today, a bulldozer would be used.

The loose waste rock was flushed away downhill, either creating mounds like landslides on the valley floor or being washed away by subsequent river floods. Once the surface material had been stripped away, the miners could work the exposed mineral vein with pick and hammer. The process was sometimes repeated many times along the same vein, creating the large hushes which are visible today as deep gullies on many hillsides in the lead-mining areas.

2. Dressing: Once the mixture of lead ore and other material (the bouse) had been extracted, it was necessary to separate out the valuable ore from the waste (which was called 'deads'). The material was first stored in a 'bouse team' (a three-sided compartment with stone walls, open to the front), usually close to the main extraction site. From there it was 'dressed', in two stages. Stage one involved crushing the bouse on a 'dressing floor' until it was about the size of a small pea. This was originally done by hand by women and boys using a heavy hammer (a 'bucker'), but since about 1800 it was done by roller crushers driven by water wheels. Stage two involved separating out the heavier ores from the lighter mineral waste either in settling tanks or on mechanical sieves ('hotching tubs') under a flow of water. The clean lead ore ('bing') was collected and sent to the local smelt mill.

Spoil heaps grew up close to the dressing floors, because the waste material was heavy to transport and had no commercial value. These spoil heaps provide useful indicators in the landscape of where historic lead processing activity took place. Bouse teams have also survived, such as the Sir Francis site in lower Gunnerside Beck.

3. Smelting: Once the lead ore had been dressed (crushed and separated from the bouse) it was ready to be smelted. Smelting involved heating the ore in a fire in order to free it from sulphur and other minerals, and to make metallic lead which could then be used in roofing and so on.

REMAINS OF OLD GANG LEAD SMELTING MILLS, OLD GANG BECK.

Remains of Old Gang peat store, Old Gang Beck.

In medieval times the lead in Swaledale was smelted in simple furnaces called 'bales' – fuelled with wood from nearby woodlands and blown by the wind – which were built near the mines on exposed hillsides.

More substantial, permanent and efficient smelt mills were introduced in the late sixteenth century, initially near Richmond but from the late seventeenth century near the lead mines. In these, the fickle wind, which could vary greatly in strength and direction, was replaced by reliable and powerful bellows driven by water wheels, allowing them to be used under any weather conditions.

As with dressing, smelting in a mill was a two-stage process. Stage one involved burning a mixture of crushed lead ore and fuel (initially dried wood, later replaced by peat) in a small 'ore-hearth', which produced a slag (vitrified cinder) rich in ore. Stage two involved burning that slag again at a much higher temperature (around 750°C), with charcoal, in a 'slag-hearth', in order to release the lead. Molten lead then ran from the slag-hearth into a collecting vessel (a 'sumpter pot'), from where it was poured into moulds and allowed to cool to make 'pigs' (ingots or bars). Each pig weighed between one and one and a half hundredweight (112–166 pounds).

At the peak of the lead-mining industry in Swaledale, in the early nineteenth century, there were around 40 smelt mills working in Swaledale and Arkengarthdale. As with other stages in the winning and processing of the lead, there are numerous surviving remains of smelt mills in the dale, including those at Beldi Hill, Blakethwaite, Grinton, Marske, and New Mill in Arkengarthdale.

On the remains of the Old Gang lead mines, Bogg (1909) elaborates:

> The mine galleries are all below, but the surface works have a
> character all their own, as unlike a coal-pit with its wheels and cage
> and engine-house as can be. The long slim smoke-shaft or arched
> tunnel runs up the face of the hill. There is a very long low shed,
> with a thatched roof, this being the peat-house where the fuel has

to be stored, since it can only be dug out – with cutting spades for the purpose – at certain seasons. The shed was built large enough to contain a whole year's supply.

4. Distribution: The lead pigs were stamped at the smelt mill with the mark of the mining company that made them, and then transported by horses called jaggers – small, sturdy, compact ponies bred in Swaledale especially for the purpose. Each pig weighed one and a half hundredweight (166 pounds), and a pony carried two of them in wicker baskets, one on each side. At their peak, single mines could produce up to two thousand pigs a year, and there were scores of mines working in Swaledale during the nineteenth century.

The lead pigs were carried to Richmond, where they were stored in a lead yard while awaiting sale and distribution. From Richmond they were sent to Newcastle, London or the Continent; transport was greatly assisted by the arrival of the railway in Richmond in 1846.

lead miners

In Swaledale a lead miner was traditionally known as 't'owd man' (the old man). Richard Muir (1998) explains: 'Until the eighteenth century 't'owd man' was a part-timer who also worked a farm or small-holding. Once the rights to exploit lead belonged to the prospector but after the Norman Conquest mining rights passed to the lords of the manors. Then lords took up to a quarter of the yield of a mine. In the seventeenth century mining companies, like the London Lead Company which was organised by Quakers, were formed and they leased lead-mining rights from the manorial lords. As mining became a more highly capitalised and technological undertaking, t'owd man gradually became a full-time wage-earner.'

As the industry developed in Swaledale, it attracted miners from across much of England. Cooper (1973) tells of how during the late eighteenth

REMAINS OF SURRENDER LEAD SMELTING MILL, OLD GANG BECK.

OLD GANG MINES. COPYRIGHT COURTESY OF ANDREW EATCH.

century experienced miners migrated in from Derbyshire and Cornwall, and how in prosperous times the dale also attracted miners from across the Pennines from Westmorland and Cumberland.

Life was tough for the miners and their families, who survived by hard graft: not for them the luxury of fine housing and high living enjoyed by the mine owners. Although some miners lodged in houses in villages like Muker and Reeth, most lived in thatched cottages that were small, cramped, dark, damp and poorly ventilated, often close to the workings. Pontefract (1934) writes of a miner and his wife and their 17 children and 5 lodgers who lived in a tiny cottage on the fells near one mine.

Working conditions within the mines, on the dressing floors or at the smelt mills, were difficult and dangerous, with risk ever present. Shifts were long and tiring, and work continued throughout the year, no matter what the weather.

'These men had an arduous existence. They sometimes had to walk six or seven miles to their place of work and their wages were very small. They lived mainly on porridge and brown bread – white being a great luxury – and tales are told of how they filed down into the darkness of the shaft with the last man closing the door behind him. Occasionally they lost their footing and plunged to their deaths … ' James Herriot (1979)

Pontefract (1934) notes that women and children also worked at the lead mines 'doing what was called "kibbling", washing and gathering up the bits of lead ore left in the streams and near the openings of the levels. They wore straps fixed across their shoulders to hold the buckets they carried, which were called "kibbles".

Although most miners' families were very poor and lived barely above subsistence level, some were granted small allotments free of rent, in which they could grow their own food. Poor health was widespread among the mining community, which was highly susceptible to contagious diseases like typhus. Debilitating and often fatal lung diseases like consumption (TB) were particularly common amongst the miners; average life expectancy for a Swaledale miner in the mid-nineteenth century was 46, fifteen years shorter than for all other occupations. Thomas Armstrong's novel *Adam Brunskill* (1952) captures the hardship of the lead miner's life in Swaledale during the early nineteenth century.

decline and fall

At its peak in the early nineteenth century, the lead-mining industry in Swaledale and Arkengarthdale produced up to 5,500 tons of lead a year, employed thousands of workers (many more than were employed in farming) and formed the backbone of the economy of these two dales. It had developed over many centuries, and had attracted great inward investment in exploration and new technology.

The boom years were not to last because Swaledale lead was proving costly to extract, process and transport to market. The industry in Swaledale fell into sharp decline from about 1870 onwards because of competition from the Continent and elsewhere. Imports of cheaper lead from Spain and Italy in particular made Swaledale lead uneconomic and killed demand for it. One by one the mines shut down: almost all of them had closed by 1890.

The collapse of the industry triggered a mass exodus of former miners and their families – between 1875 and 1885 the population of Swaledale above Richmond fell from about 7,000 to around 2,000 – and this in turn led to economic decline and stagnation in the upper dale which would persist for many decades. Herriot (1979) describes how many former miners stayed, 'and in Swaledale became smallholders and sheep-farmers with a few cows. They bred the tough little horned Swaledale sheep who can live on the bleak uplands where others would die. They are like their owners, the dalesmen, spare, durable and eminently well respected.'

'Attempts were made about 1850 to revive the ... industry, and met with partial success. Machinery was introduced for crushing, riddling [separating] and washing the ore, for driving the bellows in the smelt mills, and for pumping out accumulations of water. But all this was expensive and increased the cost of production'
Edmund Cooper (1973)

legacy

The mining industry has left its mark on the landscape – including structures such as ruined smelt mills and peat stores, along with hushes, spoil heaps and old miners' tracks, as described in Richard Muir's *The Dales of Yorkshire: a Portrait* (1998): 'tumbling chimneys, crumbling bouse teams, the litter and pockmarks of old workings and roofless cottages all add their touches of starkness and pathos to the desolate fells of the lead-working areas.'

The industrial archaeology attracts many visitors to the dale, and many walkers view the lead workings as interesting additions to the landscape. Wainwright (1989) is less forgiving about the environmental impacts the industry left behind, which he calls 'dismal wreckage':

In the triangle of land between Swaledale and Arkengarthdale particularly, the scene today is of sterile devastation, decay and despoliation. There is no beauty in these unsightly remains ... The ravines carved by streams have been further torn asunder by man, as have the hillsides and even the summits; the ground is pierced and pockmarked by shafts and levels; petrified rivers of stone litter the steep slopes; barren gullies make ugly scars in the heather; the skeletons of abandoned and derelict buildings stand gaunt and grey amid a chaos of debris and spoil heaps.

Chapter Six

TRADITIONAL FARMING & LAND MANAGEMENT

'We may be thinking of the people of Swaledale's 'traditional' landscape of walls and field-barns is no more than three or four hundred years old.' Andrew Fleming (2010)

Physical constraints – relatively high altitude, exposure to heavy storms, harsh winters, high rainfall and a short growing season – have meant that land use in the dale has traditionally been dominated by pastoral farming, and this remains true today. 'Most farms have sheep with a few cows,' writes David Leather in *The Walker's Guide to Swaledale* (1992), 'and it is the keeping of cows that is responsible for the scenic field barns and flowery meadows in the bottom of the valley. Sheep also affected the landscape by their constant grazing which did not allow young trees to survive, so the moors and fells today are treeless.'

enclosure

Whilst most evidence of human activity in Swaledale dates back only a few centuries at most, there are some signs in the landscape of much older activity. Traces of rectangular Iron Age field systems survive, for example, on Reeth Low Moor, Grinton Moor, Harkerside and Marrick Moor. Interestingly, they extend much higher up the hillsides than the dry-stone walls in use today, suggesting that climate was milder and

drier when they were created. They are believed to have been part of a managed Iron Age landscape, which included woodland and open grazing land, as well as the enclosed fields.

The next settlers to leave their mark on the dale were the Norse invaders, who built rough rectangular houses of stone and turf. They also cleared the adjacent ground to make small enclosures (which they called 'garths' or 'closes'), to provide shelter for their pigs, goats and cows at night or in bad weather. The animals would initially have been allowed to graze freely on the hillsides during summer months, but as population numbers grew it would have become necessary to control the grazing to prevent exhaustion of the common land. Each owner of a dwelling within the village was permitted to graze ('stint') an agreed number of animals on the common land, the number based originally on the money value of his dwelling and enclosed fields.

This form of land tenure persisted largely unchanged in Swaledale until the eighteenth century. Over the centuries, some parcels of common land were enclosed by agreement or sometimes by force, and disputes

SHEEP SHEARING, GRINTON SMELT MILL. COPYRIGHT LUCIE HINSON.

over boundaries were common and often long-lasting. Successful farmers and land owners were keen to consolidate the strips in the common land and enclose it, and add it to their existing holdings in order to increase output and the value of their estate.

After 1750 the government passed laws under which common land could only be enclosed by a Special Act of Parliament. The first land in Swaledale to be divided up this way was Fremington Edge and moor, under the Fremington Enclosure Act of 1778, as Cooper describes in *A history of Swaledale* (1973):

> At least three [public] meetings to allow for objections were held before the … [Fremington Enclosure Act] could be carried into force … The commissioners got busy. First of all the boundaries were ridden or perambulated. Public or private ways and roads were set out, also common quarries, wells, water-courses and watering-places for the use of the proprietors and made accessible from their future allotments. Accommodation roads were planned, the herbage of which was to be used by those who farmed the adjoining allotments. Having defined the access roads, the remaining ground was pegged out and allotted to the various owners, always taking into consideration the quality and situation of the division. Any doubts as to the fairness of the allocations were brought before the commissioners, who were required to look into all claims and examine all witnesses on oath … Upon the evidence submitted, the commissioners judged as they thought right. Within six months of the execution of the award, the participators were each required to give his assent or acceptance at a public meeting, notice of which was given out after [the church] service upon some suitable Sunday. Owners of the new allotments were obliged to fence and enclose them at their own expense.

Under the Act, existing rights of way up to and across the moors were protected, and the king retained current and future mineral rights on the enclosed land. Stone walls had to be built around each new

Hay meadows, dry-stone walls and stone field barns in Gunnerside Bottoms.

enclosure (allotment) within 12 months, and small farmers who could not afford to do so lost their grazing rights and had no option but to sell their share of the land and seek work in the towns or support from the parish poor rates. As in other areas in England, the parliamentary enclosure movement between 1750 and 1850 spread through Swaledale, and by the early nineteenth century the common land around Muker, Keld, Reeth and Grinton had all been enclosed. Not all of the land along Swaledale was enclosed though; large areas on both sides of the upper valley, such as Gunnerside Pasture and the large area of moorland on Grinton Moor, still remain as open land.

The new enclosures were larger, straighter and more systematic than the much earlier enclosures of small irregular fields adjacent to the villages and hamlets, which often date from the sixteenth or seventeenth century. They are typically square or rectangular in shape, with straight dry-stone walls that run at right angles to the hillslope and stretch up the hillsides to the 'intake walls', which marked the upper boundary of cultivation, with open moorland beyond. Stone field barns were often built at the edge of many of these enclosures. The contrast between the early and late enclosures is clearly seen at Angram in the upper dale; the small (early) fields below Angram look very different to the large rectangular (later) fields higher up on Angram Pasture. The enclosed fields in upper Swaledale tend to be smaller and less regular in shape than those in the middle section of the dale.

After enclosure, most land owners invested in improving their land in order to increase productivity and output, and thus both profitability and capital value. This would typically involve digging out or burning off the old vegetation, draining the soil and adding lime to reduce the natural acidity and increase the fertility of the soil. Many small lime kilns were built, in which limestone was heated to create lime (calcium oxide), an alkaline substance used in 'sweetening' the new pastures. Many of these stone-built kilns have survived.

STRAIGHT DRY-STONE WALL ENCLOSURES ON ANGRAM PASTURE, UPPER SWALEDALE.

TRADITIONAL DRY-STONE WALL.

NEW DRY-STONE WALL BUILT IN THE TRADITIONAL STYLE.

STONE FIELD BARN, BETWEEN ANGRAM AND THWAITE, UPPER SWALEDALE.

dry-stone walls

One of the most characteristic features of the Swaledale landscape is the dry-stone walls, most of which were built between about 1750 and 1850, as a direct result of the enclosure movement. Bill Mitchell (1990) regards them as 'among the Seven Wonders of the Dales'.

The walls serve many purposes, as well as marking the boundaries between fields and properties. They keep stock out of the meadows where hay is growing, and keep stock in while grazing stubble or autumn grass. They provide shelter for the farmers' stock but also for a wide variety of wildlife, and a habitat on which many types of mosses and lichens grow. They take up less space than hedges, require lower maintenance than fences and hedges, and last longer than both.

The walls are called 'dry-stone walls' because no cement was used in them. Each wall tapers with height from two to three feet wide at the base to about a foot at the top. Pontefract describes (1934) how the walls were traditionally built:

To keep his line and thickness the waller uses a wooden frame like an easel without the back leg. This he fixes into the ground a little distance from the wall on to which he is building, keeping it straight with a plumb-line. Strings are carried from the frame to the sides and top of the wall. Choosing stones which fit on to each other, he works from both sides, filling in the cavity with rubble. About twice in the height of the wall he places large stones which he calls 'troos' (throughs), to strengthen it. The stones meet in one layer at the top, and on this he puts a row endways for a finish. A good waller will build seven yards in a day.

The stones used in building the wall would usually come from river beds and nearby rock outcrops or small quarries, but sometimes stones from old walls and buildings were also re-used. Local material was used, because the stones were heavy (and thus expensive) to cart around. Most walls in Swaledale are made of sandstone, gritstone or limestone – the local rocks in the Yoredale Series – which weather to produce the dark-grey appearance we see today.

'Those wonderful walls,
often the only sign
of the hand of man,
symbolise the very soul
of the high Pennines,
the endlessly varying
pattern of grey against
green, carving out ragged
squares and oblongs,
pushing long antennae
to impossible heights till
they disappear into the
lapping moorland on the
summits.'
James Herriot (1979)

CRACKPOT BILL.
COPYRIGHT LUCIE HINSON.

79

Traditionally, farmers repaired their own walls, usually during June when other jobs on the farm were less pressing. Some still do repair their own walls, but in recent decades the art of dry-stone walling has been at risk of dying out. A small number of contract wallers – either specialists, or skilled farmers with a side-line – has preserved the skills required to build new walls and repair existing ones.

stone field barns

Stone field barns – also known as laithes, field houses or cow houses – are another typical feature of the Swaledale landscape. Indeed, they are perhaps the most distinctive feature of the dale. Stone barns are found in all of the Yorkshire Dales, but the greatest concentration of them is in Swaledale, particularly in the upper dale between Keld and Reeth.

Most stone field barns were built at the same time as the dry-stone walls, between about 1750 and 1850, and are similarly constructed without the use of cement. Robert White (2002) explores the history of the field barn in *The Yorkshire Dales: a Landscape through Time*:

> Just when field barns became a common feature of the dales is unclear, but was probably nearly contemporary with the rebuilding of dwelling houses in the seventeenth century … The earliest reliably dated barn identified in a comprehensive survey of Swaledale and Arkengarthdale is a much altered and extended barn near Ivelet dated to 1713.

Many barns are believed to have been rebuilt or restored during the nineteenth century, when the original turf or heather thatch roofing was replaced by stone flags. Several good examples of these small field barns survive, sometimes one in almost every meadow, particularly between Gunnerside and Muker. Many of the barns are in a good state of repair thanks to the success of initiatives by the Yorkshire Dales National Park to protect them.

Whilst they remain as interesting features in the landscape, the barns were built for a very particular purpose and were a key element in the traditional pastoral farming system of the dales. The harsh and often prolonged winters typical of this exposed upland setting made it impossible to keep stock out grazing freely on the high pastures throughout the year, so farmers built barns where their small herd of three or four cows could be safely housed during the winter months, from November onwards. As Robert White (2002) points out, in the barns 'they were visited by the farmer at least once, and sometimes as many as three times a day, to be fed and watered and, where necessary, milked'.

The most common sites for the barns were on the valley floor, which provided flat land and access to a reliable supply of water. It was also easier to gather hay from the valley-floor hay meadows and store it

VARIETY OF PLANT SPECIES IN A TRADITIONAL HAY MEADOW.

TRADITIONAL HAY
MEADOWS NEAR THWAITE,
UPPER SWALEDALE.

Visitor management in a hay meadow near Thwaite, upper Swaledale.

The sign reads:

MEADOW LAND PLEASE KEEP IN SINGLE FILE

in the barns, to provide winter feed for the cows in the barns and the sheep which were brought down from the fells and wintered in the meadows.

But as well as providing shelter the barns were also a valuable source of free fertiliser. During the summer months, when the cows had returned to graze on the pastures from May onwards, the manure which had accumulated in and around the barn was spread over the surrounding meadows to fertilise the next crop of grass, which provided the hay for winter feed. It was a very efficient and sustainable system of grassland management, which met the needs of the stock, the pastures and hay meadows, and the farmer, over many generations.

hay meadows

Closely associated with the stone field barns and dry-stone walls are the hay meadows, which similarly contribute to the special character of Swaledale. They are concentrated within upper Swaledale and Arkengarthdale; particularly good examples can be seen around Muker. Farther down the dale many of the traditionally managed hay meadows have been replaced with improved grassland that is cropped and turned into silage by fermenting it in a silo.

Hay meadows can also be found in upper Wensleydale, upper Wharfedale and Littondale, although nationally they are becoming rare as farmers make more intensive use of their land by ploughing and re-seeding their meadows and using chemical fertilisers on them to increase grass yields.

Ella Pontefract (1934) describes haymaking methods in the 1930s:

> The dale methods of haymaking are different from those of lowland districts. The hay is raked into ridges, after which a wooden contrivance, something like a snow plough and pulled by a horse,

is often used to push it together. If it is not to be led [stored] immediately, it is made into large cocks called 'pikes'. If the hay is far from a barn it is piled on to a wooden sledge for leading ... There are no haystacks, unless there has been an unusually good crop with a mild winter preceding it so that not much hay has been used for the sheep, when the farmer might make a very small, round stack in a sheltered corner. Practically all the hay is stored in the barns ...

Much has changed over the eight decades since she wrote that, and Robert White (2002) explains how the meadow management system in the dales typically works today:

> In the spring, grass is encouraged to grow almost to seed in the hay meadows. Controlled grazing and manuring in some traditionally managed meadows [by ewes until mid May, when the flocks with their lambs are taken up to higher grazing in the rough pastures] enables over thirty different plant species per square metre [three per square foot] to flourish. In July the grass is cut, traditionally with a scythe, and left to dry in the sun. Drying is hastened by occasional turning, formerly by hand but now with tractor-drawn rakes. When dry the hay is swept up and stored in the barns.

Hay meadows managed in traditional ways support a rich variety of wild flowers; up to 80 different species of plant have been counted in some fields. During the summer months they provide colour, variety and interest to the landscape, which changes as different plants come into flower – first the yellow buttercups, followed by the white and purple of the ox-eye daisies, pignut and wood cranesbill. Orchids grow in some meadows, and clover is widespread.

As well as creating attractive scenes, traditional hay meadows are important to nature conservation, providing important habitats for a diversity of wildlife as well as plants. Nature conservation bodies and the Yorkshire Dales National Park now work closely with land owners and farmers to preserve those meadows that remain, and to conserve their botanical diversity, by encouraging traditional farming methods, including through grant support.

SWALEDALE SHEEP.

COPYRIGHT COURTESY OF MARK FARRELL.

Many of the hay meadows in upper Swaledale and Arkengarthdale are designated as Sites of Special Scientific Interest (SSSIs) and the Yorkshire Wildlife Trust's Yellands Meadow Nature Reserve at Muker is one of the twelve SSSIs collectively known as the Muker Meadows. Conserving the hay meadows is an important objective of the Environmentally Sensitive Area scheme.

Many of the hay meadows lie on popular walking routes through upper Swaledale and a project (jointly undertaken by the Yorkshire Dales National Park, the Yorkshire Dales Millennium Trust and local farmers) to lay stone flags on footpaths through these meadows has been successful in protecting plants from being trampled and opening up access for wheelchair users.

Swaledale sheep

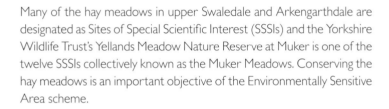

Swaledale's most famous residents are doubtless the mountain sheep which graze freely on its fells. Sheep farming has long been at the centre of the Swaledale economy. The best known, naturally, are the Swaledale sheep, which are tough and well adapted to the harsh conditions of the fells and moorland surrounding the dale that lent its name to them.

William Marshall (1794, quoted in Cooper 1973) comments on the Swaledale sheep which 'live upon the open heaths the year round. Their food, heath, rushes and a few of the coarsest grasses; a pasture on which perhaps every other breed of sheep of this Kingdom would starve'.

The Swaledale sheep are smaller and neater than many other breeds, and they have black faces with white or pale grey noses (as shown on the logo for the Yorkshire Dales National Park) and black legs with a white stripe down the front. Both the male sheep (tups or rams) and females (ewes) have horns. Swaledales produce good, fat lambs for lowland farmers when they are crossed with mutton sheep such as Leicesters and Wensleydales.

The Swaledales are the most common of the breeds of sheep in the dale and on the fells, but they share the fells with Dalesbred (a cross between the Swaledale and the Scottish black-face, which looks like the Swaledale but usually has two white patches on its black face) and rough fell breeds (which have large white patches on their face and long, straight fleeces).

All of the upland sheep breeds have thick weatherproof fleeces, which produce good quality wool ('staple') of medium length. Swaledale wool is mostly white but with a small amount of grey.

The different breeds of mountain sheep are well suited to the Swaledale environment because they share two important characteristics. First, they are extremely tough and sure-footed, and with the protection of coarse wool and an ability to cope with poor grazing they can survive long hard winters outdoors in bleak, exposed places. Second, they have a natural ability (learned over many generations) to keep to their own part of the open fell, and even to return to it if sold to farms elsewhere, just like migrating birds returning home each spring.

The fell top where the sheep are born is traditionally known as their 'heaf', and the in-built homing tendency – which lambs learn by grazing with their mothers – is referred to as 'hefting'. This ability makes it possible for the farmer to let their sheep graze freely on the open fells, and it also means that on tenanted farms the hefted flock stays with the farm when there is a change in tenant.

Traditionally, sheep have dominated the farmer's work and calendar, as we see in an excerpt from Pontefract's *Swaledale* (1934).

> Today, nearly every man has to do with sheep-farming, and his thoughts and conversation are of sheep … From the moment when the first lambs appear, through shearing and dipping, and the excitement of the local shows and sales, to the final oily dipping as a protection against winter storms, the farmer's work is all with the sheep. And when winter sets in there is the constant watchfulness, and the tedious carrying-up of hay to the moors if it is frosty or snowy … From the end of June until haymaking the time is taken up with shearing. Here again, as with dipping, two or three farmers help each other, so as to get the sheep back on the moors quickly … The women often help at shearing-time by rolling up the fleeces as they are [hand-] clipped off, ready for storing until the wool-buyers come round.'

She also painted an affectionate and now long-gone picture of the traditional shepherd who looked after the sheep grazing on the open fells, with his constant companion the sheep dog – 'As the shepherds come down from the fells with the rolling gait they develop, theirs seems the kind of life man was meant to live.'

wool and hand knitting

The long tradition of sheep farming in Swaledale is reflected in the development of a woollen industry centred upon Richmond, which can be traced back to the eleventh century. Early records mention a tailor in Richmond – called Richard son of Gunnild – and three fullers, who helped make cloth by causing fibres to felt together, by shrinking and hammering it with wooden hammers. The development of the monastic estates during the thirteenth century promoted the growth of the woollen industry in Swaledale, where Rievaulx Abbey owned extensive sheep-grazing land.

The woollen industry continued to grow nationally. The wealth and prosperity of Richmond between the twelfth and nineteenth centuries likewise depended heavily on the wool trade. One Thomas Caesar surveyed the knitting industry in the county of York in 1595 and found more than a thousand hand-knitters within 20 miles of Richmond, including in the villages of Marske, Grinton, Marrick, and Downholme. Cooper (1973) concludes that 'From the beginning of the fourteenth century the wealth and prosperity of Britain depended upon its exports of wool and woollen cloth to the Continental countries. Until the Industrial Revolution of the late eighteenth century, wool, and therefore sheep, were the main pre-occupation of the men of rural England.'

By the eighteenth century Swaledale was famous for its hand-knitted woollen goods, particularly stockings, gloves and sailor caps. It was a thriving cottage industry carried out at home by men, women and children throughout the dale as a way of supplementing meagre family incomes. Many lead miners would knit as they walked to and from the mines. Knitting was a traditional craft, and the skill was passed on from one generation to the next. Richmond and Kendal became the main hand-knitting centres in England, although the industry survived longer in Kendal. In *The Old Hand-knitters of the Dales*, Marie Hartley and Joan Ingleby (1978) write that 'Most of the stocking trade was with London merchants or army contractors who bought up large quantities … Knitted goods from Richmond and Swaledale were exported to the Netherlands … '

In Richmond 'all was cloathing, and all the people clothiers, here you see all the people, great and small, a knitting.' Daniel Defoe (1724)

The industry declined with mechanisation and changing fashion (for example, men started to wear long trousers rather than breeches and stockings). The international market changed too, as reported by Christopher Clarkson in *The History of Richmond in the County of York* (1814). He states that Richmond 'had formerly a large trade in the exportation of knit yarn stockings and seamen's woollen caps to Holland and the Netherlands, which through the fluctuations of trade and the vicissitudes of war, is now very much upon the decline, and indeed almost entirely banished out of the country.'

Unfortunately for Swaledale, the decline in the hand-knitting woollen industry happened at much the same time as the collapse of the lead-mining industry, and this 'double-whammy' had a devastating effect on the local economy and population. By the close of the nineteenth century both traditional industries had all but gone, leaving the dale with upland farming as the backbone of its economy.

Traditional hand-knitting skills were not lost completely, and since the 1970s the local industry has been revived on a small scale by Swaledale Woollens in Muker, which sells locally knitted woollen products, mainly to tourists.

woodland and hunting forest

After the end of the last ice age, as climate warmed and soils developed, forest grew across the whole of Britain, including Swaledale. The prehistoric people who migrated into the area and settled in and around the dale cleared small patches of forest, and gradually the forest cover shrank as the clearance continued. By medieval times much of the land in the dale was being farmed, including both for livestock (mainly sheep with some cows) and as arable (mainly corn and hay).

The Norman Conquest (1066) brought major change to the pattern of land ownership and use across the country, and in the case of Swaledale

SCATTERED WOODLAND ON THE WEST SIDE OF KISDON HILL, PREVIOUSLY PART OF A MEDIEVAL DEER FOREST.

this included the setting aside of much of the upper dale west of Reeth as a royal game reserve, used for the hunting of wild deer, bear, boar and wolves by the Earls of Richmond. The 'chase' or 'deer forest', which covered a vast area from Wensleydale across to Stainmore, included both natural woodland and open country. It was subject to forest law, usually surrounded by a fence or a bank and ditch, and guarded by resident forest wardens against poachers and trespassers. However, as W. G. Hoskins (1970) points out, 'The existence of forest law over wild, unsettled country did not entirely stop peasants from making clearances [small clearings or 'assarts' in which new fields were enclosed] in places and paying a fine for doing so.'

Wolves were hunted in the Swaledale deer forest until 1369. The deer had gone by the early 1820s through a combination of over-hunting (including poaching) and loss of habitat, with much of their traditional browsing woodland felled to provide fuel for the lead smelt mills, and much of the rest damaged by toxic fumes from the smelt mills. In *An History of Richmondshire in the North Riding of the County of York*, Whitaker (1823) explains that 'Swaledale, which was carefully protected by the Wharton family, became the last refuge of the persecuted [red and fallow] deer, which remained in considerable numbers northward from Muker as late as the year 1725'.

Woodland management in Swaledale also included managing hollies for winter fodder and the pollarding of elms from medieval times onwards. Pollarding involved cutting the stem of the tree at about six feet above the ground, to encourage the growth of lateral branches and avoid damage by browsing animals such as rabbits or deer.

Relatively little natural woodland survives in upper Swaledale, and most of it is small patches of semi-natural broad-leaved woodland on the

CUTTING LOGS. COPYRIGHT LUCIE HINSON.

'The hill-side [between Keld and Crackpot Hall] is covered with stunted trees, their trunks and branches thickly grown with lichen; elm, hawthorn, mountain ash, yew, silver birch, oak, ash, sloe, and bird cherry ... This is all that remains near Keld of the forest which at one time covered the land here.' Ella Pontefract (1934)

steeper slopes and limestone scars, and in the narrow valleys. Common tree species include sycamore, ash, birch, rowan and bird cherry. Birbeck Wood and Rowleth Wood, both near Gunnerside, are among the few woodlands in the dale that are ancient in origin. Some woodland, such as that on Gunnerside Pasture, is now carefully managed to ensure the conservation of its character and composition.

The largest areas of semi-natural ancient woodland in Swaledale — home to a wide variety of species including ash, pedunculate and sessile oak, birch, alder, wych elm, hawthorn, hazel and planted sycamore — are to be found just above Richmond.

moorland management

The fells surrounding Swaledale are an important element not just in the landscape of the dale, but also its character. Emily Brontë's *Wuthering Heights* was inspired by the moorland around Haworth, farther south in the dales, but the Swaledale fells have much the same feel and character. The open fells provide extensive grazing for the sheep which have grazed freely there over many generations.

The open nature and unspoiled character of the fells, the extensive views within and from them, and the diversity of habitats they offer, have helped to make them attractive for walkers and hikers in great numbers in recent decades. Their location at the junction of the Pennine Way and the Coast to Coast Walk ensures that a great many feet tread across the moors, which of course can damage vegetation and thus requires careful management to conserve wildlife and preserve the quality of the walking experience.

Great patches of heather (*Calluna vulgaris*) – a typical moorland plant in Britain – cover many of the fells and hillsides, and as it changes colour through the seasons (from brown and green, to purple and light grey) it provides a constantly changing backdrop to whatever is going on down in the dale itself. Whilst heather dominates in many places, the

IVELET WOOD BY THE RIVER SWALE, IEWED FROM THE EASTERN SIDE OF KISDON HILL.

HEATHER MOORLAND ON CALVER HILL, VIEWED FROM GRINTON MOOR, MIDDLE SWALEDALE.

HEATHER REGROWTH AFTER CONTROLLED BURNING, MARRICK MOOR NEAR REETH.

fell vegetation also includes bracken (*Pteridium aquilinum*: tall, coarse ferns), rushes (*Juncaceae*: slender marsh plants), bilberry (*Vaccinium myrtillus*: a hardy dwarf shrub), cowberry (*Vaccinium vitis-idaea*: a low, creeping evergreen shrub, also known as mountain cranberry), cotton grass (*Eriophorum*: wet-loving rush-like plants that produce tufts of long, white silky hairs) and blanket bog. This diversity of plant species offers a wide variety of natural habitats for adders and for birds such as grouse, curlew, golden plover, snipe and redshank.

Extensive areas of the heather moorland, particularly around the head of the dale, are actively managed for grouse shooting. This provides valuable employment for gamekeepers and beaters, ploughs money back into the local economy, and preserves the character and appearance of the open fell tops. Whitaker writes (1823): 'After the nobler pursuit [of deer hunting] had ceased, hawking and netting for grouse was in use to the year 1725, when shooting-flying was introduced, to the great astonishment of the dalesmen.'

During the 1960s and '70s drainage ditches were dug across many moorland areas in the dale – a process known as gripping – to reduce water-logging and improve the habitat for grouse and sheep. Tell-tale signs of moorland management in upper Swaledale include the patch-work of green (established) and grey (recently burnt) heather, the lines of stone shooting butts (the walls behind which shooters hide), and the new roads and tracks across the fells which provide access for the lucrative shooting parties in four-wheel-drive vehicles.

juniper scrub

Swaledale differs from the other Dales in having a number of patches of juniper scrub. Juniper (*Juniperus*) is an evergreen tree or shrub that has pointed leaves and aromatic, bluish-grey, berry-like cones. Patches occur and are protected within Sites of Special Scientific Interest (SSSIs) at Thwaite Stones, Scar Closes on Kisdon Side, and at Feetham Holme.

The patches of juniper scrub might be glacial refugia (survivals from the end of the last glaciation), or remnants of former land management by settlers in the dale, as Speight writes in *Romantic Richmondshire* (1897):

> The juniper has been very extensively grown in [upper] Swaledale from time immemorial, and down to the beginning of the [nineteenth] century there were many hundreds of acres of juniper and brier in the townships of Reeth, Healaugh and Muker. The chips at one time were extensively used for fumigating, and during seasons of plague and sickness no house was without them. The berries, moreover, were used as a spice and were also employed medicinally. The plant grows best on open elevated limestone country, and consequently flourished amazingly in the thin limey soils of upper Swaledale.

STONE GROUSE-SHOOTING BUTT.

Grouse shooting has been a popular and profitable pursuit in upper Swaledale since the 1850s, and continues to be today. Moorland management includes periodic controlled burning of patches of heather, which encourages the growth of fresh shoots (a source of food) whilst preserving more mature plants which provide cover for the birds.

SWALEDALE GROUSE.
COPYRIGHT COURTESY OF GLENN HAWORTH.

'This shire most of it lieth very high, with ragged rockes and swelling mountaines, whose sloping sides in some places beare good grasse, the botomes and vallies are not altogether unfruitfull. The hilles themselves within are stored with lead, pit-coale, and coper.'

William Camden (1607)

UPPER SWALEDALE, LOOKING NORTH FROM THWAITE TOWARDS KELD WITH KISDON HILL ON THE RIGHT.

PART II
down the dale

'It is a land of pure air, rocky streams and hidden waterfalls. In the winter the roads are often impassable when the heavy snow falls and the high fells are a white wilderness where a man could easily lose his way and die. But on summer days when the sun beats down on the lonely miles these uplands are a paradise, the air heavy with the sweetness of warm grass, the breeze carrying a thousand scents from the valley below.'

James Herriot (1979)

Top of Birkdale, by the B6270 road from Kirkby Stephen to Richmond.

Chapter Seven
UPPER SWALEDALE: SOURCE TO GUNNERSIDE

'One can easily ... believe that one has come into a solitude which nothing has ever disturbed and nothing can ever transform.' Joseph Fletcher (1908)

UPPER SWALEDALE STRETCHES from the headwaters of the dale on the border between North Yorkshire and Lancashire, downstream to Gunnerside. The location is remote, far from the nearest town of any size, and served by twisty country roads. The landscape is open and varied, dominated in this part of the dale by open heather moorland and grass uplands, with dry-stone walls and stone field barns on the flatter, less exposed slopes, along with scattered stone farmhouses and a few small hamlets (probably of Norse origin). Hay meadows add variety and colour on the valley floor downstream from Thwaite. The scenery also contains pockets of woodland, some dramatic limestone scars, and tumbling rivers and waterfalls. None of the settlements in upper Swaledale is mentioned in the *Domesday Book* (1086), probably because the surveyors never ventured this far up the dale, most of which they described as 'waste'.

The lower portion of this stretch of the dale, between Thwaite and Gunnerside, was described as 'Alpine' by a number of nineteenth-century writers. Two things that are not in dispute about upper Swaledale are its isolation and its bleakness; Herriot (1979) describes the wild country at the head of Swaledale and the surrounding dales as 'the bleakest country in England', while Pontefract (1934) writes that 'the dale starts on vast tracts of moorland, out of sight of cultivation or human dwellings'.

Opinions differ on how attractive this rugged landscape is. Certainly, early visitors had little positive to say about it. In 1607, for example, William Camden wrote that 'amongst the mountaines it is in most places so wast, solitary, unpleasant, and unsightly'. Two hundred years later, Christopher Clarkson (1814) was equally uncomplimentary: 'In this quarter there is nothing to attract the traveller's attention, the views being dreary, barren, and seemingly destitute of every idea of improvement ... to the traveller, who only wishes for the variegated scenes of mountains, wood, and water, it can have but few charms.' *Black's Picturesque Guide to Yorkshire* (1874) warns that 'Only they who can endure fatigue, and philosophically content themselves with such accommodation as the somewhat primitive people can afford, should undertake to explore this remote part of Upper Swaledale.'

Views on landscape are clearly a matter of taste, and whilst many walkers find upper Swaledale an attractive and inspiring place, it does not appeal to everyone, even today. Perhaps it is appreciated most by

UPPER REACH OF THE RIVER SWALE BETWEEN FIRS AND HOGGARTHS,
UPSTREAM FROM WHITSUNDALE.

those who are called by the lure of the wild and are prepared to go off the beaten track. For those who make the effort, the rewards are good and plentiful.

Dale Head

The river Swale, from which the dale takes its name, rises on the high fells that define the boundary between North Yorkshire and Lancashire, and the north-western limit of the Yorkshire Dales National Park. These fells are part of the watershed that provides the backbone of England.

Running anticlockwise, and starting at Rogan's Seat (2,204 feet above sea level) to the north-east of Keld, this arc stretches west to Nine Standards Rigg (2,171 feet), then south to High Seat (2,328 feet), south-east to Great Shunner Fell (2,348 feet) and east to Lovely Seat (2,217 feet). The hills are quite rounded and generally boggy on top.

Nine Standards Rigg is a series of tall stone cairns just to the west of the watershed of the Swale, overlooking the river Eden. They have been carefully constructed of small stones of local rock, and vary in shape and size: some are the shape of a high dome, while others have large square bases and taper upwards towards a rounded top. They are marked on eighteenth-century maps as the 'Nine Standards', but their age and origin are lost in the mists of time. Pontefract (1934) mentions several theories, including that they were built to appease a pagan god or to celebrate a battle fought there, but she prefers to think of them as 'built by shepherds as a landmark, and to occupy the long hours they had to spend on the ridge when there were several sheep-folds there; the ruins of these sheepfolds still remain.' Wainwright (1989) mentions a common theory that they were built 'to give marauding Scots advancing up the Eden valley the false impression that an English army was encamped there', but he concludes that they were probably 'boundary markers (the county boundary formerly passed through them) or beacons'. The mystery over who built them and when and why, adds to the enigma surrounding them, and these silent sentries remain a curious but impressive sight.

The Coast to Coast Walk passes by Nine Standards Rigg, but the Yorkshire Dales National Park Authority now encourages walkers to use a slightly different route during the winter months, to prevent serious erosion of the fragile peat moorland in the surrounding area.

At 2,348 feet the summit of Great Shunner Fell is the highest point in Swaledale and the fourth highest point in Yorkshire, and on clear days it offers spectacular views in all directions, including south to the summits of Ingleborough and Great Whernside. The name Shunner comes from the Norse *sjon* and *sjonar*, meaning a look-out hill. Today the Pennine Way runs straight over the top of the fell, on its way between Hawes and Thwaite.

Lovely Seat, to the east across the Buttertubs Pass from Great Shunner Fell, was once called Luina Seat or Lunasit. The name is thought to be derived from the Scandinavian word *luin*, which means a sound or alarm, and it is taken to indicate that 'warnings were signalled from it to the Norse settlers in Thwaite', as Pontefract (1934) notes.

The River Swale rises in 'a crescent-like rampart of lofty mountainous ridges, enclosing wide radiating moorland of elevated and dreary character, the birthplace of many river heads, the cloud waters of a vast area of skyland.'
Edmund Bogg (1909)

Pontefract in *Swaledale* (1934), 'there seems to be a little of everything which is found in the valley: the fells, a few meadows with a stone barn, a ford, a sheepfold, the remains of a mine. It is as though the whole life of the dale sprang up here with the start of the river.'

Birkdale

The view from the B6270 into Swaledale from Kirkby Stephen in Cumbria to the west shows just how broad and barren the moorland tops are that surround and envelope Swaledale. The road cuts across moors as bleak, broad and inhospitable as anything described in Emily Brontë's *Wuthering Heights*.

source of the Swale

The source area of the river – what Bogg (1909) calls 'the nest-hollow of the Swale … the cradle of the clouds that give life' – is relatively high and exposed to the weather systems that typically blow from the west. It receives high rainfall, which flows through the peaty moorland over impermeable rocks and gives rise to numerous small streams (locally called 'becks') which, as Speight (1897) describes, 'sometimes whip up the river below into mighty and almost inconceivable proportions'. Leyland (1896), a contemporary of Speight's, described the 'grandeur in [the] sources [of the rivers Swale and Ure], in the recesses of the dark central mass of the Pennine chain, where they rush through lonely dells in angry torrents, eating slowly deeper their rocky beds'.

The river becomes known as the Swale at Lonin End – from the Old English *loan* (a lane) – where Great Sleddale Beck flows off Shunner Fell into Birkdale Beck. 'At this junction which makes the Swale,' writes

DALE HEAD, LOOKING WEST FROM KELD UP BIRKDALE TOWARDS HIGH SEAT

Tom Bradley (1891) insists that, upstream from Keld, 'there is absolutely nothing of interest beyond the wild mountains', and he was clearly not impressed by 'the uninviting path that for eleven weary miles winds its treacherous way across the blustering moors, now amidst the clouds'.

Such a remote and desolate place inevitably struck fear into the heart of those who had to cross it on foot or by horse, particularly at night or in a raging storm. Pontefract (1934) recalls the salutary tale of a local merchant who crossed this way in 1664, en route from Askrigg in Wensleydale to his home in Kirkby Stephen, 'his two ponies laden with stockings and other knitted garments which he had bought from farmers' wives in the market at Askrigg, [who] was murdered near [Hollow Mill Cross] by a Westmorland farmer. Although the farmer was suspected of the crime, strong enough evidence could not be produced to condemn him. Two years later, while returning from a funeral at Muker in a thunderstorm, he saw the ghost of his victim by the cross. He started back in terror, and his horse, already frightened by the storm, plunged and threw him; and he was dashed to death against the stone cross. His widow found the parcels of stockings which he had stolen under the floor of their cottage.'

From Kirkby Stephen the road climbs over the long, flat expanse of open moorland between High Seat and White Mossy Hill, exploiting this natural gateway. On its exposed summit the road is surrounded by open moorland, with posts to mark the edge of the road when heavy snow blankets everything on the ground.

In the 1930s two standing stones marked the boundary between Yorkshire and Westmorland, and an old inscribed stone known as Hollow Mill Cross also once stood at the border there, shown as a cross on maps as early as the sixteenth century. This area is shown on old maps as 'Lamps Moss'. The road descends eastwards down Birkdale and follows Birkdale Beck down to its junction with Great Sleddale Beck, where the river takes on the name Swale. The road down Birkdale is twisty and narrow, and certainly not for the faint-hearted, as Pontefract

writes (1934): 'doggedly and courageously it goes, now mounting the fell, now running round it to avoid a hill, surmounting obstacles simply, perhaps a little crudely, as befits its primitive beginnings; a persistent mountain pass, finding the quickest way to the border.'

In this upper section of the dale the road crosses the river over a number of narrow, high, single-arched stone bridges. The river flows swiftly, rises fast after rain and floods regularly, so all the bridges at least as far downstream as Ivelet Bridge below Muker are built to allow for the rapid passage of high volumes of water. In 1899 a heavy storm on Great Shunner Fell caused a great flood in upper Swaledale, which wrecked a farmhouse at the bottom of Great Ash Gill (behind Hoggarths Bridge) but also damaged many other low-lying buildings and numerous bridges over the Swale, as well as drowning many sheep and other farm animals.

Whitsundale

At Hoggarths the road crosses over the Swale and continues downstream, hugging the river until it reaches Keld. Below Hoggarths the moorland is separated from the road by enclosed fields bounded by dry-stone walls, and there are scattered isolated traditional stone farmhouses. The moorland on the fells in this area is home to many species of bird, including grouse, lapwing, curlew, oystercatcher and golden plover.

Whitsundale Beck opens up to the north, just past Hoggarths Bridge. The valley leads north-westwards over White Mossy Hill towards Nine Standards Rigg, which remains stubbornly hidden from the main road along Birkdale. Nearby the Coast to Coast Walk passes through Whitsundale Beck on its way between Nine Standards Rigg and Keld.

A metalled track leads north from the B6270, past Hill Top Farm to the small hamlet of Ravenseat, where Wainwright loved to pause for tea and scones and which he described as a 'lonely outpost, comprising a sheep farm and a few cottages'. Ravenseat now consists of a few farmhouses, but Pontefract (1934) tells us that 'eleven families once lived here, most of the men being employed in a coal-pit at Tan Hill … The surplus cottages have long been turned into barns, and the same fate has befallen the little chapel, which is now only distinguishable from other barns by one or two tiny pointed windows … the chapel … is thought to have belonged to the Inghamite sect [a small Nonconformist sect of Protestant Dissenters founded in 1754 by the Rev. B. Ingham, 1712–72, who accompanied the Wesleys on their missionary journey to Georgia], and to have served the outlying farms also, but it had no resident minister.'

One feature of interest near the entrance to Whitsundale is Birkdale Tarn, a lake created by artificially damming a small stream, designed to provide a reliable source of water for lead-mining operations at Lonin End. Like the rest of Whitsundale, however, the tarn has an air of being forgotten about. Herriot (1979) describes 'something inexpressingly lonely about this little-known tarn in its desolate surroundings'. Nonetheless, it provides a valuable water habitat for birds such as the Canada goose, the mallard and the tufted duck.

A track over the moor to the north-east of Ravenseat leads to Tan Hill, at the top of West Stonesdale. The track goes past Robert's Seat

Whitsundale Beck.

Wain Wath Force, upstream of Keld.

STONESDALE BECK, LOOKING SOUTH TOWARDS WEST STONESDALE.

West Stonesdale

A mile below Whitsundale, West Stonesdale runs northwards off from Birkdale, taking with it the road to Tan Hill four miles away. The road starts with a very tight, steep, twisty section just above Park House to the south of Cotterby Scar, making it impossible for large vehicles to enter the dale. As the road climbs up from Swaledale, there is a very clear view of Kisdon Hill to the east, but Keld – half a mile away, to the east – remains hidden, almost bashfully hiding its face from the outside world.

Half a mile up the road is the small hamlet of West Stonesdale, the only settlement in the dale. It contains little more than about eight well-kept stone buildings, mostly traditional farm buildings clustered together with the road meandering its way tightly between them.

From here the road continues up to Tan Hill, keeping some way above the narrow valley floor. The eastern side of the valley, which is often quite steep, is mostly grassed and grazed, with some scattered trees, dry-stone walls and stone field barns, and isolated farmsteads. The western side is poorly drained open moorland, freely grazed by sheep and cattle. The road crosses two small single-arched hump-backed bridges (doubtless both former packhorse bridges) near Lad Gill, about two miles south of Tan Hill.

There are no farms, houses or enclosed fields above this point; the land is all open moorland, with extensive patches of peat erosion by water and wind. Much of the fell is incised with deep gullies, which are probably the result of forest clearance by settlers over the last two thousand years. The gulleys are often deep, with steep bare sides. Looking west towards Robert's Seat, one of the deeply incised gullies is called Thomas Gill; the path from Ravenseat to Tan Hill runs down it then proceeds up Stonesdale Beck. Opposite Thomas Gill, on the eastern side of West Stonesdale Beck, is

House, which Pontefract (1934) describes as 'a ruined hut in which a gamekeeper lived just before and after the shooting season, in the days when poaching was common'.

Between Whitsundale and West Stonesdale, on the north side of the river and road, is Cotterby Scar, an imposing limestone cliff. Here, too, is Wain Wath Force (force being Norse for waterfall), the first of the striking waterfalls on the river Swale above Keld. The solid rock sandstone bed of the river is also visible at this point, which makes a very picturesque scene. This is a popular spot for picnics and paddling, being easily accessible from the road. The river water here and downstream often looks more like tea than water, stained brown after having drained through the peaty catchment after heavy rain. An old disused lime kiln can be seen on the south side of the road and river, opposite Wain Wath Force.

West Stonesdale, 'one of the remotest hamlets in England'. Ella Pontefract (1934)

the Mould Gill Coal Level, from where in the past low-grade coal was extracted and sold throughout Swaledale and adjacent dales, mainly for domestic use.

The road splits at the top of West Stonesdale, one branch running north-west for six miles to the village of Barras, and the other heading east and then down Arkengarthdale.

Tan Hill

Tan Hill, at the head of West Stonesdale, effectively marks the northern limit of Swaledale. The name comes from the Celtic word *tan*, meaning fire, probably because the site was used in the past for a warning fire, or perhaps as a religious site. Behind it in the distance, far off to the west, Nine Standards Rigg peeps over the skyline. From here you can see the arc of fells that enclose the top of Swaledale itself, but the landscape here is a vast, rugged, exposed stretch of open moorland. North of Tan Hill, writes Cooper (1973), is 'one of the largest expanses of rough grass and heather-clad moorland in the North of England'.

Traditionally this was a good area for cutting peat, for use both as domestic fuel and in the lead smelt mills. Pontefract (1934) describes how it was done in the 1930s, in the dying days of the practice. Peat was cut in June:

> First the grass and heather are pared off the peat-bed, then the peat is dug out, cut into convenient sizes, and left to dry. In a few days, when they have hardened a little, the pieces are reared against each other and left until they are dry enough to bring away and stack. In a wet season the peat never dries, and cannot be gathered. Not nearly so much peat is cut on the moors to-day. Like the burning of lime for the land, the practice seems to be dying out.

Tan Hill Inn.

The Tan Hill Inn, 1,725 feet above sea level, has long claimed to be the highest inn in England. Bogg (1909) calls it 'the highest placed, loneliest inn in England' and Speight (1897) writes that Tan Hill 'stands in as wild and as bleak a situation as is to be found anywhere in England … The house, in spite of its yard-thick walls, suffers most from the high winds and beating rains which sometimes rage with tremendous fury about these desolate moorlands.'

The pub is very popular with walkers – providing a welcoming oasis roughly halfway along both the Pennine Way and the Coast to Coast Walk – and with day visitors arriving by car and bike. It is not uncommon in the winter for guests to get snowed in for several days, but few are disappointed so long as the beer and food do not run out. The existence of Drover Hole and Drover Hole Hill just to the west of the inn are reminders that Tan Hill lies on one of the traditional cattle drovers' routes across the North Pennines.

Keld

Back on the main road (the B6270) down Swaledale, Stonesdale Beck flows into the Swale over Currack Force, the second of the attractive Keld waterfalls. The third, Catrake Force, is found a short distance downstream, hidden from sight from the road. About a mile below Park House, which has a caravan park and camp site, is Keld Green.

The tiny hamlet of Keld Green signals the presence nearby of Keld, but Keld itself remains hidden from sight across a field to the north, its seclusion little changed since the time of Ella Pontefract (1934): 'Those who keep along the road [by Keld] … see only a high, gaunt shooting-lodge, a shop, a cottage, and a Wesleyan [Methodist] chapel, comparative new-comers.'

The Keld Methodist Chapel was built in 1841 of local stone, a solid building with sandstone flags on the roof. It closed some years ago,

its glory days over. Today it sits by the side of the road looking rather neglected, its doors locked and its windows boarded up. Beside it a few farmhouses and buildings have been restored and made into private houses.

The 'high, gaunt shooting-lodge' has gone through various incarnations. For generations it was an inn, once called the Cat Hole Inn (allegedly named after wild cats which lived in the area). During the lead-mining years it was renamed the Miners Arms, and it subsequently reverted to the Cat Hole Inn. More recently it was a youth hostel, serving walkers along the Pennine Way. It is now a restaurant and small hotel called Keld Lodge.

Keld is a small village tucked away in a hollow with the river Swale running through the bottom of it. It is reached by taking the road which drops down past the war memorial at Keld Green. The narrow road winds its way between the closely spaced stone walls of the houses, which huddle together for protection against the elements.

Whitaker (1823) is alone in thinking that Keld was named after 'some cold spring by which it was watered'. The name Keld in fact comes from the Old Norse *kelda*, meaning a spring or stream, a legacy of the Norse settlers who chose the site for its shelter and defensibility. Pontefract (1934) comments that 'raiders sweeping down from the north would see nothing of the hidden settlement just off their line of march'. This is one of several settlements across England with the same name, although it is believed that it was once called Appletrekelde (the spring near the apple trees).

Speight (1897) rather fancifully refers to Keld as an 'Alpine village'. It is the last village heading up the dale; the first heading down dale. The shops that Pontefract described in the 1930s have long since closed, along with the school, through lack of permanent residents. Today Keld has the air of the original Sleepy Hollow.

KELD, WITH BLACK MOOR AND EAST GILL BEHIND.

Views about the merits – or otherwise – of Keld have been mixed. Tom Bradley, writing in 1891, for example, saw it as 'an old-fashioned country village with nothing of interest in it beyond, perhaps, the chapel ... ' While Edmund Bogg, writing less than 20 years later (1909), was full of praise for the little village: 'No other place ... can equal [Keld] for river and hill scenery, sternly grand, sublimely beautiful, and even to the folk-lore lover's eye, romantic; there is the gloom of mountain form, the picturesque commingling of overhanging wood and precipices.'

'Keld has little beauty in itself,' writes Jessica Lofthouse (1950), ' ... but it tucks its cottages in odd, out-of-the-way corners, scatters its farms in an apparently haphazard way over all its many surrounding fell-slopes, making an altogether bewitching community one would not exchange for any of the beautifully planned villages in other counties.'

Alfred Wainwright was not impressed with his first visit to Keld in 1938, writing: 'Keld is like Buckden in Wharfedale, the last outpost in the valley, but where Buckden is cosy and comfortable, Keld is by comparison barren, and appears far less hospitable.' His views mellowed through

time, and by 1989 he was able to describe Keld as 'a welcome oasis encompassed by bleak moorlands, a friendly refuge in an unfriendly landscape. It is small, its stone buildings straggling its only street in a haphazard yet tidy arrangement, many of them, even the chapel belfry, bearing proud dates and the names of proud men.'

Keld serves walkers along the Pennine Way and the Coast to Coast Walk, which cross just north of the village. For a short distance they share the same path, crossing the river and ascending the slope beside another waterfall – East Gill Force. The Pennine Way then continues up the eastern side of Stonesdale Beck towards Tan Hill, while the Coast to Coast Walk turns right and heads east, following the north bank of the Swale past West Wood towards Muker.

Park Lodge, in the heart of the village, is a welcome oasis that provides for the needs of walkers and visitors through its small shop and its camp site in an adjoining field, with a car park, toilets and shower facilities.

Traditionally, the village hall was the centre of village life in Keld, as else-where. Concerts, dances and meetings were held there, and during the 1930s a travelling draper used to hire the hall and sell his goods there. Pontefract (1934) recalls that 'in the cottage below the village hall lived Richard Alderson, known as Neddy Dick, who was famous for his "musical stones". These he had collected from the Swale, and he played tunes on them with two big wooden sticks.'

The other building that was much used in the past was Keld Chapel, whose origins are uncertain. It was once a Church of England church – Leland mentions it in 1538 – but was closed and fell into ruin, probably after the Anglican church was built at Muker in 1580. It was restored as a Calvinist place of worship in 1745, but within four decades had once again fallen into a poor state of repair. In 1789, independent preacher Edward Stillman arrived in Keld, after wandering through upper Swaledale for two years preaching in barns. He settled there, vowing to rebuild the chapel and preach the gospel, which he did after raising money by begging as he walked to London. Stillman preached there for 48 years. He died in 1838 and was succeeded by James Wilkinson, who – amongst other notable achievements over the following three decades, when poverty increased with the collapse of the lead-mining industry – suggested the building of Keld village institute, directed the building of a chapel at Thwaite, founded a Mutual Improvement Society for the young men of the district and encouraged the people of Keld to cultivate vegetable plots and improve their diets. With no Anglican or Catholic church in Keld, and thus no consecrated burial ground, the people of Keld and surrounding area traditionally had to carry their dead along the Corpse Way and bury them at Grinton parish church.

'The sublime water and crag scenery here . . . [is] amongst the finest in the country.' Harry Speight (1897)

Keld Chapel was rebuilt in 1860 and is now the Keld United Reformed Church. Its grounds include a small and very picturesque graveyard and the Keld Well-being Garden, which is run jointly by the church and the Keld Resource Centre and was opened in 2010. This is a small quiet patch of grass and natural flowers, with wooden seating where people can sit and contemplate, in a peaceful setting with wonderful views of the river and surrounding hills, including Kisdon Hill.

Proud of the village's heritage, and keen to share it with as many visitors as possible, the former church manse, school, Keld Literary Institute and Methodist Chapel have recently been converted into the Keld Countryside and Heritage Centre, which is also run by the Keld Resource Centre.

The Swale drops 30 feet as it flows over Kisdon Force and through a deep gorge just after Keld. The gorge was carved by torrential floods of meltwater from the great glacier that occupied the dale during the last ice age, which caused the path of the river to shift from the west side of Kisdon Hill to the east side. Kisdon Force, writes Pontefract (1934), 'comes in two falls over high rocks with a pool between them, where it seems to gather strength for the second effort. Cliffs shut it in on either side, and around it there is complete solitude.'

One of the very oldest areas of lead mining in Swaledale, the Beldi Hill Mines, is located on the moor just to the north of Kisdon Force.

KELD CHAPEL.

Keld to Muker

There are a number of ways of getting down dale from Keld to Muker, a section which L. F. Feaver (1937) thought was 'Swaledale … at its best'.

The road passes to the west of Kisdon, following the valley that was abandoned by the Swale in post-glacial times and now contains the small stream called Skeb Skeugh (from the Norse *skogr*, meaning a wood). Along the way it goes past the hamlet of Thorns Green and a few houses at Aygill, and then twists through the hamlet of Angram and on to Thwaite.

It is also possible to walk over Kisdon Hill. This is another popular route, which follows part of the old Corpse Way and offers striking views up and down the upper part of Swaledale.

There is also an attractive and popular walk on the eastern side of Kisdon past Kisdon Force and on to Crackpot Hall, where the valley opens out to give a spectacular view downstream along the Swale past Ivelet Wood towards Muker. In 1891 Tom Bradley wrote: 'If we would enjoy the weird, wild, stern beauties of this time-wasted, pine-clad ravine, and view the rush of waters that flow down Kisdon Force to the river's darksome bed, we must follow this path [past Crackpot Hall].'

The curious name Crackpot (in 1298 the place was called Crakepot) has two parts, with different origins. 'Crack' comes from the Old English *kraka*, meaning a crow, and *pot* is an Old Norse word meaning a cavity or deep hole. So Crackpot means a crevice where crows nest. There is another place called Crackpot in Swaledale, farther downstream opposite Gunnerside.

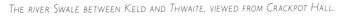

THE RIVER SWALE BETWEEN KELD AND THWAITE, VIEWED FROM CRACKPOT HALL.

THE RUINED REMAINS OF CRACKPOT HALL.

Crackpot Hall was built in the early eighteenth century as a shooting lodge for Lord Wharton, a comfortable base from which he and his guests could hunt the deer which roamed this part of Swaledale in those days. After the deer disappeared and hunting ceased, the hall had a chequered history. For many years it was a farm, but the building became unstable after its foundations were damaged by mining beneath it. The hall was still inhabited and being used as a farmhouse when Ella Pontefract was writing in the 1930s. She noted that 'the foundations of Crackpot Hall slipped many years ago, and now the tops of the doors and windows are at all angles, and the bedroom floors tilt like the rolling deck of a ship'. The hall was abandoned not many years later, and has gradually fallen into ruin. Today the roof is long since collapsed, no bedroom floors survive, few external walls stand intact, walls and windows lean at precarious angles, and the ground in and around the hall is a pile of tumbled stones. To Herriot (1979) 'the place is a ruin but it still has sad splendour'.

Swinner Gill

Just past Crackpot Hall a rocky valley opens up to the north; this is Swinner Gill, the scene of much lead-mining activity in the past. The Coast to Coast Walk follows this route heading east after it leaves Keld, hugging the southern flank of Rogan's Seat before dropping down into Gunnerside Beck near Bunton Hush.

Pontefract's (1934) description of Swinner Gill as 'a grim, treeless valley' is apt, because the landscape here is dominated by the extensive remains of lead-mining activity. These include the ruins of a smelt mill and the entrance to a mine level beside a waterfall on East Gill.

One interesting feature of this side valley is a cave beside Swinner Gill Falls called Swinner Gill Kirk. Local folklore has it that early Nonconformists (who by law were not allowed to hold meetings) used to meet there regularly for worship, with a scout stationed on the fell above to keep watch and warn of people approaching, at which the Dissenters would run and hide in the cave. Although the story is told by Ella Pontefract (1934) and others, Bill Mitchell (1990) describes it as 'vague in folk memory and unsubstantiated in any texts'.

Between Keld and Angram the road is narrow and hilly, with lots of twists and turns and some close encounters with stone field barns adjacent to the road itself. Angram is a tiny hamlet comprising little more than a handful of stone houses and farm buildings on both sides of the road. Again, Pontefract (1934) comes up with a fitting description – 'the houses cluster on the top of the hill [at Angram] as if they have been blown up there from both sides' – while Speight (1897) considers Angram 'a quiet spot … the good folk passing their lives rustically and peacefully, excluded from the business and excitement of the world.'

The name Angram comes from the Old English angr, a meadow or clearing, and ham, a home or hamlet. This ancient description tells us that this area was being farmed long before the Norman Conquest and the long, straight dry-stone walls marking out individual fields in Angram Pasture, on the fellside to the west of the hamlet, confirm that farming has been practised here probably continuously since then.

Pontefract (1934) writes: 'The grazing for the farms at Angram is of tremendous area, stretching six or seven miles on to the moors as far as Great Sleddale. Most of the pastures are around the houses, but there are a few meadows enclosed from the fells at Sleddale where grass is grown for hay.'

Swinner Gill Kirk by R. Rodwell.

Swinner Gill viewed from the east side of Kisdon Hill.

The road between Angram and Thwaite passes down the abandoned valley now occupied by Skeb Skeugh. The view of Kisdon, to the east, is probably one of the most characteristic and attractive in the whole of Swaledale: it contains all of the typical features including dry-stone walls, stone field barns, isolated farmhouses, small patches of woodland, traditional hay meadows on the valley floor and open moorland on the fell top. Nestling snugly at the bottom of the Buttertubs Pass is the tiny village of Thwaite.

Kisdon Hill

At 1,637 feet above sea level Kisdon is not particularly high, but this isolated hill, named rather dramatically by Edmund Bogg in *Regal Richmond and the Land of the Swale* as 'Mount Kisdon', dominates the scenery in upper Swaledale. It is quite striking, with grey limestone scars, a heather-covered, gently rounded gritstone summit, and gulleys cut into some of the lower slopes and meadows on the valley floor.

The name Kisdon is aptly descriptive; it comes from the Celtic *kis* (little) and *dun* (a detached hill). It is labelled Kisdon Island on Jefferys' 1771 map of Yorkshire, although it was never truly cut off from the land around it. The 'island' was formed after the glacier diverted the course of the river Swale to the north of Kisdon during the last ice age, leaving the abandoned valley of Skeb Skeugh to the west and the post-glacial valley of the Swale to the east. To the south it is defined by Straw Beck, which carries the water from Skeb Skeugh, Thwaite Beck and Cliff Beck into the Swale, just east of Muker.

Kisdon has enchanted many of the people who have written about Swaledale, and rightly so. Bogg (1909) called it 'the Table Mountain of Swaledale' and Gordon Home (1906) viewed it as 'one of the finest portions of the dale'. Ella Pontefract (1934), too, was taken in by its beauty. On Kisdon, she writes:

> Its heather-topped summit, a darker patch among the surrounding hills … Wild flowers fill its lower meadows – splashes of marsh marigolds, sheets of buttercups; bluebells and wood anemones creep up to the wild orchis and the mountain cranesbill; and yellow and purple pansies in their turn peep courageously up to the heather. Now a patch of woodland is enclosed by crumbling walls, now juniper trees crouch like dwarfs upon it, now it breaks out in limestone scars.

KISDON HILL VIEWED FROM THWAITE.

the Corpse Way

The Corpse Way in upper Swaledale is one of the oldest 'roads' in the dale, although it is really a well-trodden path; flint arrowheads found along its route point to a prehistoric origin. Its course can be traced from Keld to Grinton, running along the sunnier (thus warmer) northern side of the dale. It avoided marsh land in the valley bottom and the thick forest which covered the lower slopes, and forded the river in several places. The one in Swaledale is one of three Corpse Ways in the Yorkshire Dales: the other two are in Wensleydale and Wharfedale.

From the head of the dale, the path ran via Keld and Birkdale and over Kisdon Hill to Muker. A second branch ran from West Stonesdale, via Frith, Smithyholme and Ravenseat, and kept to the left bank of the Swale before it met the Keld path at Calvert Houses. From there it went into Gunnerside, crossed Gunnerside Beck, continued east through Healaugh to Reeth, and then crossed the Swale at Grinton Bridge.

The path gets its name from its traditional use – as the route along which bodies of the dead were carried down the dale to their final resting place at the parish church in Grinton. As Geoffrey Wright (1985) explains, 'Such routes [as the Corpse Way] were not used exclusively for that purpose, but most probably saw the normal traffic of packhorses, driven stock, lead miners, and dales folk going to and from market.'

Stories about the carrying of the dead along the Corpse Way have become part of the folklore of the dale, as Pontefract (1934), Cooper (1973) and others have recorded. Relatives kept watch over the body of the deceased in the family home, and it was then placed in a simple wicker basket. A fleece of wool would be put in the coffin of a shepherd, so that 'his occupation could thus be proved on Judgment Day, so that his irregular attendance at church would be forgiven'. A funeral party would follow the wicker 'coffin' – carried by family members and pall-bearers supplied by the hamlets it passed through – the twelve miles or so to Grinton. The journey from the head of the dale would take up to two days, including an overnight stop at Feetham, where the coffin was stored in a small stone 'dead house' (of which only traces now remain) while the funeral party went to the Punch Bowl Inn for rest and refreshment. At intervals along the route there were flat resting stones, about six feet long, where the procession could lay the coffin for a while and take a break. Two resting stones survive on Kisdon Hill.

After the new church was built at Muker in 1580 with a consecrated burial ground, the dead from the upper dale (down to Gunnerside) were taken there for burial. People who died downstream from Gunnerside continued to be buried in Grinton, as before.

The Corpse Way is now a popular walking route, which passes through some of the most attractive scenery of upper Swaledale. Bogg (1907) considers the way to be 'an uplifting of the spirit as well as a bracing of the sinews to follow this literal highway, accompanied every step by forms of quiet beauty, set in the frame of graceful scenery'.

Thwaite

Thwaite is a small village like Keld, but it is slightly less cramped. It occupies a flatter location with more accessible flat land – Tom Bradley (1891) insists that Thwaite 'nestles sweetly in the hollow' – and it sits beside the Swale. Unlike Keld, Thwaite has a shop, tea shop and hotel (the Kearton Country Hotel). The road through Thwaite is wider than that through Keld, but it still creeps around the edges of the stone buildings that huddle together and crosses the river over a narrow, twisty, single-arched stone bridge at the eastern side of the village. Herriot (1979) writes that Thwaite was 'a typical Dales village if ever you saw one; the inevitable hump-backed bridge, the massive houses of grey stone, the whole clustered atmosphere suggesting a nearness to the head of the Dale'.

The name Thwaite comes from the Old Norse *thveit*, meaning a forest clearing or meadow, again indicating an early Scandinavian settlement and a long history of farming. Like most of the villages in upper Swaledale, Thwaite suffered badly in the late nineteenth century with the mass out-migration of people caused by the collapse of the lead-mining industry. Speight (1897) writes of 'the retired hamlet of Thwaite', and Bogg (1909) calls it 'grey and sombre, with the beauty of age and decay over it, rugged but a little ruined'. The village never died completely, partly because it was a popular place for farmers and their families to retire to, but it struggled to find a new role for itself after the end of the lead-mining industry. None of what Pontefract describes from the 1930s exists today, but Thwaite has been given a new lease of

life by the restoration and conversion of many former miners' cottages and farmhouses into holiday cottages. A good example is the old stone chapel at the northern entrance to the village, which retains a small bell in a simple stone tower as a reminder of its former use.

Thwaite is probably best known these days as the birthplace of the Kearton brothers, Richard (1871–1928) and Cherry (1871–1940), famous sons of upper Swaledale who were pioneers of wildlife photography (both still and motion). They went to school in Muker. Whilst – as Pontefract (1934) points out – 'it was in exploring its gullies and the moors above them that they developed the love and interest in nature which was to make them famous', their careers took them all round

Thwaite.

'These days a drowsy lethargy hangs over Thwaite, but it wakes to life as the children come tramping home from school, and as the shepherd comes down from the moor, and the farmer appears from his walling or haymaking or fetching down loads of dried bracken or rushes from the fells. Rushes are used for bedding as well as bracken, and for thatching hay and bracken stacks.' Ella Pontefract (1934)

the world, although they returned regularly to upper Swaledale both to capture the area and its wildlife and to visit family and friends.

The main road down Swaledale between Thwaite and Muker is not suitable for long or wide vehicles, being narrow and winding, with some steep twisty bridges over the river Swale. Downstream from Thwaite the valley floor becomes much flatter and wider overall.

Buttertubs Pass

The road that climbs up from Hawes in Wensleydale and heads north six miles over the open fells to Thwaite in upper Swaledale, generally referred to as the Buttertubs Pass, is one of the most popular routes into Swaledale. It is also one of the most scenic. It is a well-established route, having been 'a foot-track in pre-Norman times, becoming a cart-track upon the intro-duction of wheeled traffic many centuries afterwards', as Speight (1897) points out. In *Wensleydale and Swaledale Guide,* Leyland (1896) writes how the Buttertubs Pass 'involves a stiff climb that is exhilarating, and the magnificent views it affords … cannot but entrance the wayfarer.'

After leaving Hawes, the road runs up the eastern side of Fossdale Gill, a long deep valley whose river eventually flows over Hardraw Force and then into the river Ure. The Pennine Way runs along the western side of Hearne Beck, to the west of Fossdale Gill, as it climbs up Great Shunner Fell, the path having been stabilised in recent years by sandstone flags which protect the fragile peat moorland from excessive erosion.

Towards the top of Fossdale Gill the road crosses a fairly flat pass, a scenic natural gateway into Swaledale. At 1,725 feet above sea level, this is one of the highest and bleakest mountain passes in England. The summit is dominated by open moorland, with eroding peat hags, purple heather in August, and grouse shooting during the season. It offers grand views in clear weather. The gentle summit of Great Shunner Fell dominates the view to the west and to the east is Lovely Seat. To the north-east

KISDON HILL VIEWED FROM THE BUTTERTUBS PASS, LOOKING NORTH.

the view is truly panoramic: it includes Kisdon with Rogan's Seat behind it. To the north, the view extends towards Nine Standards Rigg. The backdrop looking north is the Stainmore Gap, with the Howgill Fells and the Lake District in the distance off to the west.

Once over the summit of the pass, the road descends northwards into Swaledale, slowly at first but then gathering pace as the slope increases. Near the start of this descent are the Buttertubs, after which the pass is somewhat enigmatically named, beside the road on both sides. The Buttertubs are six deep, round vertical shafts – varying in diameter from 3 feet to 20 feet and up to 100 feet deep – that have been worn into

OPPOSITE: THE BUTTERTUBS.
COPYRIGHT COURTESY OF ALAN GREEN.

'From the summit of the
[Buttertubs] pass ... there
is one of the grandest
panoramic views of the
peaks of the Pennine chain
and surrounding moors to be
had in this part of England.'
Harry Speight (1897)

COTTAGE GARDEN IN MUKER.

the limestone by the action of water over many centuries. Some suggest the name comes from the fact that the shafts have a shape like wooden barrels, others that it comes from an ancient tradition of storing barrels of butter at the bottom of the shafts to keep them cool. Although – as Tom Bradley (1891) points out – 'the regularity of their sides gives them the appearance of being man's handicraft', they are entirely natural in origin. Flowering shrubs and plants and mosses grow on the stone columns and sides of the shafts. Pontefract (1934) notes how 'at one time these swallow holes were a danger to travellers in the dark or fog, but most of them are now railed off from the road'.

Arthus Norway (1903) describes the Buttertubs as 'cool dark, and cavernous, they are deep, black pits, walled by very strangely splintered limestone, standing now in crumpled pillars towering out of sheer depth, now breaking into fantastic shapes of every kind, with here and there a flowering alder, or a mountain ash growing out of a crevice, or some sweet white flower straying fearlessly down into the abyss'.

From the Buttertubs one gets a sense of the harshness of the upper Swaledale landscape and the isolation of its farms, hamlets and villages. The view is dominated by the open moorland of the fell tops, with

113

MUKER VIEWED FROM KISDON HILL.

fields on the valley sides and meadows on the valley floor, and scattered pockets of woodland. From here it is very difficult to catch a glimpse of any of the villages which lie nestled along the bottom of the valley, such as Keld, Thwaite and Muker. The descent into Swaledale provides a very clear view of Angram Pasture to the north. L. F. Feaver (1937) describes the surrounding landscape at this point: 'As the traveller passes the screes, the rills, the precipices, the rock-strewn ghylls of the Buttertubs, and observes the scanty vegetation, and sees no sign of human dwellings, far-flung scenes open out; river courses, dales branching out of dales, hills sweeping up and down in switchback lines, come and go whilst he toils at different elevations.'

The Buttertubs Pass road joins the main road along Swaledale just east of Thwaite.

Muker

Muker is little larger than Thwaite but has a more open location and a welcoming face. The road heading down dale passes straight through the village, with the river Swale on the right (south) and buildings on the left. Like Thwaite, Muker tests the courage and resilience of drivers, with a tight, narrow, zigzag stone bridge at the downstream end of the

village. There are car-parking spaces by the roadside and a pay-and-display car park by the river just over the bridge.

The name Muker means a narrow field or small piece of land. It comes from the Old Norse *miór* (narrow) and *akr* (field) and was first recorded in 1274 as Meuhaker. The name evolved over the centuries, from Muaker in 1577 and Mewker in 1606, to Muker today. The Norse naming shows that the village was settled by Norse people, but evidence of earlier people comes in the form of a number of Neolithic artefacts which have been unearthed around the village.

Early writers, viewing it after the decline of the lead-mining industry and mass migration, had little good to say about Muker; according to *Black's Picturesque Guide to Yorkshire* (1874) it was 'a small and uninteresting market-town … [which] may form a convenient central point for those who wish to penetrate the still more remote portions of Swaledale', while George Radford (1880) describes it as 'miserable, almost squalid … a small town about which it is impossible to speak enthusiastically'. Tom Bradley had little better to say when he wrote in *Yorkshire Rivers. No 4. The Swale* (1891), that Muker 'possesses neither regularity of construction nor architectural beauty'.

MUKER LITERARY INSTITUTE.

of security about it. It has placed itself so well under the shelter of the fell, and raised above the beck, not clustering round it as Thwaite does, but holding itself aloof … ' Jessica Lofthouse (1950) writes: 'Everything in Muker was perfect: the little beck running past the houses crooning so soothing a song as twilight fell, the cottages stepped, one behind the other, up the slope … it is very cosy, for one house borrows shelter from the wall of another; so must the first builders have arranged it.'

Sir Nikolaus Pevsner (1966), however, rather blandly describes Muker as 'a grey village built up against the green hillside with the church in the highest position'.

On his first impressions of Muker in 1938, Wainwright (1986) writes that it 'struck me as being one of the oddest places I had ever seen. I cannot say it was out of place, for Swaledale abounds with surprises, but it seemed to me first of all that I had walked into the Tyrol, for here was a flowery Alpine village, a jumble of ill-sorted houses along a rushing mountain stream, a charming picture, almost a fantasy.'

Muker must be one of the smallest villages in England to have earned the honour of a book about its history. Edmund Cooper's (1948) *Muker: the Story of a Yorkshire Parish*, recently republished, is an informative and fitting tribute to the place. He insists that 'from the earliest times Muker was the centre of the social life of Upper Swaledale'.

On the left-hand side of the road, soon after entering Muker, is the former Wesleyan chapel, a simple, plain stone building constructed in 1934–35 to replace one originally built in 1845 to serve the local lead-mining community. It closed as a chapel some years back and has been converted into a bed and breakfast.

Farther along the road on the same side is the former Muker school, originally established in 1678 but enlarged several times since, including in 1879 when it was recognised as a national school. Two stone tablets on the outside wall commemorate the school's two most famous pupils

Muker has a rather different feel to it than Thwaite, although the history of the two villages is very similar. Bogg writes in *The Wild Borderlands of Richmondshire: Between Tees and Yore* (1909) that Muker is 'perhaps the most compact huddle of dwellings in the dale; a motley conglomeration in stone of walls and roofs, set higgledy-piggledy yet in complete accord with the laws of picturesqueness'.

Muker has retained much of its rustic charm, with little substantial change in its fabric or layout since the turn of the twentieth century. Pontefract (1934) writes endearingly about Muker: 'there is a feeling

– Richard and Cherry Kearton. In the 1970s the building was converted into a craft gallery and the Swaledale Woollens shop. Next door is the popular Farmers Arms pub, and farther down is the small village store and tea shop.

Without doubt the most intriguing building in Muker is the Literary Institute with its quirky, tall Flemish gable end. Sir Nikolaus Pevsner (1966) describes it as 'tiny but with a portly shaped gable'. It is not known why this unusual style was adopted for Muker; there is nothing else like it in the whole of Swaledale. The Literary Institute was built in about 1867 from public subscriptions, contained around 600 books and served as a local library and meeting place, for both the social and educational benefit of the largely mining community of the day. It ceased operating as a literary institute in the 1950s. Since 1994 it has been the practice room for the Muker Silver Band which was formed in 1879. It is one of a number of such bands throughout the dale in the old lead-mining villages, encouraged by the lead companies to promote the welfare of their employees.

Up the steep hill in front of the Literary Institute is a small, open flat space known as The Green, where a market was held in days gone by. There, just behind the church, is the public hall which was built in 1922 and is used for a variety of activities. Around The Green are numerous old cottages and farmhouses, many of which have in recent decades been converted into holiday cottages and bed and breakfast establishments.

Dominating the skyline of the village and located beside The Green is the church of St Mary the Virgin, the small stone-built parish church. It has a square tower, which Nikolaus Pevsner (1966) describes simply as 'quite tall', which rises above the small cottages huddled around it. The church is sixteenth century in origin, having been built in 1580 initially as a chapel-of-ease under St Andrew's down dale in Grinton (thus ending the need to carry the deceased down to Grinton along the Corpse Way), but soon afterwards it was licensed for baptisms, marriages and burials. It was

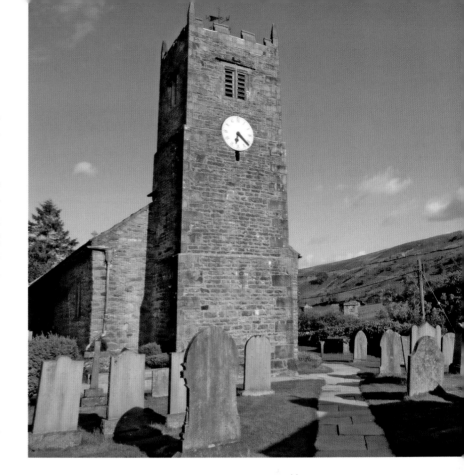

MUKER PARISH CHURCH.

restored in 1761, when the thatched roof was replaced by stone slates, and wooden pews, a gallery and a pulpit were added. By the late nineteenth century it had again fallen into disrepair; in 1880 George Radford noted 'it is strange that tombs should be more cheerful than the House of God itself'. The church was restored in 1890 and in 1892 the township of Muker became an independent parish (previously it had been part of Grinton parish). It is alleged that the church bells were brought from Ellerton Priory after the dissolution of the monasteries. Cooper (1948) describes Muker parish church as 'a small picturesque building consisting of a continuous nave and chancel, a west tower and a porch, built solidly of stone'.

The church, writes Pontefract in *Swaledale* (1934), 'is a simple building, but it achieves beauty and charm from being in perfect keeping with its surroundings. The rough tower and walls are of the essence of Swaledale.'

Like Keld and Thwaite farther up the dale, Muker is a popular base from which to explore upper Swaledale and a much-appreciated stopping-off point for walkers.

Muker to Gunnerside

The views between Muker and Gunnerside are amongst the finest in Swaledale.

Over this stretch, the valley floor is relatively wide and flat, with many dry-stone walls and some field barns, scattered trees and small copses. The fell tops tend to be lower here, particularly on the southern side. To the north there are good views of Kisdon Hill and sightings of Rogan's Seat over Black Hill. The road continues past Ivelet Bridge and Ivelet village, and on past the hamlet of Satron. The river Swale flows eastwards on the north side of the road, which stays high above it, running along a terrace. To the south, by Crow Trees, a side road turns off to Askrigg; it continues past High Oxnop, then drops down over the open moorland of Askrigg Common into the village of Askrigg, five miles south in upper Wensleydale.

'The scenery in this locality is especially inviting to the hardy and industrious pedestrian.'
Harry Speight (1897)

After Crow Trees the road passes Low Oxnop, to the south. At the entrance to Oxnop Hall there is a millstone dated 1681. The hall,

which Pontefract (1934) describes as sitting 'with a fine, unstudied ease', is now a bed and breakfast establishment, with some holiday cottages available to rent on site. It sits proudly above the main road, looking over the valley towards Ivelet and Gunnerside Lodge, the local residence of the owner of the Gunnerside Estate and its shooting rights.

The road continues eastwards towards Satron and Gunnerside New Bridge. Just out of sight to the north is Ivelet Bridge, the much-photographed narrow, high, stone, single-arched former packhorse bridge over the river Swale, which Pontefract (1934) calls 'one of the gems of Swaledale, a perfect specimen, unspoilt by flood or storm'. Nikolaus Pevsner describes the bridge in *Buildings of England: Yorkshire – The North Riding* (1966), as 'the most romantic of the Swaledale bridges. One arch, rising very high and never widened. The bridge is in the trees, in a place where a splashing beck [Ivelet Beck] meets the Swale.'

The tiny hamlet of Ivelet sits a short distance north of the bridge, beside Gunnerside Lodge. Just above Ivelet a small single-track road runs westwards from Gunnerside towards Calvert Houses, and then continues unsurfaced by Ivelet Side and on through Ivelet Wood, along the valley of the Swale past Swinner Gill and Crackpot Hall towards Keld.

The hamlet of Satron once contained one of the earliest corn mills in upper Swaledale, but today it is just a handful of well-kept stone cottages huddled tightly together beside the main road. It looks northwards towards Ivelet Bridge, and west towards Gunnerside Lodge.

Ivelet Bridge.

118

GUNNERSIDE VIEWED FROM NEAR GUNNERSIDE NEW BRIDGE, LOOKING NORTH.

Chapter Eight
MIDDLE SWALEDALE: GUNNERSIDE TO REETH

'The landscape ... is eminently wild and romantic ... [and] ... much exposed to the brunt of storms, and snow in winter often accumulates, in many places, to an enormous depth.' Harry Speight (1897)

THE SECTION OF SWALEDALE between Gunnerside and Reeth differs in character from the headwaters and upper dale. Here the valley is broader and flatter, and land use is dominated by farming. The scenery is very attractive and includes numerous well-kept dry-stone walls, field barns and hay meadows. Two side valleys to the north of the river Swale – Gunnerside Beck and Barney Beck – contain extensive remains of the former lead-mining industry, and provide fine walking country with added interest from the industrial archaeology.

Gunnerside

The approach to Gunnerside New Bridge carries the road from Muker (three miles upstream) over the river Swale from the south to the north side of the valley. It offers clear views to the north of the old lynchets on Gunnerside Pasture above Ivelet, and of the village of Gunnerside and Gunnerside Beck. This whole area gives a good sense of the antiquity and continuity of human use of the land in the dale.

The name Gunnerside, like many other place names in upper Swaledale, is of Norse origin. It has two parts – the name Gunnar (probably the Norse chief who settled here) and the word *saetre* which means a hill pasture, so Gunnerside means Gunnar's pasture.

Gunnerside has a very picturesque setting, huddled at the mouth of Gunnerside Beck. Tom Bradley (1891) describes the 'grey stone buildings [that] sit almost by the brink of the river, hemmed in by high hills, for the valley has narrowed down to a marvelous degree, and the huge mountains rise precipitously on each hand, while right in front, blocking up the head of the dale, as it were, is the giant hill of Kisdon'.

Gunnerside Beck was one of the most important centres of the lead-mining industry in Swaledale, and Gunnerside was the gateway to it and its main local service centre. The development of Gunnerside owes much to the development of the lead industry, and at its peak during the eighteenth and nineteenth centuries lead mining dominated the local economy and society. The decline and collapse of the industry,

Gunnerside Old Smithy.

Gunnerside Bottoms, looking upstream towards Great Shunner Fell.

therefore, had a particularly strong impact on the village, which, as Pontefract (1934) records, 'showed it in its look of ruin and desolation'.

The houses in Gunnerside are 'thick walled, snug, and warm-hearted as their indwellers … [but it is] a curiously grey, grim, hard featured townlet', wrote Bogg in 1907. Many of the cottages and houses, having been built by miners, were subsequently abandoned. Since the 1960s, however, many have been restored and brought back to life, often as holiday cottages, and modern Gunnerside has emerged, in the words of James Herriot (1979), as 'a most appealing village with pretty little houses climbing up the hillside and a glorious view along the valley'.

Gunnerside is a larger village than those farther up the dale, with buildings at all angles but less squashed together, because it occupies a flatter and more extensive site. The main road runs right through the middle of the village, across a stone bridge over Gunnerside Beck. Gunnerside is also less sleepy than the other villages up the dale; it has a primary school, a large Methodist chapel with its own graveyard, a popular pub (King's Head), blacksmith's metal-working shop, and a café-cum-tea shop. The Gunnerside Literary Institute, a fine stone building beside Gunnerside Beck in the centre of the village, was built in 1877 and restored in 2000. It is now a community centre (locally referred to as Gunnerside Village Hall) with an active programme of social activities for all ages. Gunnerside also contains a number of bed and breakfasts, and a good proportion of the small restored cottages are holiday cottages or rental properties. The village is a popular base from which to explore Gunnerside Beck, which contains the remains of the Sir Francis Mine and other mining sites on Melbecks Moor.

To the east of the village on the floodplain of the Swale is Gunnerside Bottoms, which has the most extensive and best preserved hay meadows and associated dry-stone walls and field barns in Swaledale. This is part of the Environmentally Sensitive Area (ESA) scheme which provides grants to farmers to enable them to continue using traditional farming practices, designed to preserve the characteristic appearance of the landscape and the diversity of natural habitats.

On leaving Gunnerside and heading east towards Reeth, and ultimately to Richmond, the road runs along the north side of the river.

Gunnerside Beck

Gunnerside Beck flows southwards through Gunnerside and joins the river Swale by Gunnerside New Bridge. It drains the eastern side of Rogan's Seat and the former lead-mining area of Old Gang and Bunton Hush, and Blakethwaite Gill.

The whole valley of Gunnerside Beck is rich in old lead-mine workings. Much remains of the Blakethwaite lead mines at the head of the valley, including remnants of the smelt mill and the long flue which extends up the hillside, as well as kilns, levels and extensive spoil heaps.

Farther down the beck the Coast to Coast Walk comes in from Swinner Gill to the west. The walk descends down the western side of the valley past Lownathwaite lead mines, crosses the beck by Blind Gill, then climbs up the eastern side past Bunton Hush, continuing over Melbecks Moor past the Old Gang Mines before dropping into Old Gang Beck and Barney Beck. The exposed moorland crossing over Melbecks Moor passes through a flat, Martian landscape dominated by gravel from the spoil heaps of the adjacent mines. As Wainwright (1989) emphasises, 'not a blade of grass nor a sprig of heather is visible in a vast desert of stones'.

'A century ago, the . . . [upper part of the valley] was a scene of intense mining activity and although now a place a deathly quiet, with only the stream showing movement, it is easy to imagine from the many evidences remaining, the animation and noise that once prevailed here and understand the methods of operation ... This is a tortured landscape, appearing as if bombed on a massive scale, yet the ravages were done by men working with bare hands and primitive tools. The picture is without any vestige of beauty ... '
Alfred Wainwright (1989)

Wainwright (1989) describes a walk along Swinner Gill as a 'grim trek amidst the debris of a dead industry, amidst the skeletons of a past enterprise that once flourished exceedingly and then, in the space of a few years, withered and was abandoned ... The scene is one of utter man-made devastation stripped of all natural beauty.'

Gunnerside to Low Row

Between Gunnerside and Low Row the road is narrow, twisty and has switchback hills and dips. In places it runs very close to the river Swale, and it can flood under high flow conditions. In *James Herriot's Yorkshire* (1979), Herriot describes the river here as 'a curving avenue of constant enchantment, a long delight of unfolding views of green fells, scattered grey barns and always the pebbly river at its heart ... The river, widening into shallow loops, the waters glittering and dancing as they played between their banks of white pebbles ... '

The road runs through some wooded areas, and then past a small cluster of buildings called Strands. Strands House, Strands Farm and Strands Cottage have fine views looking south across the floodplain of the Swale. The road continues through Rowleth Wood and past isolated houses on its way eastwards to Low Row. Just past Isles Bridge, on the south side of the main road, is Hazel Brow Farm, a tourist development with camping ground and farming attractions for the whole family.

The main road along Swaledale runs north of the river Swale between Gunnerside and Grinton, but there are some interesting places south of the river which can be reached from the main road. A small

GUNNERSIDE BECK.

side road turns off the main road (the B6270) heading south, over Isles Bridge. It continues up Haverdale Beck past Crackpot to Summer Lodge. Pontefract writes in *Swaledale* (1934) that the name Haverdale, 'coming from the Norse *halfri*, oats, suggests that in medieval times oats were grown in the district. Until comparatively recent days corn was grown on the level ground near the river.'

Recall that there is also evidence of grain having been grown between Ivelet and Gunnerside, and also to the east of Haverdale at Harkerside. Records show that there was once a watermill at the bottom of the beck where oats were ground to make oatmeal, a staple food product through history, though no traces of it remain. A new mill called Haverdale Mill was built nearby to replace it, which had a variety of uses including as a worsted mill for making carpets, then a flour mill, and later as a concert venue. There was also a small fulling mill a bit farther upstream, to which the dales people brought their knitted items (mainly socks, jerseys and coats) to be fulled (shrunk and cleaned in soapy water) before being sold.

The road up Haverdale Beck runs through the tiny hamlet of Crackpot, a small group of houses. The origin of the word Crackpot is the same as that of Crackpot Hall between Keld and Swinner Gill, but this hamlet gets its name from a cave in the beck above Summer Lodge, known as Crackpot Cave or Fairy Hole. Crackpot can also be reached by the road that runs east from Gunnerside New Bridge, past Hag Wood and Spring End.

The Haverdale Beck road ends at Summer Lodge.

Harkerside

The road that runs west from Grinton south of the river Swale goes past Harkerside, Maiden Castle and How Hill. It then climbs up over the moorland past Summer Lodge Pasture, over the fell top at Windgates Currack, and drops down into Askrigg in Wensleydale.

Harkerside is a hamlet at the foot of High Harker Hill, on the south side of the Swale opposite Healaugh. The name Harkerside comes from the Old Norse word *akr*, meaning an open field. This district was cultivated in the Anglo-Saxon period, like Haverdale Beck and the area between Ivelet and Gunnerside. In Roman times there was a ford across the Swale near here, close to Feetham, which the foot soldiers used as they marched between the camp at Bainbridge in Wensleydale northwards to the fort at Greta Bridge, on the important trans-Pennine route from what is now Scotch Corner to Carlisle. It is thought that a track also led up from the ford to the earthwork known as Maiden Castle.

In recent years, detailed surveys by the Swaledale Ancient Land Boundaries Project have uncovered evidence of organised systems of prehistoric field systems in the area around Harkerside and Calver Hill, over the river to the north. Archaeologists have long been intrigued by a series of embankments and ditches in this area. One theory is that these are part of a hill fort used by the Brigantes, possibly after their defeat by the Romans at Stanwick near Gilling in about AD 71–74.

The embankments start just below the brow of the eastern side of High Harker Hill, and, in Cooper's words, they 'seem to continue northwards in the Reeth direction until they reach the downward slope. Then there is a break of 1000 yards and an embankment appears again, ending almost at the edge of the river Swale. Another similar earthwork runs parallel to this lower one and also ends near the Swale, but it can be picked up again on the north side of the river near Fremington. It then runs up through that village and finally ends one third of the way up to Fremington Edge … The dyke … has its bank thrown up on the higher side of the ditch, suggesting that it is a defence against people advancing up the slope.' (1973)

Maiden Castle

The most striking archaeological site in Swaledale is the major earth-works known as Maiden Castle at Harkerside, which landscape archaeologist Robert White (2002) calls 'enigmatic'. The site, located just over a mile west of Grinton at the base of High Harker Hill, has attracted much speculation and more than its share of folklore. The site is covered in heather and bracken, and is well marked on maps. According to Pontefract (1934), 'Tradition has it that a chest of gold lies buried beneath the first mound, and many have searched for it.'

The main feature of the site is a large, irregular circle about 300 feet in diameter – 'as nearly circular as the ground will admit' as Whitaker (1823) puts it – surrounded by earthworks, which may have had a rampart wall on top. Below the earthworks is an external ditch originally between 10 and 15 feet deep, which on the upslope side is cut into the hill and the downslope side follows the contours. The entrance is on the eastern side of the site and it is marked by an avenue of stones about 330 feet long and 16 feet wide. Piles of dressed sandstone blocks at the entrance suggest that there might have been a gateway or gatehouse here. There is a round mound like a tumulus (burial mound) just outside the entrance, and an oblong one at the western end of the site. Cooper (1973) notes that 'there are traces of 2 or 3 hut circles in the south-east corner [of the inner circle] and one near the north east'. Robert White (2002) debates the purpose of the avenue: 'It could have been of only limited use for driving stock as the walls do not form a funnel, and is perhaps best explained as a high status entrance to the enclosure.'

The name Maiden Castle offers clues to the origin of the site. Speight (1897) notes that Maiden might be derived from the Celtic *mai-dun*, meaning a great ridge, but he preferred a Celtic-Roman origin based on the Celtic *meadhon* and Latin *medius*, both of which mean middle. He pointed out that 'wherever these Maiden Castles occur we find them midway between two or more important stations; thus Maiden Castle on Stainmore stands midway between the stations of Bowes and Brough, and Maiden Castle on Harkerside stands midway from the camps at Bainbridge and Greta Bridge.'

The best known Maiden Castle in England is the large and well-preserved one in Dorset, which was first occupied during the Neolithic period, then abandoned, then enlarged and strengthened during the Early Iron Age, and finally abandoned again around AD 70, shortly after the Roman invasion. The age and detailed history of the Swaledale Maiden Castle remain shrouded in mystery. The general consensus is that it was built during the Late Neolithic or Early Bronze Age; a few writers agree with Speight (1897) that it was later 'occupied as a guard and rest-station by the Roman troops, but not as a permanent camp'.

The purpose of the site is as uncertain as its age. Cooper (1948) believes that the site was probably used as a place of assembly for ritual worship, but most writers note its defensive position and explain it as a fort. It was clearly not a castle in the traditional sense of the word, which is usually applied to structures built by and since the Normans. The general consensus is, as Bogg (1907) suggests, that 'it may have been utilised by the Romans as a temporary camp', but it was built by early British people as a place of safety, where they could defend themselves against attack. Flint arrowheads have been found on the surrounding moors, suggesting an early origin.

Maiden Castle, writes Pontefract (1934), 'was a secure site, either as a fortress or a halting-place, with the river below and the boggy moor behind. Keen eyes would watch from this hidden ridge for figures moving over Mount Calva [Calver Hill] or along Fremington Edge beyond Reeth, another Roman way, and wonder were they friends or foes … [today] there is little left of the forest which the Romans saw.' Whoever built it, and when and for what purpose, constructing earthworks on this scale must have required a huge amount of work by a large number of people over a long period of time, which itself would need great organisation, communication and co-operation. Our ancestors were clearly not always the barbaric warriors as painted by some historians.

Low Row

Back on the main road to the north of the Swale, Low Row, just over two miles east of Gunnerside and three and a half miles west of Reeth, is a classic strip village. Bogg (1907) describes it as 'rather a long broken street than a group of houses'. It has old, traditional stone buildings spread out along both sides of the road that runs straight through it. The houses here are much more spaced out than in the more compact villages farther up the dale. The village sits above the river Swale, and enjoys extensive views across the dale. Low Row, continues Bogg, is a 'tapestry on which many pleasant vignettes are embossed, such as clustering or grazing cattle – clutches of feathered fowl and 'bits' of human life'.

Low Row has a few buildings of note, in addition to the numerous holiday cottages and bed and breakfasts. On the left of the road, heading down the dale from Gunnerside, is Low Row United Reformed Church, which Pevsner (1966) commends for its 'round-arched windows'. It is twinned with Keld United Reformed Church and has a small grave-yard attached to it. The church was built in 1810 as a Congregational chapel to replace the small, crumbling Smarber Chapel. Low Row also has Holy Trinity Church – the Melbecks parish church – built in 1810 'with bellcote and a short chancel', as recorded by Pevsner in 1966. It is located adjacent to the Punch Bowl Inn, north of the main road, and has its own small graveyard. The large and impressive Punch Bowl Inn, traditionally a stopping-off point along the Corpse Way, enjoys pano-ramic views up and down the dale.

A minor road turns north off the main road just after Low Row, climbing over Feetham Pasture, crossing Barney Beck at Surrender Bridge, and continuing north of Calver Hill towards Langthwaite, four miles away in Arkengarthdale. This would have been the main route down to Low Row from the Old Gang Smelt Mill in Barney Beck.

Between Feetham and Healaugh 'the whole prospect … is one of enchanting loveliness'.
Tom Bradley (1891)

Low Row to Reeth

Swaledale grows broader downstream from Low Row. The valley floor is fairly wide and relatively flat, with fields and farms, dry-stone walls and scattered patches of trees. The moorland fellsides are lower here than farther up the dale and the scenery has a different feel to it. Much of the small patchwork of landscape elements that is characteristic of farther up the dale has by now disappeared, but open moorland still creeps over the tops of the hills and reaches down to the top of the enclosed areas.

Between Low Row and Feetham a minor road turns off to the north, and heads up towards the small hamlets of Blades and Smarber.

Like most of the villages upstream from Reeth, Blades is a former lead-mining village. Like them, it also suffered badly when the industry declined. Perhaps Blades' only claim to fame is the fact that funeral processions heading down dale to Grinton along the Corpse Way often left their coffins overnight in a small stone barn known as the dead house at Riddings Farm, while the bearers themselves called in at the nearby Punch Bowl Inn to slake their thirst.

Less than a mile west of Blades, Smarber Hall Farm contains the remains of a hunting lodge built by Lord Wharton in the days of deer hunting, like Crackpot Hall near Keld. At Smarber there are also the remains of the Nonconformist Smarber Chapel which was built and endowed by the Dissenter Philip Lord Wharton in 1691. At that time it was illegal to build a chapel within five miles of a church: Smarber lies just outside that limit from Grinton, where the main church for the dale stood.

Back on the main road heading down the dale into Reeth, a short distance from Low Row (in fact the two merge together) is the tiny hamlet of Feetham. The name Feetham was recorded in 1242 as Fyton; it comes from the Old Norse *fit* which means a river meadow. The collapse of lead mining devastated Feetham as it did other villages, and at the turn of the twentieth century Bogg (1907) reported that 'many houses are desolate and fast falling in'. Most if not all of them have since been restored as comfortable dwellings, with impressive views south across the floodplain of the river Swale. Somewhere near Feetham was the foot ford across the river Swale which was used by the Roman infantry passing between the camps at Bainbridge and Greta Bridge. Speight (1897) writes that 'the Roman ford of "stepping-stones" [near Feetham] was doubtless used for many centuries down to and beyond Norman times'.

The main road hugs the north bank of the Swale for much of the way between Feetham and Healaugh. Halfway along that section is How Hill, a mound (moraine) of glacial sediment that was deposited across the valley floor as ice retreated at the end of the last ice age, and has since been reshaped by river action. Just past How Hill, Whita Bridge crosses the Swale and joins with the minor road that runs west from Grinton past Maiden Castle to Summer Lodge and on to Askrigg.

Healaugh

The village of Healaugh is very compact, just like the other villages up the dale. It comprises a group of traditional stone buildings, huddled together, through which the road threads its way tightly. As elsewhere, Healaugh was badly affected by the decline in lead mining, leading Speight (1897) to describe it at the close of the nineteenth century as a 'ruinous and conspicuously-fallen, old-world village'. Healaugh, writes Pontefract (1934), has a 'peaceful, but rather mournful air, as though it remembered former greatness, and harboured just a little discontent. It seems slightly alien in Swaledale.'

Today it is quite a discrete and peaceful place, devoid of facilities like a church, school or pub. There are no obvious signs of holiday cottages for rent or bed and breakfast establishments. Most of the houses in Healaugh, particularly those on the south (right) side of the road, have grand views across the wide valley of the Swale at this point, looking south across the river to Harkerside Moor, and east towards the remains of Grinton Smelt Mill above the village of Grinton.

The name Healaugh was recorded in 1200 as Helagh in Swaledale. It comes from the Old English word *heah*, meaning a high forest clearing. Dense forest, which has since been felled and converted to farmland, covered most of this area in medieval times.

Barney Beck and Old Gang lead workings

Barney Beck gives access to some excellent walking up Hard Level Gill and over Melbecks Moor to the west, past the Old Gang Mines and Bunton Hush into Gunnerside Beck. The Coast to Coast Walk passes south-east down Barney Beck to Surrender Bridge, then hugs the base of Calver Hill and heads east into Reeth.

There is no road above Surrender Bridge, but there are three ways to reach it: one small side road runs north from Low Row over Feetham Pasture, one runs north-west from Healaugh past Park Hall, and a third runs south from Langthwaite in Arkengarthdale past Tottergill Pasture to the north of Calver Hill.

Barney Beck flows south into the Swale just west of Healaugh. The lowest section of the river is called Barney Beck, but above Surrender Bridge it is called Old Gang Beck, and above the Old Gang Smelt Mill it is known as Hard Level Gill. These last two names give strong clues about the importance of this small valley to the lead-mining industry – Old Gang was an important lead mine, and 'level' was a vein of galena (lead ore) that the miners worked. This was one of the most heavily worked areas for mining and smelting lead, up to the late nineteenth century,

Meanders on the river Swale near Reeth.

and the evidence survives in the remains of structures which are dotted along the valley above Surrender Bridge.

The name Old (or Auld) Gang comes from the Old English *gang*, meaning a road. This early origin indicates that the tracks, and probably the lead mines themselves, date back at least to the sixth and seventh centuries when the Saxons settled in this area.

The Old Gang Mines on Melbecks Moor were worked for many centuries and were very productive. The enormous spoil heaps from them, on which nothing will grow, extend over much of the top of the moor, giving what Ella Pontefract (1934) calls 'an almost terrifying desolation to the moor'. But she concedes that 'the moor is too vast for even so great an upheaval to spoil; rather does the dreariness emphasize the surrounding beauty'. The Coast to Coast Walk drops into Barney Beck (here called Hard Level Gill) at Level House Bridge, and then follows the well-worn miners' path along the north side of the river down to Surrender Bridge.

Halfway between Level House Bridge and Surrender Bridge, what Herriot (1979) describes as the 'massive, haunting remains' of the Old Gang Smelt Mill come into view. Wainwright (1989) refers to them as 'another melancholy reminder of past glories'. The remains of the Old Gang lead workings 'add to the grandness of the stretch of moor as a ruined abbey adds to the beauty of riverside meadows'. Ella Pontefract (1934)

The site is a treasure trove of industrial archaeology, and very photogenic in the right weather conditions. It is dominated by the ruined remains of the stone complex of the smelt mill, whose four furnaces can still be seen, along with a tall upright chimney. There are also remains of a long chimney, built of stone in the nineteenth century, which run up the moor side and end as an upright chimney on the moor half a mile from the smelt mill. Between the smelt mill and Surrender Bridge are the striking remains of the peat store, which was large enough to keep a

year's supply of locally dug peat which was burned with hard coal (from the Kings Pit near Tan Hill) in the smelting furnaces. Its tall stone gable ends and pillars have survived; the long building used to have a thatched roof, with open sides between the support pillars. The ruins of another smelt mill can be seen just downstream from Surrender Bridge, on the north side of the beck.

Reeth

From Healaugh heading east the road climbs up above the Swale on its northern side until it reaches Reeth. As it approaches Reeth the road commands extensive views across the valley, looking over a tightly meandering section of the river, with Grinton Moor as a backdrop. Downstream the view is towards Marrick and Marrick Priory, and upstream it is towards Low Row and beyond. Reeth lies at the centre of Swaledale, marking the boundary between the upper dale and the lower dale. For tourists and walkers arriving from the east, it represents a gateway to the hills farther up the dale.

Although quite modest in scale, Reeth is the largest settlement in the dale upstream from Richmond. Indeed, it is the only town along that 20-mile stretch. It looks and feels very different from the other villages and hamlets throughout the dale, with a charm of its own. Throughout history Reeth has served as a hub in the centre of the dale; the main road along the dale passes through it, and the road along Arkengarthdale joins it there.

Since the late seventeenth century Reeth has been a market town, and for many centuries it was a supply base for lead-mining operations, and home to many mining families. The town's reputation these days is as a walking centre and a popular destination for day-trippers arriving by road.

The name Reeth means 'place by the stream', derived from the Anglo-Saxon *rip*, meaning a stream. The stream it was named after was

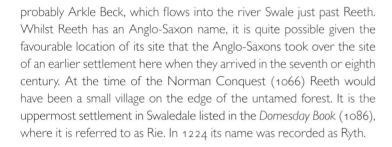

Reeth Green, with Fremington Edge behind.

Calver Hill viewed from Arkle Town.

probably Arkle Beck, which flows into the river Swale just past Reeth. Whilst Reeth has an Anglo-Saxon name, it is quite possible given the favourable location of its site that the Anglo-Saxons took over the site of an earlier settlement here when they arrived in the seventh or eighth century. At the time of the Norman Conquest (1066) Reeth would have been a small village on the edge of the untamed forest. It is the uppermost settlement in Swaledale listed in the *Domesday Book* (1086), where it is referred to as Rie. In 1224 its name was recorded as Ryth.

Reeth's setting – on a ridge at the junction of Arkle Beck and the river Swale – is both dramatic and strategic. It provides a natural gateway into both Arkengarthdale and upper Swaledale. It sits snugly, almost complacently, between two major hills, which frame it neatly, topped with their colourful fells. To the north-west is Calver Hill (Mount Calvy to the Victorians), and to the north-east is the imposing cliff of Fremington Edge, 'with its limestone scars and dappling of juniper-trees'

as Pontefract (1934) emphasises. Speight (1897) describes Calver Hill, whose 'bare yet picturesque summit stands out boldly by reason of the scars of Main Limestone that encompass it'. This setting creates striking scenery, which has long been appreciated by travellers. In 1950 Jessica Lofthouse wrote that Reeth was 'a town in miniature – and how we like it … it is high-placed with higher fells not far away and constantly swept by winds'. Tom Bradley (1891) had previously described the town as 'standing on a slight sloping eminence like an Alpine village at the foot of fir-lined mountains', a sentiment echoed by Edmund Bogg in 1907, when he compared Reeth with 'the townlets of Switzerland, secluded and hemmed in by hills, and of limited resources [as with Reeth], there is a charm which grows on one upon further acquaintance'.

Despite its setting and scenic assets, Reeth has enjoyed mixed fortunes through its history, as is true of all of the settlements in Swaledale. It prospered with the development of the lead-mining industry, and suffered with its collapse. Reeth was also a thriving centre for hand-knitted stockings, and felt the impact of the declining knitting industry. Since 1695 it has been an important market town, after a charter was granted to Lord Philip Wharton to hold a market there every Friday and four fairs a year.

During the nineteenth century Reeth was also an important communications hub; Cooper (1973) reports that in 1840 there were three carriers based in Reeth, ferrying people and goods to Leeds, Richmond and Barnard Castle, and the new turnpike road between Richmond and

Reeth was constructed in 1836 to speed the movement, particularly of lead, to the main depot in Richmond.

By the close of the nineteenth century Reeth had lost much of its economy and many of its people, and it looked and felt like a pale shadow of its former self. A reflection of its decline is the fall in the number of inns in Reeth from seven in the 1840s to three in 1897. 'In this solitary townlet,' complained Arthur Norway in 1903, 'I could find nothing worthy of comment save a pig.' A more optimistic impression of the town was recorded by Edmund Bogg (1907): 'Although

REETH IN SNOW. COPYRIGHT COURTESY OF MARTIN EADON.

the population has diminished and roofless or ruined cottages are to be seen here and there, the Reeth township to-day wears on its face quite a clean smiling prosperous look.'

Whilst its economic woes at the end of the nineteenth century were serious and persistent, Reeth nonetheless continued to serve the communities in central and upper Swaledale. Speight (1897) mentions that Reeth had a union workhouse (for the poor), a mechanics' institute with an extensive library, an independent chapel (built in 1783), a Wesleyan chapel (built in 1797) and a Quaker school (built in 1780), as well as a post and telegraph office, and a printer and stationer's shop.

Like some of the other settlements in Swaledale that were adversely affected by the collapse of the lead-mining industry, Reeth has been able to find a new sense of direction and purpose, developing a reputation as a centre of tourism, particularly relating to outdoor pursuits like walking, painting, photography and industrial archaeology.

The town's attractions for tourists were already apparent in the late nineteenth century. *Black's Picturesque Guide to Yorkshire* (1874) points out that Reeth 'may serve as a station for the tourist who wishes to devote some time to the examination of neighbouring scenery', and Speight (1897) describes Reeth as 'the "Mecca" of visitors'.

Reeth, wrote Gordon Home in 1906, 'is glad of the fact that its splendid situation, and the cheerful green which the houses look upon, have made it something of a holiday resort … '

The striking scenery surrounding Reeth, and the historic features preserved in the townscape – particularly the grand eighteenth-century

stone houses and hotels clustered around the triangular village green, with views southwards towards Grinton Lodge and the expanse of Grinton Moor – attract many day visitors, and those who spend time in the town's hotels and holiday cottages. Herriot (1979) recognised its attraction: 'Make no mistake about it, Reeth is beautiful. Its setting on the slopes of Calver Hill is perfection, the ring of houses with fascinating little alleys wandering among them seem to beckon to the stranger – "come and seek us out".'

Today Reeth is a market town, with a broad range of support services including a primary school, fire station, petrol station and Post Office. Around The Green sit the three remaining pubs (the King's Arms, the Buck Hotel and the Black Bull) and the Burgoyne Hotel and restaurant. There is also a newspaper shop, ice-cream parlour, gift shop, Christian book shop, bakery and cake shop, several cafés, a pottery and a Yorkshire Dales National Park Information Centre (Hudson House). There are two churches in the centre of the town – the Grade II listed Wesleyan Chapel and Reeth Evangelical Congregational Church – along with numerous holiday cottages and bed and breakfasts. On the western side of town a new arts and crafts centre (the Reeth Dales Centre) provides 12 purpose-built workshops and studios. A small market selling local produce (meat, vegetables and dairy products) is held on The Green on Fridays throughout the year.

One of Reeth's most popular attractions is the Swaledale Folk Museum which is housed in the former Methodist day school, built just off The Green in 1836. This independent museum is run by volunteers, opened in 1974 and re-opened after refurbishment in 2005. It tells the story of life and heritage in Swaledale and Arkengarthdale through the ages via a lively programme of displays, talks, workshops and events.

Chapter Nine
ARKENGARTHDALE

'the country of old lead-mining industry ... Here and there you come across gaunt, abandoned workings, and villages that seem to live in the past.' Alfred Brown (1952)

ARKENGARTHDALE IS ON THE LARGEST TRIBUTARY of the river Swale. Although Ella Pontefract (1934) argues that it 'has not the romantic beauty of Swaledale', Alfred Brown (1952) was struck by its 'stark beauty'.

Arkengarthdale

The name Arkengarthdale was recorded in 1199 as Arkillesgarth, and this gives strong clues to its origin. The name comes from the Old Norse *garthr* (garth), which means an enclosure or high pasture, so Arkengarthdale means 'Arnkell's enclosure'. The river that flows along the dale, which rises on the north-west side of Water Crag, is called Arkle Beck. It was recorded in 1226 as Arkelbek, the name being derived from the Old Norse *bekkr*, meaning a stream; Arkle Beck is 'Arnkell's stream'.

Arnkell was apparently a common Viking name, and the one who gave his name to this valley is believed to have been the son of Gospatrick, a Norse settler (or a descendent of one) who held this land before the Norman Conquest. There is continuity in naming, because as Herriot

(1979) points out, 'the farmers [in Swaledale] still call their fields garths'. Neither Arkengarthdale nor any of its few small settlements are recorded in the *Domesday Book* of 1086.

Throughout most of history the valley remained largely covered by forest with a few settlers clearing patches to make smallholdings, these patches scattered across a wide area. Arkengarthdale was part of the extensive hunting forest managed by the Normans. 'The old Forest of Arkendale,' wrote Speight in 1897, 'was ... part of an extensive chase that abounded in wolves, boars, and wild deer.' The road down Arkengarthdale follows the route of an old drovers' road, along which drovers would drive their large herds of cattle from beyond Tan Hill down to market in Reeth and beyond.

lead mining

Arkengarthdale was the scene of much lead mining, particularly in the eighteenth and nineteenth centuries. This was the second most important lead-mining area in Swaledale, after the Old Gang complex. According to Christopher Clarkson (1814), in the early nineteenth century the mines in Arkengarthdale were contributing around two-thirds of the total annual output from the Swaledale mines – about 3,000 tons of lead. Bogg (1907) reports that in the middle of that century there were more than 300 miners working in Arkengarthdale alone.

Given the scale and duration of lead mining in the valley, it is no surprise that the landscape here preserves abundant remains of old workings. But the impact of mining stretches way beyond the mines and the smelt-mill sites, to include numerous large hushes (such as North Rake Hush above Booze) and spoil heaps (for example, along the limestone cliff of Fremington Edge). The mining legacy also includes the few scattered

NORTH RAKE HUSH AND LEAD-MINING SPOIL, SLEI GILL, ARKENGARTHDALE.

villages and hamlets and their small, stone former miners' cottages. Each settlement had its local mines, usually some distance away on the fells. Pontefract (1934) describes the 'faint atmosphere of the industrial [that] still hangs over its villages. Mine-tippings mar the fells, and ancient levels look out from them like black windows.'

Reeth to Langthwaite

The road up Arkengarthdale branches off the main road (the B6270) along Swaledale on the north side of Reeth village green, beside the Buck Hotel. The imposing cliffs of Fremington Edge to the right and the rounded summit of Calver Hill to the left dominate the view and provide a natural gateway to the bottom of the dale. Fremington Edge – capped by moorland, littered with remains of old lead mining and crossed by numerous walking paths – overlooks the valley bottom of Arkle Beck, which is dominated by grazing land and scattered woodland.

Within a mile north of Reeth the view starts to open up on both sides as the valley grows wider. The road climbs above the bottom of the beck on the western side, below Calver Hill. On this western side of the valley the landscape is dominated by boggy open moorland on which sheep graze freely. Lower down the fellside are a few small scattered stone field barns and fields marked out by dry-stone walls. There is grazing land for sheep and cattle on the relatively narrow, flat valley floor. Across the beck, on the eastern side of the dale, there are scattered isolated farmhouses, fields surrounded by dry-stone walls, but few if any field barns. Along Fremington Edge between Reeth and Booze the slopes are too steep and inhospitable for grazing. At the northern end of Fremington Edge there are remains of old lead-mining works in and around Slei Gill, particularly on Fell End Moor and at North Rake Hush.

The first settlement up Arkengarthdale is the tiny hamlet of Arkle Town, just to the east of Langthwaite. Like the dale and the beck, this settlement is named after Arnkell and is Norse in origin. The collapse of the lead-mining industry badly affected the hamlet, made up of little more than a handful of miners' cottages, but river erosion also took its toll. Pontefract (1934) describes the original parish church in Arkle Town: 'The foundations were undermined by the Arkle Beck, and a new church was built at Langthwaite in 1818. Nothing is left of the old building but its graveyard, with forlorn-looking tombstones, bent at all angles.'

Across the beck from Arkle Town, sitting quietly, high on the sloping fellside below Low Moor, and overlooking Slei Gill to the east, is the equally tiny hamlet with the enigmatic name, Booze. Pontefract (1934) writes that Booze 'means the house by the bow or curve, the curve being either Arkle Beck which flows below it, or Slee Beck which runs at the side of it. Its name in 1473 was Bowehouse, which has gradually changed to Booze, most inappropriately, for it does not possess an inn.' It comprises no more than about a dozen stone buildings, and around it are scattered isolated stone farms with some field barns and dry-stone walls.

Langthwaite to Dale Head

A short distance up Arkengarthdale from Arkle Town, the road drops down steeply, with tight twists and turns, into Langthwaite. Small as it is, this is the only village of any size along the dale.

The name Langthwaite comes from the Old Norse words *lang*, meaning long, and *thwaite*, meaning a clearing or meadow (the same as the village in upper Swaledale called Thwaite), so it describes a long meadow. The name was recorded in 1167 as Langethwait. The village, until the end of the nineteenth century being at the heart of the lead-mining area, is now a sleepy retreat with a small community scattered over a wide area, including the outlying hamlets of Whaw and Eskeleth to the north. The Red Lion Inn sits proudly surrounded by small stone cottages on both sides of the road and beck. On the west side of the road just before the village is the solid, serious-looking Wesleyan Chapel, described by Pevsner (1966) as 'large; debased Italianate with windows in two

LOWER ARKENGARTHDALE, LOOKING UPSTREAM PAST LANGTHWAITE.

REMAINS OF THE CHURCHYARD IN ARKLE TOWN, BY ARKLE BECK.

THE CB INN, TOWARDS
ESKELETH BRIDGE,
ARKENGARTHDALE.

storeys and a pedimental gable'. It was built in 1882 to serve the needs of the Nonconformist miners, and continues in use today. Towards the northern end of the village, on the opposite side of the road, is the parish church – the Church of St Mary the Virgin – built in 1818–19 to replace the damaged church at Arkle Town (whose font it houses). Pevsner (1966) describes it as 'quite a big church to serve Arkengarthdale, with quite a high W[est] tower. The church … is tall for its width, and has thin buttresses all along its sides and a lot of pinnacles.'

A short distance farther up the dale is the site of the CB Yard, the administrative centre of the CB Lead Mining Company which contains the remains of the joiners' and blacksmiths' workshops, a peat store, sawmill, and offices and houses for the agent. All of the buildings, dating from the early eighteenth century, are now private homes. Opposite the yard on the other side of the road are the ruins of the New Mill Smelt Mill, the remains of whose long flue are still visible.

The CB Lead Mining Company and mines were

*The upper part of Arkle Beck
flows through the branching dale
of garths hemmed in by scarred
and seamed moorland upland.'
Edmund Bogg (1907)*

owned by Charles Bathurst, whose father Dr John Bathurst had been a scholar at Richmond Grammar School until 1631 and was Oliver Cromwell's physician and a Member of Parliament for Richmond in the 1650s. Charles Bathurst opened many new lead mines in the dale in the eighteenth century.

Leaving Langthwaite, heading north, a narrow side road turns off to the west, heading for Low Row three miles away in Swaledale, crossing over Surrender Bridge in Barney Beck along the way.

Just under a mile up the dale from Langthwaite village, past the Church of England school, is the CB Inn, which Pevsner (1966) describes as 'Georgian with two symmetrical bow-windows'. He points out that 'the inn, the chapel and the church are all on such a generous scale because of Arkengarthdale lead mining … [which] was at its height early in the 19th century'.

A safe distance from the CB Yard, in a field just past the inn, Bathurst built a powder house in

1725, gunpowder being an important mining tool. The striking six-sided building survives by the junction of the road that runs north across the north edge of Windegg Moor past Stang House towards Barnard Castle, ten miles to the north-east. This road was used by the Romans for transporting lead from the mines in Arkengarthdale.

The fellside on the west side of the dale near Eskeleth Bridge, running up towards Great Pinseat, contains the deepest scars of mining activity, including Hungry Hushes and Stoddart Hush, which thankfully are not visible from the road up the dale. Eskeleth itself is a hamlet clustered around a stone bridge over Arkle Beck, which carries the road to Barnard Castle.

A short distance farther up Arkengarthdale a side road on the right leads to the hamlet of Whaw, the uppermost settlement in the dale. Like most other hamlets along the dale, Whaw is very small indeed, consisting of little more than about eight cottages (including a bed and breakfast), with neither a pub nor any other services. On the fellside above Whaw, to the east, are isolated farm buildings with fields enclosed by dry-stone walls. On the western side is open moorland.

Dale Head

The road continues round, along the northern edge of the Yorkshire Dales National Park, for a further five miles or so until it arrives at Tan Hill.

Open moorland dominates the Dale Head area. The heather moorland here, with purple heath and blanket bog, is recognised as being of international importance, and is part of the Pennine Dales Environmentally Sensitive Area. It provides a valuable habitat for populations of breeding waders, including the golden plover, curlew and snipe, and birds of prey such as merlin and the short-eared owl.

SLEIGHTHOLME MOOR, HEAD OF ARKENGARTHDALE.

Like many other moorland parts of Swaledale, Arkengarthdale is criss-crossed with footpaths which are well signposted and clearly shown on maps. After it passes Tan Hill, the Pennine Way heads north-eastwards across Washfold Rigg and Sleightholme Moor towards Stainmore and Barnard Castle.

The most northerly section of Arkengarthdale – which feels like the top of the world – overlooks Slightholme Moor, a wide and relatively featureless expanse of open moorland that stretches north to the Stainmore Gap and the A66, which crosses the North Pennines between Brough in the west and Scotch Corner in the east. Part of the moor is shown on maps somewhat enigmatically as 'Adjustment Ground' or 'The Disputes', probably contested border land between England and Scotland.

FREMINGTON, WITH FREMINGTON EDGE
BEHIND, VIEWED FROM GRINTON MOOR.

Chapter Ten
LOWER SWALEDALE: REETH TO RICHMOND

It is 'one of the finest nine or ten mile drives in Yorkshire, and combines the merit of interest and picturesqueness with accessibility.' Harry Speight (1897)

THE SECTION OF SWALEDALE between Reeth and Richmond is wider and more subdued than that above Reeth, and the land use is dominated by pastoral farming which usually extends well up (if not completely over) the fellsides. The river Swale is wider and deeper, and it meanders sleepily across its wide floodplain except when swollen by heavy rain.

Key elements of the traditional farming landscape that dominate the scenery above Reeth – the stone field barns and hay meadows – largely disappear below Reeth. In this section of the dale the fields are larger but still surrounded by dry-stone walls. The fields tend to be more regularly shaped, indicating more recent enclosure than many of the fields farther up the dale.

Many writers have commented on the marked change of character of the dale below Reeth. Speight (1897) describes the road between Reeth and Richmond as a 'very romantic highroad', but warns travellers to 'take proper care that your horse, trap, gearings, or other belongings of the expedition are in safe and sound condition, as the attractions of the scenery may keep your attention constantly withdrawn'. *Black's Picturesque Guide to Yorkshire* (1874) contrasts the 'wildness and grandeur' of the upper dale with 'the features of rich and gentle beauty' of

the lower dale, which it regards as 'some of the most delightful scenery in Swaledale'. Furthermore, it continues, 'there are numberless points in this, the richer and more wooded part of the dale, that may well tempt the artist to pause and employ his pencil'.

Alfred Brown (1952) notes that below Reeth 'the scenery changes and becomes more wooded and picturesque, if less wild … the scenery is enchanting.' After going over Melbecks Moor and down Barney Dale, the Coast to Coast Walk continues through Reeth, then along lower Swaledale north of the river to Richmond. Meanwhile, Wainwright (1989) describes this stretch as 'a scenic delight, with the lovely Swale and its wooded valley in sight or close by throughout'.

old road and new road

The old road between Reeth and Richmond, which Speight (1897) calls 'the old mountainous highway', runs along the northern edge of the lower dale, starting at Fremington then heading eastwards five miles towards Marske. From Marske it climbs up above Applegarth Scar and Whitecliffe Wood, where it offers extensive views across the lower dale and Richmond, and farther east across the Vale of Mowbray to the North York Moors and Teesside. The road, which for much of history was the only route along the dale, enters Richmond through Westfield. In many places the old road is little more than a narrow lane, with some very steep hills and tight bends to negotiate, so it must have posed major challenges for the transport by packhorse of heavy ingots of lead, particularly in bad weather.

The old road is 'a road of ups and downs,' writes Jessica Lofthouse (1950), 'of lonely cross-roads and long, unpeopled stretches where we can imagine the days of hold-ups and highway robbery.' Little wonder that in the nineteenth century local merchants were keen to fund the building of a new road in 1837. The new road (now the main road, the B6270) follows a flatter, straighter and more sheltered route along the valley floor, through Grinton, past Marrick Priory and Ellerton Priory, entering Richmond along what is now Reeth Road. It links up with the Marske road at Downholme Bridge.

Fremington

As the road along Swaledale leaves Reeth it passes over a narrow hump-backed stone bridge over Arkle Beck, then within less than half a mile it passes traces of an old terraced field system (lynchets) to the north, below Fremington Edge. It continues through the small hamlet of Fremington, which is recorded in the *Domesday Book* (1086) as Freminton. A small road turns off to the north to High Fremington, a few hundred yards away, and a track extends north from it up the side of Fremington Edge and over Marrick Moor to the former lead-mining hamlet of Hurst, three miles away.

The main road passes the very imposing Draycott Hall, secluded behind a tall stone wall. The hall was built in the late eighteenth century for Sir George Denys, owner of Old Gang Smelt Mill, but is now a Grade II listed building divided into apartments. The former mine offices and

mine agent's house adjacent to the hall have also been converted to residential use. The road continues past the Dales Bike Centre then swings south towards Grinton Bridge.

The small hamlet of Hurst lies at the heart of the oldest lead-mining area in the dale, if not the whole of England. Speight (1897) notes that the Hurst mines were 'of great depth and have been worked from remote times'. A Roman bar of lead was found in this area, testifying to its long heritage.

Hurst was the only settlement in Swaledale that looked directly over its mines, as they were so close by. The collapse of lead mining seriously affected Hurst, as Pontefract noted in 1934: 'Hurst is a broken village, left bewildered, its reason for being gone. It too is long and straggling, but it has not the grace and dignity of Marrick. There are ruins everywhere, and the houses that are left intact seem to weep with them.' Today many of the abandoned cottages have been restored, but the hamlet remains remote, secluded and quiet.

Grinton

After Fremington the main road crosses over the river Swale into the village of Grinton via Grinton Bridge, past Blackburn Hall and St Andrew's Parish Church on the right and the Bridge Inn opposite them on the left.

Grinton appears in the *Domesday Book* (1086) as Grinton, and in 1180 it was recorded as Grentone. The name comes from the Old English *tun*, meaning a fence or enclosure, which suggests that in Anglo-Saxon times this place was a cultivate spot, probably surrounded by forest. Grinton is certainly very old; the church dates back at least as far as the thirteenth century, and in 1538 Leland reported that 'Grinton is a little Market Town'.

HURST, CONVERTED LEAD-MINERS' COTTAGES.

THE BRIDGE INN, GRINTON.

GRINTON PARISH CHURCH.

Just over the bridge, sitting snugly between the river and the church, is Blackburn Hall, an imposing Elizabethan residence dating from 1635. The hall was derelict for many decades and has recently been restored as a family home; it is a Grade II listed building. The traditional gardens have also been restored, but remain largely hidden from view behind a high, thick beech hedge. Bogg (1907) describes Blackburn Hall as 'the quaintest feature of the district in domestic architecture'.

GRINTON MOOR.

Like many other settlements in Swaledale, Grinton suffered badly when the lead-mining industry collapsed, but it has a charm which few others can match. This comes partly from its prominent location (straddling the main road) and unique setting (on the valley floor, beside the river). Bogg (1907) agrees: 'The bridge, church and village seen from the northern edge of the bridge, make a characteristic dale picture, both in composition and detail.'

One of Grinton's finest features is the triple-arched stone bridge over the Swale, which is strategically and practically important but also visually appealing. It is wide enough to take two lanes of traffic and has pointed stone buttresses and breakwaters to cope with the fast-flowing current and the wide river at this point of the Swale.

Grinton Lodge.

The parish church in Grinton, St Andrew's – the self-proclaimed 'Cathedral of the Dales' – sits solidly in the centre of the village and, writes Alfred Brown (1952), 'has the dignity of a cathedral'. It was founded by the monks of Bridlington Priory, was the mother church of Marrick Priory, and served as the parish church for all of upper Swaledale. Before 1580, when the church was built in Muker with its own burial ground, funeral parties would travel to Grinton from the head of the dale along the Corpse Way.

The church is surrounded by an olde-worlde churchyard with ancient headstones at jaunty angles, shaded by huge yew trees. Pevsner (1966) describes the church as 'a low, grey, spreading Perp[endicular style]'. It is Norman in origin, probably dating from the thirteenth century, but it may occupy the site of a pre-Christian temple from the Anglo-Saxon period. Little remains of the original Norman building other than part of the chancel arch, a small window over the tower

arch and the bowl of the stone font. The importance of St Andrew's through the ages is emphasised in the way the church building was successively enlarged and remodelled. A tower arch was added in the late twelfth century, and the tower was reconstructed in 1500. A south aisle was added in the fourteenth century, and a north aisle and chapel in the fifteenth century; both were rebuilt and widened in the sixteenth century, when a south chapel and small vaulted sacristy were added. Speight (1897) reports that it underwent a 'complete yet conservative restoration … [and] was re-opened in Easter week, 1896'.

A narrow road called Swale Hall Lane turns off to the left (west) past the church. It continues along the foot of Harkerside Moor past Maiden Castle and How Hill, joining up with the road over Isles Bridge near Smarber. A short distance along Swale Hall Lane from Grinton is the Grade II listed building of Swale Hall, built by the Swales, descendants of

Walter de Gant, who held the manor of Healaugh and gave the manor of East Grinton (which included Grinton church) to the priory church at Bridlington.

A road branches off the main road by Grinton church and carries on southwards up the lower part of Grinton Gill. Then it climbs up over the fell to Grinton Lodge and on over Grinton Moor to Redmire in Wensleydale. After a steep climb up from Grinton village, the road suddenly emerges onto Grinton Moor. On the left (east) is the fine turreted building of Grinton Lodge – built as a shooting lodge, later converted into a youth hostel, now part of Hostelling International – keeping watch over this central part of Swaledale, looking northwards to Reeth past Fremington Edge and up Arkengarthdale.

In *James Herriot's Yorkshire*, the writer describes a view, driving along the moor road: 'one of the gems of Grinton, the row of ancient houses and cottages which border the steep road from the village. As we climbed slowly towards the moor, it struck me again that it would be difficult to find a more picturesque line of dwellings anywhere.'

Opposite Grinton church, the main road to Richmond turns off to the east, just past the Bridge Inn. Shortly after leaving Grinton, the road passes a cemetery (believed to have been built on the site of an Iron Age hill fort), then it crosses over Cogden Gill which drains south off Grinton Moor. The moors in this area were the scene of extensive lead mining, and the preserved remains of the Cogden Gill Smelt Mill can be seen at the base of the gill, along with a long section of covered stone flue running from the mill up to the adjacent hilltop.

Swaledale grows wider downstream from Reeth and Grinton. It now has a wide, flat floodplain that provides grazing land and some small pockets of woodland. Fields enclosed by dry-stone walls extend at least halfway up the low hillsides, and above the fields are moorland on the northern slope and mature conifer plantations on the southern slope between Grinton and Marrick.

MARRICK PRIORY.

Marrick Priory

The remains of Marrick Priory sit on the floodplain of the river Swale, on its left (north) bank. They can only be reached along the old road between Reeth and Richmond, about a mile east of Fremington.

Marrick appears in the *Domesday Book* (1086) as Marige; in 1190 it was recorded as Marrich. The name is a Scandinavian form of the Old English *(ge)mur-hrycg*, meaning a boundary ridge. However, as Andrew Fleming (2010) points out, 'there is no plausible "boundary ridge" near Marrick village. In any case … this village formerly had a different name; the original Marrick was down by the Swale, where Marrick Priory was established. The "boundary ridge" must have been Rue Dyke, across the river.'

Marrick Priory, a priory of Benedictine nuns, was founded by Roger de Aske, probably in the 1150s; the exact date is unknown. It is much older than Ellerton Priory, a few miles farther downstream. The Black Nuns

at Marrick were allowed to visit the White Nuns at Ellerton, and they could climb the 375 stone steps (known locally as the Nunnery Steps) up through the woods to visit Marrick village on the escarpment above the priory.

Whilst the priory held lands granted to it by Roger de Aske and had an income from its granges (farms), it had only modest means compared with many other religious establishments of the time. One of Marrick Priory's claims to fame was that in 1536 it provided a refuge for Isabella Beaufort, one of Henry VIII's maids-in-waiting whom he wanted to marry. She, however, wanted to marry Edward Herbert, so she ran away from the court. The prioress allowed her to hide at Marrick Priory and correspond with her lover, who rescued her when the priory was closed, and took her back to Somerset, where they married.

Life in the priory is described in detail in the historical novel *The Man on a Donkey*, written by H. F. M. Prescott in 1952. During the dissolution of the monasteries Marrick Priory was surrendered in November 1540 by Prioress Christabella Cowper and sixteen nuns. Christopher Clarkson (1814) records that the prioress and nuns were given pensions, and the buildings and land were granted to John Bannister and John Uvedale (one of the king's commissioners) and were later sold on.

Like other religious establishments, after the dissolution the priory buildings were robbed of much of their stone and fell into ruin. Some of this building material was probably used to build a stone farmstead just south of the priory.

The picturesque scene attracted the attention of painter J. M. W. Turner, who sketched the remains of the priory in July 1816. David Hill (1984) describes the priory in Turner's sketch: 'set on its own prom-ontory amongst a patchwork of fields, woods, hedges and lanes, and in his drawing is punctuated by the new church tower rising from a farmyard, with smoke rising from a hearth fire in the farmhouse kitchen where dinner is being prepared in the late afternoon.' The 'new church tower rising' was the construction of a new church and tower on the site of the former priory nave, using stone from the ruined priory; unusually, the site continued in use as a parish church up to 1811 after serving as a monastic church. In 1852 William Longstaffe described Marrick church as 'a singularly patched up building, composed out of the ancient church, whose choir stands roofless and melancholy', and Speight (1897) regretted that the new church 'has evidently been built with a careless disregard for the beauty of the old stonework or of architectural fitness'. Pevsner (1966) notes that one arch and two half-arches from the former priory were used in the new church, and the tall west tower includes a re-used late thirteenth-century window.

Since the church and tower were built in the early nineteenth century, other new buildings have been added. The site is now used by the Ripon Diocese as a residential adventure centre for young people.

The small village of Marrick sits almost hidden from sight, high on the hillside north of the river Swale, two miles along the old road from Fremington to Marske. It is a small compact settlement in a secluded location on the escarpment that continues east from Fremington Edge, which endows it with extensive views up and down this part of the dale. Pontefract (1934) notes that it 'was affected like other places with the decay of the lead industry, but it has turned, without the aid of visitors, into a farming village with spacious houses'. There is no pub, nor obvious signs of bed and breakfast establishments or holiday cottages.

'The old grey abbey tower back-grounded by wild moorland on the vale's other side, the whole forming a picture of supreme beauty and symbolism, so plain for all to see. The peaceful lonely neglected God's-acre [churchyard] has a few slanting tombstones, lichen-stained and crumbling ... even they, with the lonely tower watching over them, strike a note of desolation and desertion, not without a wan charm, a wrecked beauty of its own.'
Edmund Bogg (1907)

The Coast to Coast Walk passes through Marrick after leaving Reeth and Fremington and goes past Marrick Priory; it then continues through Marske, Applegarth, Whitecliffe Wood, past Westfield and into Richmond. Just north of the village are the remains of the Marrick Smelt Mills. The road north from Marrick crosses the old road between Reeth and Richmond, then continues northwards over Marrick Moor to Hurst.

Ellerton Priory

Ellerton Priory lies beside the main road, about a mile to the east of Marrick Priory, on the south side of the floodplain of the river Swale. The isolated remains of the priory stand proud in the field beside the eighteenth-century Ellerton Lodge. Ellerton is listed in the *Domesday Book* (1086) as Alreton, and in 1227 it was recorded as Elreton. Like Grinton, the name is derived from the Old English *tun*, meaning an enclosure. According to Leland, writing in 1538, Ellerton Priory 'takes its name from the elder trees' that grew there.

Ellerton was a Cistercian priory, or as Christopher Clarkson (1814) puts it, 'a House of White Cloathed ... Nuns'. Like Marrick Priory, the date of its foundation is not clear but the first recorded prioress was Alice in 1227. The nuns lived in silence, dedicated to a life of prayer and worship, in their small isolated foundation built in a clearing in the forest; its remains are now surrounded by fields. By all accounts Ellerton was one of the humblest of the monastic establishments, much poorer than its nearest neighbour, Marrick. Cooper (1973) records, however, that it was still susceptible

little remains today other than the intact tall west tower with a round arch to the nave, and fragments of two walls. Pevsner (1966) notes that the nave had no aisle, and may be older than the tower. Three or four carved stones (including what are thought to be stone lids from the coffins of two former prioresses) have been unearthed in the nave from under piles of rubble. Stone from the former priory was doubtless used in the building of Ellerton Lodge, in whose grounds the remains are enclosed. William Longstaffe wrote in 1852: 'The church [of Ellerton Priory], of which the shell remains, is only about thirty paces long, and five broad. No aisles, no transept. The foundations of the cloister quadrangle may be traced, but not a memorial of any one is visible, save a shield with two crescents on the tower, which is at the west end of the church.'

Mature trees now grow in the priory site. It all looks very picturesque, as though constructed as a folly, to attract the interests of people passing by the river along the dale. The scene, writes Bogg (1907), ' ... is charming enough, yet there is a lonesome feeling engendered by the few fragments of the Priory shewing their forlorn and stark condition ... The site ... [is now] somewhat naked and neglected in aspect, grey fragmentary walls set in evergreen pasture-land sparsely tree-sheltered – its tower a lighthouse-like memorial to the Sisters who passed their time here in prayer and unostentatious good works.'

Downstream from Ellerton the landscape changes; the valley sides are lower, the valley is broader, and the slope of the valley side is more gentle. It is more of a gentle rolling hill-farming landscape than the typical dale countryside and rugged moorland farther west. The main road past Ellerton continues its journey down the dale, hugging the south bank of the river Swale past Downholme Bridge, Applegarth Scar and Whitecliffe Wood towards Richmond. Prominent yellow signs along the road here warn of military training grounds on both sides of the road, centred on Wathgill Camp on Stainton Moor above Downholme, in the direction of Leyburn to the south.

ELLERTON PRIORY.

to raiders: 'When the Scots made one of their raids into Swaledale in 1347, they violated . . . [Ellerton] priory and stole or destroyed its charters and writings.'

In 1537, during the dissolution, Ellerton was surrendered without resistance by Johanna, the last prioress. The site came into the hands of one Ralph Closeby, and in 1601 it was sold to the Drax family, who held it for more than three centuries. The buildings fell into ruin and

Marske

Marske is one of the most prominent villages in lower Swaledale, and it captured the attention of most of Swaledale's nineteenth-century writers. Before the new road was built from Reeth to Richmond, all the traffic along the main road (the old road) passed through Marske; it was the only settlement directly on the route. Today it can be reached either along the old road, or via a sharp turn off the new road over Downholme Bridge, just east of Ellerton Lodge and the junction with the A6108, which comes from Leyburn and runs down past Downholme.

The most picturesque way of approaching Marske is over Downholme Bridge, a very solid, high, triple-arched stone bridge built in 1773, which offers extensive views across the valley floor. The landscape here is open parkland – including Bushy Park and the Deer Park Wood – with abundant trees, large fields and (unusual for Swaledale) hedges, as well as dry-stone walls. The scenery contrasts sharply with the more rugged moorland and marginal farmland landscape typical of the rest of the dale. The road is lined by hedges, and the Hutton Monument is visible on a hilltop to the south-east of Marske. The village of Marske, which nests snugly in a hollow at the southern end of Marske Beck, remains hidden from view until you almost tumble into it, no matter which road you approach it from.

The name Marske comes from the Old English *merscum*, meaning a marsh. The Marske in Swaledale is not mentioned in the *Domesday Book* (1086), although another Marske near Saltburn is recorded as Mersche.

Victorian writers were particularly impressed by what they saw as the 'Alpine' setting of Marske. Whitaker (1823) describes the valley as being 'one of those Alpine valleys, which, though nature has not adorned, she has furnished with features capable of being adorned by the hand of man'. Bogg (1907), meanwhile, depicts 'a delightfully rural dale village, reminding one of a Swiss hamlet, hid away … among woods and the folds of the hills, a very place of dreams – a sleepy hollow in the wooded hills', and Wainwright (1989) portrays Marske as a 'charming village … snugly sequestered among handsome trees in a side valley of Swaledale … The charm of the place is its natural scenery … '

Marske lies at the bottom end of Marske Beck, just upstream from where it flows into the river Swale. The village surrounds a narrow, single-arched stone bridge over the beck, which Pevsner (1966) believes was probably built in the fifteenth century. The bridge most likely started life as a packhorse bridge; it is only about five feet wide and has no side walls, which would have impeded the passage of ponies carrying heavy side-packs, typically containing lead ingots.

Marske village consists of a number of stone cottages and houses, comfortably spaced out. They are well maintained, with tidy and colourful gardens and well-kept hedges, creating the feeling of a quiet, genteel, well-loved place. The village has a tea shop but no pub or signs of holiday accommodation.

MARSKE HALL.

Pride of place in the village goes to Marske Hall, an imposing residence at the end of a wide drive, surrounded on the roadside by a high stone wall. Pevsner (1966) suggests that the hall was probably built in the middle of the eighteenth century. Opposite the hall, with its grand vista, are the remains of large formal gardens which include specimen trees and an ornamental lake. Pontefract (1934) outlines the history of Marske since the Hutton family acquired the manor in 1596: 'Matthew Hutton who bought the estate for his son was Archbishop of York; and a later Matthew Hutton, born at Marske, became Archbishop of York in 1747. The obelisk [Hutton Monument, 60 feet high] on the hill to the west of the village covers the grave of another Matthew Hutton who died in 1814. He had a racing-stable near, and the horses were exercised on the hill. Marske people say that he asked to be buried where he could hear the tramping of the horses.' The hall was converted in the twentieth century into apartments, following the sale of the estate.

The other jewel in Marske's crown is the parish church of St Edmund the Martyr. The original church – of which only the south door, a blocked north door and traces of the nave remain – was built in Norman times and was heavily restored in 1863. The church is surrounded by a small but well-kept graveyard, heavily shaded by overhanging trees, creating a rustic scene reminiscent of Jane Austen's novels.

MARSKE PARISH CHURCHYARD.

To the north of Marske, on the eastern side of Marske Beck, sheltered by woods and high cliffs, is the site of the former manor house of Clints. The house was pulled down by the Hutton family when it added the Clints estate and the Skelton estate (on the opposite side of the beck) to its Marske estate in 1842. Once again the vivid imagination of Victorian writers led them to compare a part of Swaledale with the Alps, exemplified here by Speight (1897), describing Clints as 'a most romantic spot, strikingly picturesque at any season, but to see the glorious summer sunshine flood the verdant slopes, towering scars, and overhanging woods is to awaken memories of those perched-up out-of-reach châlet-homes in the flower-spangled Alps of Switzerland or the Tyrol.'

From Marske one road heads east, climbing up over Applegarth Scar and past Whitcliffe Scar, and on to Richmond. The Coast to Coast Walk follows the foot of the escarpment that runs to the south of the road, overlooking lower Swaledale. 'The scenery,' writes Wainwright (1989), 'is now rich in variety and interest and of high quality … between a long limestone escarpment and a canopy of foliage shrouding the river.'

Another road leaves Marske and heads north, up the eastern side of Marske Beck over Marske Moor. It passes a series of large fields in an area called Cordilleras, which was created by the Hutton family in 1809 as a model farm on newly enclosed land, and named after South American mountains. The Cordilleras are now owned and managed by

DOWNHOLME PARISH CHURCH.

the Ministry of Defence, which uses the nearby Feldom Ranges as military training grounds. The road eventually winds its way south-west past Holgate to the hamlet of Hurst, above Fremington Edge.

Downholme

Over the river Swale from Marske, on the south side of the dale, about a mile up the main road (the A6108) between Richmond and Leyburn, is the small village of Downholme. It sits on the western slope of Downholme Moor, at the eastern edge of the Yorkshire Dales National Park, on the watershed between Swaledale and Wensleydale. The name Downholme comes from the Old English *dun*, which means a hill. It is listed in the *Domesday Book* (1086) as Dune and was recorded in 1231 as Dunum.

The first visible sign of Downholme, going uphill from the river Swale, is the parish church of St Michael and All Angels. This small stone church, well set back to the west of the road in a field of its own, is very picturesque and well kept. It occupies an idyllic setting overlooking the lower part of Swaledale. A Norman doorway and some features remain of

EAST APPLEGARTH.

the original church, which was built in the twelfth century, but the north aisle and chancel arch were rebuilt in the Early English Gothic style.

Downholme parish church, writes Whitaker (1823), 'stands on a knoll commanding wild and striking views of the Swale, with its rocky and sylvan banks, up and down, improved by the collateral valley of Marske, with its widely extended plantation to the north'.

On entering the church, Pontefract (1934) describes how 'it is easy to shut out the world. Nothing mars its restfulness. Sufficient for simple needs, it has also a beauty which uplifts and makes humdrum lives forgotten for a time.'

Curiously, Downholme village lies half a mile east of the church, hidden from sight from both the church and the road, halfway up the hill. It is little more than a small group of well-kept houses and cottages with tiny neat gardens, and the Bolton Arms Inn. Behind the inn, Pontefract (1934) tells us, there 'was once a stately hall of which only the vaulted cellars remain. It is said that an underground passage runs from them to Ellerton [Priory].'

A particularly striking building can be seen about two miles south of Downholme, along the road to Leyburn. This is Walburn Hall, which Pontefract (1934) calls 'a fine Elizabethan manor house'. Pevsner (1966) refers to it as 'a fortified house', and points out its Elizabethan east-wing and signs of an earlier sixteenth-century range (farm).

Hudswell and Hipswell

A road runs east from Downholme village towards Hudswell, south of the river Swale. It climbs up over the White Scar limestone escarpment which runs along the north-western edge of Downholme Moor, then continues over the open moorland that now serves as a military training area. The road defines the eastern edge of the Yorkshire Dales National Park.

Hudswell sits on the escarpment high above the south bank of the river Swale, overlooking the section of the river that flows through Richmond. It is quite an unusual village for Swaledale, because it is linear – strung out along the road, with buildings well spaced apart – rather than the more common cluster of buildings nesting together around or near a river crossing point. Harry Speight (1897) rather fancifully refers to it as 'the little Alpine village of Hudswell', showing a distinct lack of awareness of what Alpine villages really look like!

Christopher Clarkson wrote in 1814 that Hudswell has 'a forlorn appearance, but in a few years, from the enclosing of the Moor and Waste Lands, and from the planting of hedges and trees about it, good crops of corn will be produced, where nothing but ling and whin used to grow'.

There is little of architectural merit in Hudswell, other than St Michael's Church which was rebuilt in 1884. The village contains the George and Dragon pub, a small shop, a village hall and some former stone farm buildings that have been converted to residential use. It also contains early post-war bungalows, along with some recent barn conversions and residential infill.

A short distance along from Hudswell is the hamlet of Hipswell, birthplace of John Wycliffe (1338–84), who translated the Bible into English. Other than a handful of old stone houses, the hamlet contains St John's Church (built in 1811), a primary school and Hipswell Hall, of which Pevsner (1966) notes, 'on the tower-porch the date 1596 … the front is castellated'.

After a few miles the road then turns left and comes out at the New Holly Inn at the top of Sleegill. The steep road down Sleegill presents a glorious view of Richmond Castle, across the river Swale to the north, as Ella Pontefract (1934) describes it – 'a romantic way to enter Richmond'.

Applegarth and Whitecliffe

The lower part of Swaledale, as it approaches Richmond, is much narrower than the area around Reeth. The fringing hills are relatively low and mostly covered by trees, with mixed land use on the valley floor. The old road between Reeth and Richmond runs north of the river Swale through Marske and then climbs above Applegarth Scar and Whitecliffe Wood and continues east into Richmond.

The main road (the B6270) – the new road – down the dale joins the road (the A6108) from Leyburn to Richmond, just past Ellerton Lodge. From here down to Richmond it hugs the foot of Downholme Moor and runs south of the river Swale until it crosses a bridge south of Hudswell, then continues into Richmond on the north side of the river along Reeth Road. The road here offers good views of Applegarth and Whitecliffe Wood. By Hag Wood, about half a mile before the bridge, there is a well-screened large caravan park (Swale View Caravan Park) between the road and the river. A second caravan park, more hidden from sight from the road, is located past the bridge just outside Richmond opposite Round Howe, on the site of the former paper mill at Whitcliffe.

Without doubt the most attractive route along this lower part of the dale is along the Coast to Coast path. After leaving Marske it continues along the base of the escarpment that defines Applegarth Scar and Whitcliffe Scar, often passing through woodland, on its way to enter Richmond via Westfield. The name Applegarth – from the Old Norse *garthr*, meaning a small field or enclosure (page 20) – recalls a time when a small, simple hut was built here in a clearing in the forest, with fruit trees around it.

Whitcliffe Scar and Whitecliffe Wood are named after the white limestone cliff or escarpment that overlooks the north side of the river Swale. Tom Bradley (1891) describes the 'grey seared limestone crags, crowned with sable yew and sad tinted fir'. Below Whitcliffe Scar, near Applegarth, is the site of an ancient British camp.

On the top of Whitcliffe Scar, halfway between Marske and Richmond, is a monument known as Willance's Leap. Three stone pillars commemorate an accident that occurred here in 1606, when Robert Willance (a draper in Richmond whose wealthy father owned lead mines) was out hunting one day when a thick fog descended. Confused about exactly where he was, Willance accidentally rode his horse over the 200-foot-high cliff. The horse died instantly, but Willance is said to have kept himself alive by cutting open the dead horse and sticking his broken leg inside it to keep the limb warm until he was rescued. Robert Willance lived a further ten years; he died in 1616 at his home at 24 Frenchgate in Richmond and is buried in the parish churchyard behind his old house. Whitcliffe Scar, writes Wainwright (1989), 'is not a spectacular precipice, as the name might suggest … [but Whitecliffe Wood beneath it] provides an enchanting walk through an avenue of mature trees bordering a farm road for a mile, and every step is a paradise.'

'This, perhaps, the most
picturesque spot in this
land of the picturesque ...'
Edmund Bogg (1907)

PART III

Richmond

'Richmond ... is a place one has dreamed of, but not hoped to find. In its own way it is as satisfying as the fells. It does not unbend, a long, proud history has given gravity and dignity, but it spreads itself out for one to imagine what one will.'

Ella Pontefract (1934)

THE MARKET PLACE, VIEWED FROM THE CASTLE KEEP.

Chapter Eleven

RICHMOND

'a place apart, rich in relics of the past, steeped in a long history that still lingers in the precincts of the castle and the narrow alleys and quaint buildings.' Alfred Wainwright (1989)

RICHMOND IS THE JEWEL IN THE CROWN of Swaledale, the gateway from the east and the terminus from the west. It is, and has always been, highly dependent on the dale; the two have been tightly interconnected and inter-dependent since Norman times, when the town was established. Pontefract (1934) notes that in Richmond 'one is conscious of those roads to the hills. They call with their promise of adventure; and one cannot stay long in Richmond and not answer the call.'

In 1952 Alfred Brown wrote that Richmond 'stands supreme among the market towns of Yorkshire and is one of the finest examples of an old market town in England'. Indeed, the town has had praise heaped upon it over many years. For example, in 1945 the British Council chose Richmond as the typical English country town as part of a global publicity campaign promoting what was best in the English way of life. In the late 1970s Sir Alec Clifton-Taylor selected Richmond as one of 'Six English Towns' in his BBC television series – and his book of the same name – which was first shown in 1978. In 2009 the Academy of Urbanism voted Richmond 'Great Town of the Year' based on its character, governance, commercial viability and sustainability.

'Richmond is ... far too good to be bypassed.' Alfred Wainwright (1989)

origins of Richmond

The impressive stone tower of the castle dominates the skyline of Richmond when viewed from any direction. English Heritage promotional material describes the castle as 'guardian of Swaledale'. 'The traveller,' writes Christopher Clarkson (1814), 'on approaching Richmond, cannot avoid being struck with admiration and wonder at the very first sight of the Castle, nor does a nearer view deceive his expectations.' The castle is not just a focal point in the town; without the castle, the town would not have been built. The castle occupies pride of place, but it also provides the reason for Richmond being there in the first place.

The castle was built between 1071 and 1091, probably in a clearing in the forest which originally covered much of Swaledale. There is no mention of either a castle or a settlement in this location in the *Domesday Book*, probably because the castle was still a work in progress at the time of the Domesday survey, and no settlement had yet grown up adjacent to it.

The castle was built by Alan Rufus, a relative of the Duke of Brittany, who had been granted the vast estate of the Honour of Richmond by William the Conqueror after the Norman invasion in 1066. Alan began the castle in 1071 but never saw it finished. After he died single and childless in 1089, the estate passed in turn to his brother Alan Niger (who died in 1093) and his younger brother Stephen (died 1135), then to Stephen's son, another Alan Niger (died 1146), and then on to Alan's son Conan the Little (died 1171). Conan developed the castle further between 1146 and 1171, adding the great stone keep (tower), the curtain wall along the south side of the site, a barbican with a dry moat and drawbridge to strengthen the northern entrance, and an enclosed court (the Cockpit) on the eastern edge of the site.

The castle and surrounding land remained in the hands of people connected to Brittany for a number of generations, and this link is preserved in the French names for some of the streets in the settlement which grew up beside the castle (such as Frenchgate and Maison Dieu).

Like the other French nobles who were granted land after the conquest, Alan Rufus quickly set about building the castle to cement his rule over the territory. It served multiple purposes. It was a conspicuous display of Alan's status, power and wealth, and provided a clear message that the area was now under new management. Pontefract (1934) notes that Alan built 'a fortress to protect the vast estates given him by the Conqueror', but Alec Clifton-Taylor (1978) adds that he built his castle here 'not so much to protect England from the Scots as to protect himself from the local Anglo-Saxons'.

Market scene Richmond by Ernest Forbes.

Alan needed protection from attacks by local people who had been disenfranchised, whose land had been confiscated, and who had been subjected to the servitude of the feudal system as a result of the Norman Conquest. They had every right to feel aggrieved.

Alan chose to build his castle not in Gilling, which had long been the local administrative centre during Anglo-Saxon times, but at a new place several miles away to the south. As well as offering a site that was more prominent and easier to defend, this move also underlined the break with the past; a new local land owner, a Frenchman chosen by the new King William, was now in charge, and the area was effectively under French rule.

Some have suggested that the castle was built at either Neuton (meaning new town or settlement) or Hindrelac (Old Norse for 'clearing of the hind'), two small settlements somewhere in this area that are recorded in the *Domesday Book*. Neuton is listed straight after Easby, Brompton-on-Swale and Skeeby, so the surveyors must have passed through it soon after those other places. Hindrelac is recorded as a small village with a church and priest, and it might have been located in the area of Richmond shown on old maps as Aldbiggin (meaning old buildings or settlement), around what is now Anchorage Hill. No trace survives of any pre-existing settlement on this site, either because there was none or because it was lost under the large structure of the castle.

The site of the castle – on a cliff overlooking the river Swale and the plains to the east – was chosen to maximise visibility and defendability. It is a

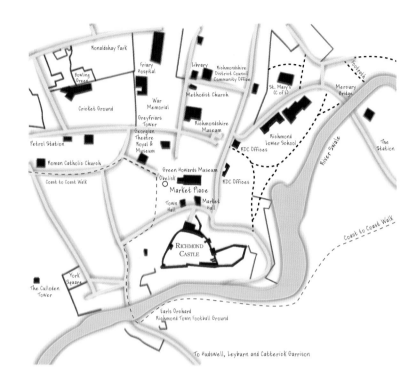

Yorkshire can produce', T. Bulmer (1890) considers it 'charmingly pictur-esque', and Joseph Fletcher (1908) writes that Richmond was 'the most romantically situated town in England'.

Pevsner (1966) saw Richmond as 'one of the most visually enjoy-able small towns of the North of England'. Two centuries earlier an American Quaker called Jabez Maud Fisher (quoted in Morgan, 1992) passed through Richmond in 1776 and wrote in his diary: 'A situation full of grandeur, and from the number of churches, towers and other objects its entrance is very striking.'

The settlement which grew into Richmond town began life as a shanty town, where the stonemasons and other craftsmen who built the castle initially lived with their families. The bailey (courtyard) of the castle

CASTLE WALK, LOOKING EAST TOWARDS GREEN BRIDGE AND BILLY BANKS WOOD.

commanding site, which is probably why Alan chose to call it 'Riche Mount' – the strong hill.

In *History, Topography and Directory of North Yorkshire,* Bulmer (1890) describes the site of the castle as 'a bluff, rising almost perpendicularly to the height of 130 feet above the Swale on the south and east, and falling away somewhat less abruptly on the west. The only possible approach was by a neck of land on the north less than 50 yards across, which was defended by a moat or ditch now filled up.'

The same factors that made this site suitable for the castle have also endowed the town with a spectacular setting. William Longstaffe (1852) describes 'the fairest spot on one of the loveliest streams which

grew into a market, but by the time the town wall was built in 1312 the settlement amounted to little more than the castle and market place. Through time it expanded, as the population grew and the market developed, with new suburbs opening up along what are now Frenchgate and Newbiggin, with further expansion along Bargate down to an industrial area near the river Swale (now The Green) and to the river crossing there.

The location, name, nature and character of Richmond were all effectively decided in Norman times, which has left an indelible legacy in the form of the castle, the Market Place, Holy Trinity Church and the remains of many religious houses, as well as street names and layouts in the town centre.

The character of Richmond also owes a great deal to the Georgian period (1714–1836), which saw the town grow in importance as an administrative, business and cultural centre, and saw many of its residences grow very prosperous. It is easy to imagine characters walking straight out of a Jane Austen novel and feeling very much at home in Georgian Richmond! They could take promenades around the new Castle Walk, dance or play cards in the Town Hall Assembly Rooms, see plays at the theatre, watch the horses and mingle with the great and the good at the racecourse.

The society of Richmond, according to Christopher Clarkson (1814), was 'good, chiefly composed of persons of independent fortunes, who at a moderate rate enjoy all the advantages of a polished and agreeable intercourse; and no where can a stranger, well recommended, find more civility and every proper attention'.

the name Richmond

The name Richmond is first mentioned in 1090 in a document which refers to the Archdeaconry of Richmond, so it appears that the new town acquired a name while the castle was still being built and shortly after the Domesday survey (1086). Unlike most other settlements in Swaledale, Richmond is French in origin, having been named by the Normans. As Pontefract (1934) points out, 'there are many examples of the name in France'.

This was the first place in England to be named Richmond, and others have since borrowed the name. The best known of these in England is the town in Surrey, which until 1499 was called Sheen, but in 1510 was renamed Richmond by Henry VII (who was Earl of Richmond) after he built a new palace there (Richmond Palace) by the river Thames. Since then the name Richmond has been adopted in former colonial countries around the world.

According to a league table compiled by *The Times Universal Atlas of the World* in 2008, there are now 55 settlements called Richmond on three continents (North America, South Africa and Australia), making it the most widely copied place name to emerge from the UK.

Richmond Castle

The castle that Alan built was huge, solid and clearly designed to impress – if not terrify. Bogg (1907) refers to it as 'the stupendous old Breton fortress', and Jane Hatcher (2004) emphasises that 'the very monumentality of it expresses the Normans' political will to dominate this part of the country'. It was designed with two things in mind: it had to be secure and it had to endure. Security was ensured by the careful choice of site and design. Richmond Castle was never besieged, and as Pontefract (1934) notes, 'it was too far from main thoroughfares to play much part in history'.

'The almost perpendicular rock, on which it stands, and the river nearly surrounding it on the South and East, must have made it, according to the mode of warfare used at that time, a strong and impregnable fortress,' writes Christopher Clarkson (1814) in his depiction of the castle.

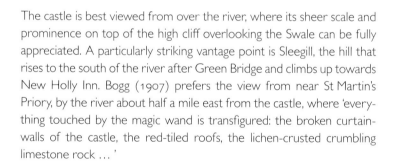

RICHMOND CASTLE BY W.R. ROBINSON.

THE CASTLE KEEP.

The castle is best viewed from over the river, where its sheer scale and prominence on top of the high cliff overlooking the Swale can be fully appreciated. A particularly striking vantage point is Sleegill, the hill that rises to the south of the river after Green Bridge and climbs up towards New Holly Inn. Bogg (1907) prefers the view from near St Martin's Priory, by the river about half a mile east from the castle, where 'everything touched by the magic wand is transfigured: the broken curtain-walls of the castle, the red-tiled roofs, the lichen-crusted crumbling limestone rock ... '

Bogg (1907) considers Richmond castle 'the Yorkshire Heidelberg! ... Bolder far than Windsor, and with less stark sternness than Edinburgh, our island cannot show its like.'

Many Norman castles were built in existing towns, but Richmond Castle was relatively unusual in being built on a new site, away from existing settlements. It was unusual, too, in that it was built with stone from the outset, and on a flat site; more typically, Norman castles were initially built on earthworks with timber outer walls and a timber keep, which could be built quickly. The only other stone buildings in England at that time would have been some local churches; houses and other buildings were timber-framed with walls made of wattle and daub (mud and straw). Richmond is one of the oldest stone castles in England, and may well have been the first one built in stone from its outset. Building Richmond Castle out of stone rather than wood would have required the service of a great number of craftsmen and specialists.

French stonemasons were brought to Richmond to do much of the intricate stonework, such as the doorway and windows in Scolland's Hall, but native workers (probably conscripted) would have built most of the stonework, particularly the long, high curtain walls.

163

Richmond Castle was built to the motte-and-bailey design typical of its time. This involved building the castle on a natural or built mound (the motte), usually surrounded by a deep ditch and defensive walls, beyond which there would be a large open space (the outer bailey) which attackers would have to cross with no protective cover. The bailey would usually be surrounded by a wooden palisade (wall) and an outer ditch (fosse), which might contain water diverted from a nearby stream.

Inside the bailey would be a variety of buildings for the people who lived and worked in the castle, such as stables, storehouses, bakeries, kitchens, cottages and soldiers' quarters. Through time the bailey would also develop into a market, where all the goods needed for the day-to-day living of the many people associated with the castle would be traded.

THE CURTAIN WALL AND SCOLLAND'S HALL INSIDE THE CASTLE.

The design of Richmond Castle is based on a large, flat, roughly triangular courtyard, or Great Court, about 5 acres (24,200 square yards) in size, with a base at the southern side, on top of the cliff overlooking the river. The court would be used for tournaments, and for grazing cattle in times of danger.

The Great Court is protected by high, stone curtain walls nearly half a mile long, which were completed within three years. The curtain wall on the south side topped the edge of the cliff and part of it has fallen down, but most of the rest remains in good condition, as described by Alec Clifton-Taylor (1978): 'At least on the east side the original curtain wall of the late eleventh century survives intact, notable for the incorporation of sections of typically French herring-bone masonry, best seen from the small enclosure known as the Cockpit.'

There are remains of a number of tall, square towers built into the curtain wall, which Christopher Clarkson (1814) describes as 'the lodgings of the principal officers … at the inside were placed the habitations of the owner and his warlike retainers'. This is another way in which Richmond Castle is untypical of Norman castles in England; it was the first to have projecting mural towers designed to improve the defences of the curtain walls. On the northern side of the eastern curtain wall are the remains of the small St Nicholas's Chapel, which include the stone barrel-vaulted roof and stone benches divided into stalls. This was the earliest chapel of the castle and was given by Alan Rufus to St Mary's Abbey at York in 1085.

Beside the chapel is the ruin of Robin Hood Tower, which projects out about ten feet beyond the curtain wall. As T. Bulmer (1890) comments, 'what connection Robin had with the tower is not known, but it has borne his name from time immemorial'. The tower, which has a small vaulted chapel at its base, is believed to have been the apartments given to the lords of Middleham. Just past Robin Hood Tower is what is now known as Fallen Tower. A short distance farther along the curtain wall are the remains of another chapel, and part of the surviving great west

windows, and beyond this are the ruins of a large apartment with a fireplace on the west side, which was probably the kitchen.

The largest remains, at the south-eastern corner of the Great Court, are those of the Gold Hole Tower and the adjacent Scolland's Hall. T. Bulmer (1890) tells us that the tower was named after some treasure that was once found inside part of its structure, although Pontefract (1934) says it was the strong-room of the castle.

Legend has it that a small underground passage led from the Gold Hole Tower under the river Swale to St Martin's Priory about a quarter of a mile to the east, 'through which the ladies of the Castle might retire for protection', as William Longstaffe (1852) puts it. John Speed's 1610 map of Richmond shows an opening in the Earls Orchard across the river to the south, which he described as 'a vault that goeth under the river, and ascendeth up into the castle', but no traces of any tunnel have been found.

Pontefract (1934) reminds us of two other local legends, both involving tunnels; one tells of 'King Arthur and his knights asleep somewhere beneath its walls, and one Potter Thompson who found the entrance to where they slept with the sword Excalibur and a jewelled horn on a table near … the potter picked up these, but was frightened when he saw the knights move, and he fled … [Another tells of] the drummer boy who bravely started out to explore the … [underground passage] to Easby, beating his drum as he went, and of how the listening soldiers followed the beat of the drum across town, down the hill, and into the woods leading to Easby, till, at a place called Clink Bank, it stopped; and the drummer boy was never seen again.'

Adjacent to the Gold Hole Tower is a chapel which was once the main one in the castle. Next to that is a great hall called Scolland's Hall. The hall was named after Scolland, Lord of Bedale, who as Earl Alan's sewer (chief steward) oversaw banquets and hospitality in the castle, and was in charge during Alan's frequent periods away at other parts of his vast estate. The area beneath the hall was used for storage. The hall has five elegant windows to the south, looking over the river Swale and the jousting field on its south bank (now known as Earls Orchard). The windows were probably fitted with wooden shutters because glass was extremely expensive at that time. Food would have been carried into the hall from an adjacent building, up a spiral staircase. According to Pevsner (1966), 'The Great Hall … is very probably the oldest in England.' Scolland Hall, writes T. Bulmer (1890), 'was the most ornate apartment in the castle, and may possibly have been the banqueting room'.

To the east of Gold Hole Tower is the twelfth-century Cockpit Court, where sports were held. This walled court is now a garden called the Cockpit Garden. At the south-western corner of the court are the remains of another tall, square tower, about 60 feet south of a former narrow postern gate which provided access into the court from the west.

The main entrance to the castle was located at the apex of the triangle on the northern end of the site, through the Barbican, a semi-circular space enclosed by a high wall. A dry moat and drawbridge were originally included, but the latter (located beside what is now the ticket office and shop, to the north of the keep) was abandoned centuries ago. Remnants of it were uncovered in a dig in 1732, but Edmund Bogg (1897) reports that a house was later built over the site. T. Bulmer (1890) notes that 'only a small portion of a retaining wall remains to mark the outline' of the former Barbican.

A century after Alan Rufus had begun building the castle, his successor Conan built the keep – the great square tower. The huge keep – over 100 feet high, 52 feet from east to west, 45 feet from north to south, with battlements on top – still dominates the skyline, and as Jane Hatcher (2004) emphasises, it also 'forms the most instantly recognisable symbol of Richmond today'. It was built between about 1150 and 1180 of dressed ashlar stone, quarried locally. It was built over the original gatehouse, to protect the weakest part of the curtain wall and at the same time to add grandeur to the appearance of the castle. Many Victorian writers wrote enthusiastically about the keep – for example, Tom Bradley (1891), who described it as 'possibly the finest in England, with the exception perhaps of the Tower of London'. T. Bulmer (1890) thought it 'a noble and majestic tower' and Whitaker (1823) wrote that it was 'of finer masonry and handsomer aspect than the rest of the building'.

Pevsner (1966) points out that 'the castle is unusual, if not unique, in having its keep not at the safest distance from the gatehouse, which is after all the most accessible part of the castle, but right over it or by the gatehouse … the original gatehouse is now the ground floor of the keep'. The walls of the keep are eleven feet thick, with a stone staircase running between the inner and outer walls, which, as Pontefract (1934) notes, is 'an unusual feature for this date'. The basement (which had a well to supply water should the castle ever have been besieged) has a vaulted roof, and there are three stories above, with battlements on the top. To make the tower as secure as possible (and thus provide refuge should the castle come under attack) the entrance was placed on the first floor, originally accessed via an external staircase, now long since gone. The first and second floors each have a large room, with small side chambers built into the thickness of the wall. Unlike other Norman keeps in England, the one at Richmond was designed solely for military purposes, as a core part of the castle's defences. Unusually, it contained no domestic accommodation, fireplaces, kitchens or chapels.

Richmond Castle was never besieged or attacked, but it has held some famous prisoners, including three kings – William the Lion of Scotland was imprisoned there in 1174 after his defeat at Alnwick, David Bruce of Scotland in 1346 on his way to York after his capture at Neville's Cross, and Charles I after his capture by the Scots.

From the top of the keep there are impressive views in all directions. Looking east, the vista extends over The Batts on the river, over the former railway station and downstream to Easby Abbey, with the Vale of Mowbray and the outlines of the North York Moors in the far distance. Looking north offers almost a bird's-eye view of the large cobbled Market Place, with shops around it and the centre dominated by Holy Trinity Church, with shops built into its outer fabric. The distant view northwards is dominated by the heavy industrial skyline of Teesside. Looking south, the view takes in the river and continues up Sleegill, including a great view of Billy Banks Wood and westwards to Round Howe just upstream of Richmond. The view westwards extends over The Green, York Hill and Culloden Tower, and over the woodlands to the lower part of Swaledale as far as Appletreewick.

The castle had been completed by the early fourteenth century. It later declined in importance and was eventually abandoned and fell into disrepair. By the early sixteenth century it was so dilapidated that in 1538 Leland described it as 'now mere ruins'. Christopher Clarkson (1814) attributes the poor state of the castle not to 'any remarkable siege or military assault, but rather to the want of repairs, occasioned by the desertion of its chief and his military followers … [it] remains a melancholy monument of the destructive hand of time'. By the 1820s Whitaker (1823) was able to write of 'a few sheep which quietly graze upon its herbage'.

Jane Goodall (2001) describes how the castle keep 'remained in [a ruinous] condition for the next three hundred years [after 1538] and became much admired as a romantic ruin. Many celebrated artists, including Turner, painted the castle and Richmond became the object of fashionable tourism.'

Paintings of the castle in the early nineteenth century show much stone missing from the bottom of the keep, which was repaired to stop it collapsing. During the nineteenth century the castle got a new lease of life, in its second spell as a military establishment. In 1854 the Duke of Richmond, who owned it, leased it to the North York Militia for use as its headquarters. The following year a barrack block was built in the Great Court against the west curtain wall, which remained there until it was demolished in 1932. T. Bulmer (1890) describes how 'the area within the walls has been levelled for a parade ground, and a row of houses for the residence of the staff of the regiment erected'. He added that 'these have been built in a style to harmonize as far as possible with the old Norman ruins', although photographs of the time suggest otherwise. Other military adaptations included building a storage block beside the main castle gate, and converting the keep for use as a depot. In 1874 Black's Picturesque Guide to Yorkshire described the keep as 'at present used as a store for the accoutrements of the militia'. In 1908 the castle became the headquarters of the Northern Territorial Army, under the command of Robert Baden-Powell (architect of Catterick Camp a few miles away, and founder of the Boy Scouts).

In 1910 the army handed over responsibility for the fabric of the castle to the Ministry of Works but kept control of the buildings, which were used as a prison for conscientious objectors during both World Wars (1914–18 and 1939–45). In 1984 English Heritage assumed responsibility for the fabric and use of the castle, which is now open to the public.

the Market Place

Without doubt one of Richmond's finest features – after the castle – is its historic cobbled Market Place surrounded by fine Georgian buildings. The Market Place is adjacent to the castle, and was originally its outer bailey, or courtyard.

The special character of the Market Place has helped make Richmond a relatively unique place. It is triangular in shape, slopes down from west to east following the lie of the land, and is said to be the largest in England. Speight (1897) describes it simply, as 'ample, well-built, and convenient', but in *A Vision of Britain* (1989) Prince Charles suggests that it resembles the historic Campo in Siena, northern Italy.

The cobbles have long been a feature of the Market Place. In 1538 Leland described Richmond as 'paved', seventeenth-century traveller Celia Fiennes found that 'the streets are like rocks themselves', and three centuries later Arthur Norway (1903) was bemoaning the fact that the Market Place is 'paved with atrocious cobbles'. Traditionally, well-rounded water-worn cobbles of relatively uniform size were collected from the bed of the river Swale and set on a base of sand, but in recent times the cobbles have been set firm in cement to carry heavy vehicle traffic. The cobbles are such an integral part of the special charm and character of the Market Place that they are Grade II listed and can only be altered legally with official planning consent.

Little remains today of the stone town wall that was built in 1312 to replace an earlier earth and wood structure which marked the outside of the castle bailey, but the semi-circular shape of the wall is preserved in the line of the buildings around the Market Place. The stone wall was about five feet thick and was designed to protect the town from attacks by the Scots. It was built under royal licence, paid for with money raised from special taxes on goods sold in the market. The line of the wall shows just how small the town was in medieval times. In 1538 Leland wrote that 'The wall, now ruinous, is not more than a half-mile around its perimeter, so that it encloses little more than the market place, the houses which surround it and the gardens behind them.'

Gateways, locally called gates or bars, were built into the town wall to allow the passage of people, horses and goods. There were two main gates, at the entrance to what are now Frenchgate and Finkle Street,

'There never was such a rambling old cobbled square, with such steep streets leading down to the river and the lower town. There never was such a quaint church as Holy Trinity, with shops and offices built into the main fabric. And there never was quite such a stupendous keep towering over the housetops across the square.' Alfred Brown (1952)

and smaller postern gates at The Bar at the top of Cornforth Hill, and in Friars Wynd. Through time they fell into disrepair, and by 1538 Leland was able to write that only 'traces of them remain'. The Frenchgate and Finkle Street gates were taken down in 1773 to make it possible for well-loaded broad carts to get into the Market Place, but the two postern gates have survived as reminders of Richmond's origins and past. Through time, as the town grew larger it spread beyond the old town wall. By the time of Leland's visit in 1538, many people were living in suburbs which had grown up in Frenchgate, Newbiggin and Bargate.

THE BAR, WITH TEMPLE GROUNDS AND CULLODEN TOWER BEHIND.

The growth and development of Richmond as a town owes a lot to the development of the market, which allowed it to become the trading hub and focal point of the dale as well as its gateway to the outside world. The right to hold regular markets and annual fairs was granted by royal charter in the twelfth century, and outdoor markets are still held weekly in the Market Place.

Through much of history the main trade was in corn and cattle and as the market grew in importance it attracted traders from as far away as Lancashire and Cumbria. David Brooks (1946) notes that 'the Cornmarket of Richmond was for centuries the largest in the North'. Corn remained important until about the eighteenth century, but Richmond's dominant position was undermined by the establishment of toll-free markets in surrounding towns (Bedale, Masham and Middleham), the loss of the lucrative markets in Lancashire and Cumbria (which by then were growing corn locally), and the 1597 plague.

Nothing tangible remains of the old corn market in Richmond, but an old map dated 1724 shows three market crosses marking the places where barley (for making beer), wheat (bread) and oats (porridge) were sold. There also used to be a stone called the Market Cross in the upper Market Place, believed to have been built when the market charter was renewed in 1440. By all accounts it was a huge structure, surrounded by walls six feet high, with stone steps up to a square platform on top of which was the massive stone cross. The old cross was demolished in 1771 and replaced by the stone pillar which still stands on the site today, on top of a water tank that used to store water piped into the town, with well-worn stone steps all round its base where generations of people have sat waiting for their buses.

Pontefract (1934) describes the scene in the Market Place: 'Butter and produce were sold within the walls of the old Market Cross, and religious meetings held. On the north-west exterior of this cross, criminals were tied to iron rings and flogged; the pillory stood near.'

As well as the corn market, there used to be separate areas within the Market Place for the sale of vegetables, geese and fresh fish. The latter area sold 'catches from Hartlepool and Redcar, and salmon in season from Stockton, Yarm and Carlisle', according to David Brooks (1946). Doubtless the smelliest and most unpleasant part of the market was the beast market and shambles (butchers' row). These originally occupied wooden stalls towards the northern side of the Market Place, were moved to the site of the present Market Hall in 1764, and were later incorporated in the covered Market Hall when it opened in 1854.

By the 1700s wool had replaced corn as the staple commodity in both the market and the local economy, and Richmond was famous for hand-knitted stockings and caps, many of which were exported. Towards the south-west corner of the Market Place there used to be a Wool House, 'where all wool, "in any manner sold within the liberties of the Corporation" was weighed', according to Speight (1897). Jane Hatcher (2004) reports that the Wool House 'seems to have gone out of use in the mid-18th century'; by the time Christopher Clarkson was writing in 1821 the building was being used as a grocer's shop.

A large, three-storey stone building can be seen in old photographs and paintings located towards the south-west corner of the Market Place, between Holy Trinity Church and the Town Hall. This was the toll-booth, built in 1744 on the site of at least two earlier buildings. On the ground floor were shops for rent – 'to encourage the town's increasing commercial success', according to Jane Hatcher (2004). Upstairs were the offices of the men who collected the tolls from market traders; the standard weights and measures used for market goods were also kept there. There was also a courtroom, where the mayor dispensed summary justice and traders and merchants could meet and discuss business. A bell was mounted on the roof, which was rung to mark the start and end of trading in the market. The building was demolished in 1948 to improve access for vehicles (particularly buses) to the western side of the Market Place.

Holy Trinity Church

The centre of the Market Place is dominated by Holy Trinity Church, with its distinctive tower. W. R. Robinson (1833) calls it 'an uncouth looking building', and whilst its architectural merits might be somewhat limited, it is nonetheless very distinctive. 'No other church in England has shops built into its walls,' wrote Ella Pontefract in 1934.

The church started life as Holy Trinity Chapel; it was built in 1150 to serve the needs of the people who lived outside the castle in what was then the town (confined within the bailey, now the Market Place). It was probably the original church in Richmond, although the chapels within the castle (which served the needs of the earl and his family and garrison) are older. Some believe that it stands on the site of an earlier Saxon church, but there is no physical evidence of this. T. Bulmer (1890) tells us that 'there were two chantries in this church, but neither the dates nor the names of the founders are known'.

As the town of Richmond grew during the medieval period, both in extent and in population, Holy Trinity lost most of its congregation to the parish church of St Mary's. Both were endowments of St Mary's Abbey. The parish church was closer to the growing suburb of Frenchgate, and had a consecrated churchyard for burials, unlike Holy Trinity which, as David Brooks (1946) puts it, was 'crabbed, cabined and confined by the town walls'.

In 1360 the original Norman Holy Trinity Church was a ruin and had to be rebuilt. It continued in use as a place of worship up to 1712, after which it again fell into disrepair. It was restored again in about 1740, although that was 'only superficial, and not in the best of taste', according to T. Bulmer (1890). Around that time, too, some shops and tenement houses were built into the south wall beneath the gallery. Whilst this gives the church its distinctive character, the innovation was not universally welcomed. *Black's Picturesque Guide to Yorkshire* (1874),

HOLY TRINITY CHURCH IN THE MARKET PLACE IN 1898. COPYRIGHT THE FRANCIS FRITH COLLECTION.

for example, is critical of 'the houses which so strangely and disgracefully encroach upon the sacred edifice'.

The wide variety of tenants around the church walls in the early twentieth century included, according to Bogg (1907), 'two tobacconists and hairdressers, a sixpence-halfpenny bazaar, and a dealer in antique wares … a saddler and leather merchant's … a dealer in corn and meal, and a decorator and picture framer.'

In the early nineteenth century Christopher Clarkson (1814) reported that 'Divine Service is now performed every Sunday afternoon to a large congregation'. The ground floor of the north side of the church had been converted to shops, and upstairs was the Consistory Court (which dealt with church affairs) and an office where legal documents were stored. In 1858 plans were prepared to do away with the unsightly shops and restore the church to its original purpose, but they were not adopted. A limited restoration scheme of the inside of the church was undertaken in 1864 under the direction of Sir Gordon Gilbert Scott, during which a large ornate window was uncovered which had probably been walled up two centuries earlier. Pevsner (1966) calls Holy Trinity 'the queerest ecclesiastical building one can imagine … Most of the features now inside are of the restoration of 1864.'

Richmond Market Place in 1908. Copyright The Francis Frith Collection.

In 1852 William Longstaffe wrote that the Holy Trinity Church was 'a master-piece of desecration. The chancel is gone, and the decorated nave actually divided from the perpendicular tower by a dwelling-house. The south aisle is destroyed, and in the arches are inserted windows.'

Pontefract (1934) comments that 'probably no other church [in England] has had such a chequered history and survived'. Over the centuries it has served many different purposes, including providing a refuge from the plague in the late sixteenth century, as well as housing the Town Hall and Court of Justice. It has also been a granary, a warehouse (for the storage of beer, china and earthenware) and the chapel of Richmond Grammar School. David Brooks (1946) notes that here also 'were lodged some of the captive followers of Bonnie Prince Charlie on their

way south to trial, imprisonment or death after Culloden'. The shops around the base of the tower of Holy Trinity Church were demolished in 1923. Today the north-west corner of the building is the regimental museum of the Green Howards, which tells the 300-year history of this famous Yorkshire regiment.

around the Market Place

The Market Place is surrounded by Georgian buildings, mostly of stone with tiled roofs, with modern shopfronts on the ground floors. Pevsner (1966) is perhaps a little unfair in writing of these buildings that 'there is very little to comment on', because many of them have great character and display some of the finest of the town's Georgian legacy. Christopher Clarkson (1814) certainly doesn't agree, writing: 'The Market Place is very spacious … it contains many well built handsome houses, with shops equal to those in any town in the Kingdom.'

The best way of describing the nature and character of the Market Place is to take a walk around the outside of it, starting at the entrance to the castle and walking in a clockwise direction. Tower Street opens onto the centre of the south side of Market Place, with Holy Trinity Church stranded in the middle, rather like an island surrounded by flows of traffic and people.

The Town Hall is located on the south side of the Market Place to the west of Tower Street, just past the Town Hall Hotel, opposite Holy Trinity Church. The two-storey building was built by the Richmond Corporation in 1756 as Assembly Rooms, on the site of the medieval Guild Hall which belonged to the Guild of St John the Baptist, 'a fraternity or society combining both commerce and religion', according to T. Bulmer (1890). It also contained a courtroom where borough sessions were held, and a card room and supper room. The building very much reflects Georgian taste and sensitivity. 'The Town Hall is a very handsome and convenient structure,' writes Christopher Clarkson (1814),

RICHMOND TOWN HALL.

'[which contains] a very large and elegant room in which Balls and Assemblies are held.' Jane Hatcher (2004) describes such scenes:

> By providing this handsome facility suitable for balls and assemblies, Richmond Corporation was following a trend set by other towns in deliberately encouraging fashionable and monied patronage … The assemblies were intended to be exclusive gatherings, and only subscribers could obtain tickets … The older generations gossiped, played cards and watched the younger folk dancing. Meeting potential marriage partners was an important function of the assemblies, which were eagerly anticipated by young men and women of prosperous local families, dancing masters coming to Richmond to teach them the latest dances in advance of the annual 'season'. Although assemblies were sometimes also held at other times of the year, Richmond's main 'season' was usually a week in early September.

The Town Hall, which is now a Grade II listed building, contains a restored Georgian courtroom and the historic Council Chamber, and is open to the public.

A short distance along from the Town Hall is the Bishop Blaize Inn, which, as David Brooks (1946) explains, 'is Richmond's surviving link with the woollen trade, once its very life-blood … [although] its age and origin, like the association with Richmond, are hidden in the past.' The inn is named after Blaizius, the Bishop of Sebaste in Armenia and patron saint of woolcombers, who was martyred for his faith by the Romans in AD 316. It is situated close to the site of the former Wool House, and was for many years the centre of the hand-knitting industry in Richmond. In *A Tour Through the Whole Island of Great Britain* (1724), Daniel Defoe writes how in Richmond 'all was cloathing, and all the people cloathiers, here you see all the people, great and small, a knitting; and at Richmond you have a market for woollen or yarn stockings, which they make very coarse and ordinary, and they are sold accordingly.'

Castle Hill opens up the south-western corner of the Market Place, at the start of the Castle Walk. There are striking views from here looking west over The Bar and Cornforth Hill, to The Green with Culloden Tower and Billy Banks Wood in the background. New Road runs down-hill from here to The Green.

The western side of the Market Place is defined by buildings of a variety of styles. Most look Georgian in origin, and were probably built as private residences but have long since been converted into shops. Most have very modern façades on the ground floor. There are also two pubs and a bank along this section.

Finkle Street leads off from the north-western corner of the Market Place towards Newbiggin. *Finkle* is a Scandinavian word meaning crooked, and its use here suggests that the Norman settlers and the much earlier Norse settlers co-existed peacefully in the early days of the new town. Finkle Bar, one of the gates in the old town wall, was located halfway along Finkle Street, where the wall changes direction near the Georgian Black Lion Inn. The gate was demolished in 1773, but a plaque marks its position. Chantry Wynd is a small shopping area on the north side of Finkle Street, close to the Market Place. The last surviving medieval timber-framed building in Richmond, now long since gone, is shown in an 1896 photograph (in Lesley Wenham, 1989) of the junction of Finkle Street and the Market Place.

Friars Wynd leads off the Market Place a short way along from Finkle Street, heading north towards the former Franciscan friary (hence the name). *Wynd* is Scandinavian for a narrow lane, and the term applies well to Friars Wynd, which is less than 10 feet wide. In medieval times it allowed townsfolk to attend church services at the friary, and to collect water from the well there, which was then the town's main water supply outside the castle. The path runs through the well-preserved remains of one of two surviving medieval postern gates (the other is in The Bar, off Castle Hill), and past one of the few remaining sections of the old town wall.

Beyond the gate was the site of the Quaker Meeting House (active between around 1677 to 1750), which Christopher Clarkson described in 1814 as 'a very plain building, characteristic of the simplicity and decency of that orderly Society'. By that date the meeting house was disused. The Georgian Theatre Royal is situated at the northern end of Friars Wynd, opposite the old friary, on what is now Victoria Road. There are sections of old metal tramlines on the path by the gate in Friars Wynd, used in the past to guide a trolley containing heavy items being pushed between an ironmonger's shop in the Market Place and his warehouse in the Wynd. King Street leads northwards off the centre of the northern side of the Market Place, towards the old friary.

THE KING'S HEAD HOTEL.

The King's Head Hotel, the most impressive of the Georgian façades around the Market Place, sits on the eastern side of King Street. It caught the eye of Pevsner (1966), who described it as 'eight bays, brick, early C18, with one original and two recent doorways'. The hotel started life as an elegant town house, built around 1718 by Charles Bathurst whose family had made a fortune from lead mines in Arkengarthdale. The town house was an unashamedly conspicuous sign of his wealth and importance; it was much larger than those around it, was three storeys high, and built in a classical style of handmade bricks (a fashionable but expensive building material in Georgian times) with stone window sills and surrounds and stone quoins (corners to the building). A large pleasure garden behind the house was landscaped with flower beds and trees. It included a bowling green and cockpit and was known as Plasingdale (Jane Hatcher, 2004, considers this a possible corruption of 'pleasing-dale').

Within two years of completing it Charles Bathurst built another town house in York and moved his family there. The house then became the King's Head Hotel, and has been the finest one in Richmond ever since.

Distinguished guests who have stayed at the King's Head Hotel include the artist J. M. W. Turner who stayed for two nights in 1816, and the pianist Franz Liszt who gave a piano recital in the ballroom on 27 January 1841.

The north-east corner of the Market Place drops away into what was known as the 'Great Channel', which leads up to Frenchgate and Station Road. In this area was the medieval town gate of Frenchgate, which was built in 1312 and demolished in 1777 (like that at Finkle Street) to open up access for carriages and wide, high-sided carts.

FRENCHGATE VIEWED LOOKING SOUTH FROM POTTERGATE.

The Grove, Frenchgate.

Number 24 Frenchgate, former home of Robert Willance.

Millgate sits at the south-east corner of the Market Place. As the name suggests this was the old road down to the former corn mills by the river at The Batts (on the flood plain) and The Foss (waterfall, Old Norse *fors*). Millgate also provides access to the eastern end of the Castle Walk, and the attractive riverside walks along The Batts. Millgate House has gardens at the back which are open to the public most days and were described in an article in *The Sunday Times* as 'one of Yorkshire's most surprising gardens'.

The Market Hall, located adjacent to Tower Street, completes the circuit of the Market Place. Although trading continued in the open stalls of the Market Place throughout the nineteenth century, Richmond Corporation built a new covered Market Hall in 1854 on the site of the old shambles. T. Bulmer (1890) describes it as 'a commodious stone building', whilst Pevsner (1966) writes of it sparingly as 'ashlar stone, three arches, three pediments'. The building is still in use today.

Frenchgate and Station Road

The north-east corner of the Market Place leads downhill into the Great Channel, which in turn leads northwards up to Frenchgate. Station Road turns off the Great Channel and runs downhill past St Mary's Church, then drops south-eastwards over Mercury Bridge past the old railway station.

The Great Channel was named after an open sewer that ran down it until the 1740s, making access difficult, as David Brooks (1946) explains. He writes that there was often 'a pool of water in the hollow [at the foot of Frenchgate] and at times a strong current, which had to be negotiated, somehow or other ... In 1746, a little bridge was built over it, and then the road was lifted to the height of the bridge to straighten out the dip.'

The steep descent down the cobbled road of Frenchgate is one reason why King Street and Queens Road were built, to make it easier for coaches and wagons coming from the north to reach the Market Place.

Ryders Wynd, on the western side of the Great Channel, offers a steep walk up to the friary, the tower of which Bogg (1907) insists offers 'a striking vignette and a graceful picture in itself'. Richmondshire Museum was opened in 1978 on the northern side of Ryders Wynd. It includes galleries devoted to the history of lead mining in Swaledale and the history of transport in the area, and the set of James Herriot's BBC television series *All Creatures Great and Small*.

Swale House sits on the eastern side of the Great Channel, just before the junction with Station Road. Since 1974 the building has been the offices of Richmondshire District Council, but it was previously the residence of James Tate and his son James who were masters of Richmond Grammar School (1796–1833 and 1834–63, respectively). During the First World War (1914–18) it housed wounded soldiers.

Frenchgate, a wide, cobbled street, runs north from the Great Channel to Pottergate and the bottom of Gallowgate. The name Frenchgate means literally 'the street of the French people', from the Old Norse *gata*, meaning street. The street dates back to soon after the castle was built in 1071; one of the four gates in the stone town wall was sited at the bottom of the street. From medieval times onwards Frenchgate served as the main route northwards out of Richmond to places such as Maison Dieu, Easby Abbey and beyond.

It appears to have developed as the town's principal street, and according to David Brooks (1946) the road has been widened at least five times through the centuries. Many of the houses along the street retain their original medieval plot boundaries. Frenchgate is still cobbled, like the Market Place and Newbiggin, which adds to its charm and character. Vehicles now have no access to Pottergate, which is much higher above the war memorial, an imposing stone pillar erected in 1921 in memory

of the fallen soldiers of the Green Howards Regiment, where it would have been seen by all those going to and from the barracks at the top of Gallowgate.

There are many fine Georgian houses along Frenchgate, but none finer than The Grove which is set back from the road at the southern end of the street, just above the Great Channel. This imposing brick-built house was erected around 1750 by Caleb Readshaw (1675–1758), a wealthy merchant who exported hand-knitted

MERCURY BRIDGE (FORMERLY STATION BRIDGE) OVER THE RIVER SWALE.

woollen goods (particularly caps and stockings) to what is now the Netherlands. The Grove in Frenchgate was named after a grove of trees that once grew in the back garden. The brickwork has clearly settled in places, giving a rather wavy appearance to the front wall of the building, which has been converted into rented holiday flats.

Dundas Street runs down from Queens Road and the old friary grounds and joins Frenchgate on its western side just above The Grove.

Church Wynd runs downhill from the eastern side of Frenchgate above Dundas Street to the parish church of St Mary the Virgin and its rustic

Richmond Grammar School, now Richmond Lower School.

churchyard. Towards the top of the street, on the same side, Lombards Wynd runs along the base of Clink Bank (below Maison Dieu), behind the churchyard. It joins Station Road opposite the old Richmond Grammar School.

Above Dundas Street, Frenchgate has quite a varied street frontage dominated by Georgian architecture. Most of the buildings are residential, although there are a few small hotels and bed and breakfasts there too. There is a mixture of two- and three-storey houses, mostly terraced, tightly squeezed together, including some small cottages. In places narrow passageways lead through arches into former back gardens, many of which are now infilled with small houses.

The houses in Frenchgate are built of a variety of materials; some are made of dressed stone and others are brick, and some now have cement rendering over the original stonework. Frenchgate is noted for its many elegant Georgian properties. Some are double-fronted, some have ornate pillared doorways, and many have nicely proportioned and well-preserved small-pane windows. Frenchgate, writes Pevsner (1966), has 'some of the wealthiest Georgian houses of Richmond'. Ella Pontefract (1934) does not disagree: 'Frenchgate, its tall houses opening on to the road, might be a residential street near the centre of London.'

It is likely that some of the buildings are pre-Georgian in origin but were remodelled and refronted in a fashionably contemporary style in the prosperous Georgian period – during the 'Great Rebuilding'. There are several interesting houses along the street, including number 24 where Robert Willance (who took the leap over Whitecliffe Scar on his horse in 1606) lived and died, and number 83 where John James Fenwick (founder in 1882 of the department store that bears his name) was born.

Most of the largest and finest houses in Frenchgate were the town houses of wealthy merchants who owned estates farther up the dale and spent the winter months in town when travel was difficult in bad weather. The top of Frenchgate offers a commanding view down the street and over the rooftops of the town centre, to the castle keep beyond; Bogg (1907) calls it 'exceedingly fine'. The town war memorial occupies a prominent position at the top of the stone steps at the head of Frenchgate, on Pottergate opposite the foot of Gallowgate.

Station Road comes off the bottom of Frenchgate at the site of the Great Channel and runs down to the former railway station, crossing over the river Swale via Mercury Bridge (originally called Station Bridge). From the bottom of Station Road you can also look south-east, along the floodplain of the Swale – here called The Batts – to the curtain walls and keep of the castle in the middle distance. The lower part of Station Road, around the bridge, offers a grand view of the parish church up the hill, surrounded by mature trees, and behind it the backs of fine Georgian houses above Clink Bank on Maison Dieu.

Remnants of Richmond Grammar School (now enlarged as Richmond Lower School) survive at the top of Station Road, opposite the parish church, overlooking The Batts. The oldest surviving part of the building dates from 1849, but it is known that there was a grammar school somewhere in Richmond as far back as 1392, and that a new school was built in St Mary's churchyard in 1567 (close to this site, before Station Road was built). The best known of the school's headmasters was Rev. James Tate, a native of Richmond who led the school for 37 years between 1796 and 1833, when he moved to London on his appointment as a canon residentiary of St Paul's Cathedral. The school's most famous pupil was probably Charles Dodgson (a professor of Mathematics at Oxford and better known as Lewis Carroll, the author of *Alice in Wonderland*), who spent two years (1844–46) there studying under James Tate while his father was Vicar of Croft and Archdeacon of Richmond.

St Mary's Parish Church

The parish church of St Mary the Virgin – usually referred to simply as St Mary's – sits between the bottom of Frenchgate and the top of Station Road, on a triangular site that slopes eastwards towards the river. David Brooks (1946) points out that 'unlike most churches, St Mary's does not stand due East and West'; it is aligned slightly north-west to south-east along the line of the slope.

St Mary's occupies a prominent site, visible from the castle keep, the former railway station and Maison Dieu. But it has not won prizes for

RICHMOND PARISH CHURCH.

its looks, described, prior to its restoration, as 'a plain and substantial structure' by W. R. Robinson (1833), while William Longstaffe (1852) wrote: 'The peculiar character of the place causes the walls to be unusually high, and the windows to appear disproportionally elevated.' Even after restoration, writes Pevsner (1966), the church 'is not conspicuous by … any exterior features. Its tower cuts less of a figure than that of the Greyfriars.'

The age of the church remains unclear, but it is known to have been in existence in 1135. T. Bulmer (1890) mentions 'an old grant to St Mary's Abbey, York, in which Earl Stephen, who died in 1137, gives to that establishment "the churches of Richmond"'. As the town grew and the settlement expanded beyond the town walls, Holy Trinity Chapel in the Market Place proved too small, so this new church was built outside the wall, in the middle of an existing consecrated burial ground which originally belonged to Holy Trinity, at the bottom of Frenchgate. St Mary's became, as Leland put it in 1538, 'the parish church which serves the whole town'.

The imposing west tower, which is 80 feet high, was added in 1399 by Ralph Nevill, the 1st Earl of Westmorland. Bulmer (1989) tells us that there were three chantries (probably altars rather than chapels) in the church before the Reformation, dedicated to the donors' favourite saints, endowed with lands given by donors, the income from which maintained the chantry priest. Many of the church's finest features, including its statues and stained glass, were destroyed during the Reformation and the period of the Commonwealth in the seventeenth century.

Much of the church was rebuilt in the nineteenth century, with a major restoration in 1859–60 and further changes in 1864 and 1892. The major restoration was directed by Sir George Gilbert Scott, who designed many Victorian churches across England as well as St Pancras

RICHMOND PARISH CHURCHYARD, WITH THE CASTLE KEEP IN THE DISTANCE.

180

Station and the Albert Memorial in London. He also restored Holy Trinity Church in 1864. Scott's work on St Mary's has received mixed views; supporter Harry Speight (1897) emphasises that 'original features [were] as far as was practicable judiciously preserved', while Pontefract (1934) argues that the church 'lost much of its character'. Pevsner (1966) simply writes that 'it is over-restored'.

Jane Hatcher (2004) describes some of the work undertaken during the 1859–60 restoration. 'The whole of the west tower, the outer walls of the east end and some other sections of the outer walls of St Mary's were retained, but the interior was totally reconstructed, with lofty new arches supporting a taller and more steeply-pitched roof.'

Most of the inside of the church is the result of nineteenth-century restorations, but some earlier items have survived, including two Norman pillars and an elaborate monument to the first Sir Timothy Hutton of Marske (who died in 1629) and his wife and children. St Mary's is best known for its elegantly carved wooden stalls along each side of the choir, which were brought from Easby Abbey when it was dissolved in 1539. The stalls, dating from around 1511, are misericord seats – wooden choir staff seats against which monks could lean during long services – and carvings on the underside of the seats depict faces, plants and mythical animals (including a pig playing bagpipes and two piglets dancing).

The churchyard pre-dates the church itself; it was originally the burial ground of Holy Trinity Church in the Market Place. It contains the grave of Robert Willance, among many others, as well as a marker stone to commemorate the communal graves of the 1,050 or so local people who died from the plague in 1597–98. The churchyard is also immortalised in the poem *Lines written in Richmond Churchyard,* which was written in 1816 by the poet Herbert Knowles, who died in 1817 aged nineteen.

THE FRIARY TOWER.

181

First three verses of *Lines written in Richmond Churchyard* by Herbert Knowles (1816).

Methinks it is good to be here;
If Thou wilt, let us build—but for whom?
Nor Elias nor Moses appear,
But the shadows of eve that encompass the gloom,
The abode of the dead and the place of the tomb.

Shall we build to Ambition? Oh, no!
Affrighted, he shrinketh away;
For see! they would pin him below,
In a small narrow cave, and, begirt with cold clay,
To the meanest of reptiles a peer and a prey.

To Beauty? Ah, no!—she forgets
The charms which she wielded before—
Nor knows the foul worm that he frets
The skin which but yesterday fools could adore,
For the smoothness it held, or the tint which it wore.

King Street and Queens Road

King Street leads north off the Market Place, along the side of the King's Head Hotel. It was opened up in 1813 on the site of the former King's Arms Inn. Plasingdale – the landscaped garden area behind the King's Head – and the surrounding area was then a popular Georgian promenade. The Richmond Corporation built the new road to link up with what is now Queens Road, in order to ease the flow of people and traffic into the Market Place from the north. Today it is a one-way street, carrying a high volume of buses and cars out of the Market Place, but for many years this narrow road allowed two-way traffic.

King Street, writes Christopher Clarkson (1814), 'has lately been made in the great improvement of the town, and forms a pleasant and

FRIARY GARDENS.

convenient road to the Market Place from the back of the Friar's, over an old piece of enclosed land called Plasingdale, some time since taken away ... '

At the northern end of King Street, at the junction with Victoria Road, is the richly decorated former temperance cocoa and coffee rooms, described by T. Bulmer (1890) as 'a neat building in the Queen Anne style ... erected by the Countess of Zetland.' The ground floor of the building is now an estate agents and the upper floor a Thai restaurant. Ryders Wynd runs downhill from that junction to the south, to join the bottom of Frenchgate at the site of the Great Channel.

Past the roundabout at the eastern end of Victoria Road, King Street leads into Queens Road (the main road – the A6108). This runs northwards past the former Victoria Hospital (now a funeral director's) situated on the left at the corner of Quaker Lane, then it swings eastwards to become Pottergate. Queens Road follows the line of an earlier road, variously called Back Flags (after the large paving stones or flags that formed its surface) or Back of the Friars (after the Friary), according to William Wise in the 1830s (quoted in Lesley Wenham, 1977), who also mentions that there were then racing stables and a stable block belonging to the King's Head along the road. The old road was widened and improved in 1887.

In the 1830s, writes William Wise (quoted in Lesley Wenham, 1977), 'there was no Dundas Street as there is today. A narrow, five-foot wide passage was all that gave access to Frenchgate. Here was the regimental store of the local cavalry, the Yeomanry. Dundas Street has now taken the place of that dark, narrow wynd.'

REMAINS OF THE ANCHORAGE, ANCHORAGE HILL.

Dundas Street leads down from Queens Road towards the bottom of Frenchgate. Along Dundas Street today are the town library, the side of the Methodist church, a building called The Parish Room (1899) and a former infants' school (1834) which are both now private business premises, and the Community Offices of Richmondshire District Council.

the Friary

'The greatest ornament of Richmond is the beautiful Tower of the Church of the Grey Friars, which ... from its handsome light appearance cannot fail to attract the attention of every stranger.' Christopher Clarkson (1814)

Variously referred to as Greyfriars, The Friarage and The Friary, this religious house was founded by the Franciscans in 1258 to the north of the Market Place, just outside the walled medieval town, through the old town gate at Friars Wynd. The friary was built on land donated by Ralph Fitzrandal, Lord of Middleham, who died in 1270 (and whose name lives on in the Wetherspoons pub over the road, in the former town Post Office. T. Bulmer (1890) tells of how 'his [Fitzrandal's] bones were laid beside those of his father in Coverham Abbey, but his heart was, by his orders, enclosed in a leaden urn, and buried in the choir of this church'. It is believed that the friary was built on the site of an earlier church made of timber.

Most of the friary buildings have long since gone, but we can get a sense of how large and important the friary was from an inventory dated 1386, which lists a series of stone buildings clustered around a cloister on the north side of what remains of the tower; these included the church, a guest house, a dorter (dormitory), a frater (refectory), a parlour, the warden's house, a room called 'the studies' which was used for teaching, and a washroom. The evidence suggests that the friary was

183

still being developed at the time of the dissolution; the central bell tower was incomplete when the friary was surrendered early in 1539. Richmond's only well outside the castle was in the friary grounds, and townspeople were allowed to draw water from it in return for the friars' right to use the wynd named after them.

The tower is just about all that remains of the fabric of the friary, but it is a striking structure

Behind Frenchgate is the grey friars, not far outside the wall, and their house, with meadow, orchard and a small wood, are also enclosed by a wall, through which a postern gate gives access from the market place. At the grey friars is the only conduit of water in the whole of Richmond. John Leland (1538)

and has been widely praised. The Friary Tower, according to Whitaker (1823), is 'lofty, well proportioned, and of the lightest and richest style of late Gothic architecture'. 'A rich composition,' writes William Longstaffe (1852), 'late but good, something in the style of the Somersetshire churches, [it] rises from four of the most gracious arches in the north.' Speight (1897) describes it as 'time-toned yet beautiful in decay'.

The Franciscan friars – who wore long, grey, hooded habits, hence their name the Grey Friars – were committed to a life of poverty, chastity and obedience. They lived off charity and owned only the clothes they stood up in. David Brooks (1946) explains how 'the friars of Richmond received various gifts of land and other property, although according to the Rule of their Order, they could only possess their own House and the meadow or close around it. There was an orchard and a tiny wood attached – about 18 acres in all – and strictly, even these did not belong to them: they were for their use, but the land was vested in the City Fathers as the temporal owners.'

Unlike most of the monastic orders at that time – including the Premonstratensian Canons (or White Monks) at Easby Abbey, a few miles down the river Swale – which were enclosed and contemplative, the Franciscans were committed to service (particularly evangelism and teaching) and they lived in open communities and travelled widely.

The friary was surrendered in January 1539 by Robert Sanderson, the last warden, and the fourteen friars who were based there. At the time of the dissolution the friary was the second richest in the North Riding. Most of the buildings and property were quickly sold off, dismantled or redeveloped, and the site passed into private ownership. It was owned

MAISON DIEU OVERLOOKING THE RIVER SWALE, VIEWED FROM THE BATTS.

by various families over the centuries until it became the responsibility of the Richmondshire District Council.

Today the grounds of the friary are a landscaped flower garden which is maintained by the Richmond District Council and open to the public. The Friary Gardens include bench seating, information boards describing the history of the site and a small stone war memorial.

above Frenchgate and Queens Road

After its junction with Quaker Lane, Queens Road becomes Pottergate, which runs eastwards towards Anchorage Hill. In the past Frenchgate was the main road to the north in and out of Richmond, but steps at the top of Frenchgate (with the war memorial on top) now prevent vehicles from passing through that way.

Pottergate is quite a short road, but not without charm. Pevsner (1966) describes it as 'another street of wealthy houses', of which the best are Oglethorpe House (at the base of Gallowgate) and Hill House. William Wise, quoted in Lesley Wenham (1977), describes how in the 1830s Pottergate 'had a few half-timbered houses, one of which was a bake-house selling the most delicious muffins and crumpets'.

Hill House, which is well set back off the road and shielded by a high stone wall and large trees, is reputed to have been the home of Francis (Fanny) I'Anson about whom the song 'The Lass of Richmond Hill' was written by Leonard McNally, whom she married in 1787. Jane Hatcher (2004) thinks it more likely 'that the words [of the song] refer to Richmond-on-Thames, which was much closer to the MacNallys' lives than the Yorkshire Richmond, and also was well-known to the London audience the song was aimed at'.

Gallowgate heads uphill to the north from Pottergate towards the Richmond Park Golf Club and the site of the old racecourse. The road is named after the site of the former town gallows, where public hangings took place; this area to the north of the town was previously known as Gallow Fields, or Gallowfields. Again William Wise describes the scene in the 1830s, quoted in Lesley Wenham (1977). He writes how the cottages at the bottom of Gallowgate were 'indescribably dilapidated, and inhabited by some of the meanest and poorest townsfolk … Over their sanitary arrangements it is best to cast a veil.'

The site of the former Green Howards barracks – which were built between 1875 and 1877 – is towards the top of Gallowgate. T. Bulmer (1890) notes that the '1st Yorkshire North Riding Regiment of Foot was originally raised here in 1688. It has served with distinction during the last 200 years in various parts of the world, including the campaigns under the Duke of Marlborough, at Seringapatam, in Ceylon, the Crimea, India, and latterly in Egypt and the Sudan.' The barracks closed in 1961 and the site was then used as a residential school, which closed in 1983. The site, renamed the Garden Village, has since been converted to residential use.

The remains of the old racecourse are on the western side of the top of Gallowgate, which continues north into Whashton Road. There are records of horse-race meetings on the High Moor in Richmond between 1576 and 1622, between 1714 and 1733, and between 1753 and 1765. A new racecourse was opened on Low Moor in 1765. In The History of Richmond in the County of York (1814), Clarkson notes how the new racecourse was on 'better ground, which, being properly levelled at great expense, is looked upon as one of the best in the North for trying the goodness of a horse's bottom. The form being oval, and the company in the middle, the spectators, with a very little interval, never lose sight of the racers.'

An imposing stone grandstand was built by public subscription in 1775, and shortly afterwards the Dundas family built its own private stand beside it. In 1814 the Richmond Corporation built a third small stand for the stewards, known as the Starter's Box, or Judge's Box. The last race meeting was held on Low Moor in 1891. The grandstand was used as an isolation hospital during the 1920s, and whilst half of it was demolished in 1948 enough survived to impress Pevsner (1966), who described it as 'of ashlar, only five bays long, and has an arcade of Tuscan columns below and larger arched openings above with an iron balcony all round'. The site offers panoramic views across Richmond and the Vale of Mowbray.

Anchorage Hill lies at the eastern end of Pottergate, at the junction with Maison Dieu. It has been suggested that near here might be the site of the pre-Norman settlement which evolved into Richmond (the 'Neuton' recorded in the *Domesday Book* of 1086). Anchorage Hill is named after a medieval anchorage (or anchorhold) – a small single cell lived in by an anchoress, a deeply religious woman who chose to live a solitary life of prayer. Hermits lived alone in forests or caves, while anchoresses lived in or near towns, their anchorage often attached to the wall of a church. In this case the French anchoress Eleanor Bowes built her cell, one of a number in Richmond in medieval times, adjacent to the twelfth-century chapel of St Edmund outside the medieval town wall. T. Bulmer (1890) reports that 'this cell is supposed to have been founded by Whyomar, sewer [steward] to the Earl of Richmond'. Leland included it in his description of Richmond in 1538, and a place called the 'Anchridge' is shown on Speed's map of 1610. David Brooks (1946) reports that 'such little property as it possessed was surrendered in 1547 by Agnes Dent the last Anchorette, but the name is preserved in Anchorage Hill'. In 1618 the site was converted into three small almshouses for poor widows and named the Eleanor Bowes Hospital. Pontefract (1934) notes that 'the blocked east window [of the hospital] can be seen outside, though nearly covered by a garage'. Whitaker (1823) writes that The Anchorage 'may be considered as the earliest endowment of a monastic nature at

From about 1900 the Hon Robert James created [at St Nicholas] a garden of historic importance, the prototype of Hidcote in Gloucestershire, and his second wife, Lady Serena, continued to live here and tend the garden until she died aged 99 [in 2000]. Jane Hatcher (2004)

Richmond, contemporary indeed, or very nearly contemporary with the town itself'.

Pottergate continues past Anchorage Hill to the roundabout from which Gilling Road (the B6274) heads uphill to the north to Gilling and the A66, and Darlington Road (the A6108) continues eastwards to Scotch Corner and the A1.

Maison Dieu turns off Pottergate at Anchorage Hill and heads east as the main road (the B6271) to Easby and Brompton-on-Swale. It runs along the top of the hill above Clink Bank and Flint Bank Wood, and offers panoramic views of Richmond's town centre and castle, with Billy Banks Wood as a backdrop. William Wise's take on Maison Dieu in the 1830s, as quoted by Lesley Wenham (1977), was that it was 'a miserable rookery of antique dwellings, some still built of wood, relics of the Middle Ages … These hovels were occupied by anthropological and entomological specimens which, in civilised cities, would only be found in asylums or museums.' Christopher Clarkson (1814), however, was much more complimentary about this area of the town: 'The view [over the town from Maison Dieu] … yields to very few places in the country, as possessing every ingredient of rural scenery. The cataract, the castle, and the town, backed by the high moorlands now enclosed, cannot fail to strike the attention of every one as a fine situation … '

St Nicholas Gardens, the site of the medieval St Nicholas Hospital, is on the south side of Maison Dieu, above Flint Bank Wood and overlooking St Martin's Priory to the south and Easby Abbey to the south-east. Like the Eleanor Bowes Hospital, the term 'hospital' used here means almshouses, not a medical establishment as such, although it did offer an infirmary for the sick. St Nicholas Hospital was founded some time in the twelfth century by black-cloaked Benedictine monks, 'for the relief of the poor and infirm' as T. Bulmer (1890) puts it, but it also offered lodging to pilgrims and lost or distressed travellers. It was endowed with land in Richmond and Skeeby, and its chaplain was paid to say mass daily in the chapels of St Edmund and St Nicholas (over the river). By 1448 the buildings had fallen into serious disrepair, and mass had long been neglected; the buildings were restored and the mass re-endowed by Sir William Ayscough of Ayscough, near Bedale. The hospital was surrendered in 1535 by Richard Baldwin, the last master, and in 1585 the ruined remains passed into private hands. A house was built on the site, adjacent to the road, which might include parts of the remains of the hospital and is believed to be the oldest inhabited house in Richmond; it was extensively restored in 1841. Pevsner (1966) describes it as 'a C17 house with a front with two projecting wings, and was given its present appearance by Ignatius Bonomi after Lord Dundas had bought it in 1813'. St Nicholas Gardens, which are of great importance in the history of early twentieth-century garden design, are open to the public.

Newbiggin

The western end of Finkle Street, which leads off the north-west corner of the Market Place, opens out onto Rosemary Lane, which in turn leads into a large cobbled square that marks the start of Newbiggin. The name Newbiggin comes from the Anglo-Saxon for new settlement or new building. The street was one of the first suburbs built outside the town walls in medieval times, and has been an important street in Richmond ever since. There is no evidence of any earlier settlement on the site.

Newbiggin is an attractive street; it is wide, flat, tree-lined and cobbled; it has one of the finest streetscapes in Richmond, framed by elegant Georgian town houses. 'Perhaps on account of its trees and the boulevard atmosphere they give,' comments David Brooks (1946), '[Newbiggin] has a serenity of its own.'

The old Unicorn Inn stands on the northern side of the cobbled square. Parts of the former coaching house, which served traffic heading up Swaledale and Arkengarthdale, date back to the sixteenth century. Around the square are houses of a variety of dates and styles, the most prominent of which (across the square from the inn) is number 11, called Christmas House, which Pevsner (1966) points out has 'a pretty Adamesque doorcase'. On the front of the house is a sign which explains that John Wesley (1703–91), founder of the Methodist movement, visited Richmond three times, on 3 June 1768, 14 June 1774 and 9 May 1786; he probably preached in this square on his second visit.

Two other notable buildings around the square are the former freemasons' hall and the working men's hall. The freemason's hall, described by T. Bulmer (1890) as 'a handsome and commodious structure', was built in 1868 for meetings of the Lennox Lodge. The Zetland Working Men's Hall nearby contained, 'besides reading and recreation rooms and library, an upper room, in which the Oddfellows and Good Templars hold their meetings', according to Bulmer.

Bargate, another cobbled street with a variety of types and sizes of terraced housing, leads south off Newbiggin and runs down the steep hill towards The Green and Green Bridge. Bargate, wrote Pontefract in 1934, 'starts out influenced by the dignity of Newbiggin, but the houses get smaller as it descends, until, near the bottom, are what would be slums in a less artistic place'.

Newbiggin is bordered by some fine Georgian buildings, including one particularly striking Georgian house – number 47 (Goodburn House). This double-fronted stone house has three bays with two attractive Gothic bay windows on the ground floor. Pevsner (1966) considers that Goodburn House 'may well be some people's favourite house at Richmond', while Alec Clifton-Taylor (1978) describes it as a 'decidedly entertaining example of Richmond's Gothick [sic]'.

The Catholic church of St Joseph & St Francis Xavier, with its interesting tall thin tower, richly ornamented with pillars, is located towards the western end of Newbiggin, on the northern side of the road. It was built in 1809 and at the time was, according to Christopher Clarkson (1814), 'suitably adapted to all the ceremonies of the religion. It is very nearly fitted up and will contain about 200 persons.' T. Bulmer (1890) considered it 'a handsome stone edifice in the Decorated Gothic style ... The nave is lofty and well lighted, and separated from the aisles on each side by an arcade of elegant pointed arches ... The windows are all of elegant Gothic form, and filled with stained glass.'

The old jail, which W. R. Robinson (1833) refers to as 'the Debtors' Goal', sits over the road from the church, on the south side of Newbiggin. David Brooks (1946) tells us that 'the "private" goal in Newbiggin belonged to the Earls of Richmond who claimed ... the power of judging any thief caught within the Liberty of Richmondshire, and to inflict the usual consequences – the death penalty. They had a gallows at the entrance to the town – Gallowgate – where those coming and going were visually reminded of the unhappy fate of sheep steelers.'

The last hanging took place in Richmond on 12 January 1613. A sign on the wall outside the jail records that Richard and John Snell, Protestant

NEWBIGGIN, LOOKING EAST.

NUMBER 47 NEWBIGGIN, GOODBURN HOUSE.

martyrs, were imprisoned here in 1558, and that Richard Snell was burned at the stake nearby on 9 September 1558 – one of Richmond's less glorious episodes.

At the western end of Newbiggin is the entrance to the former Yorke grounds. Pevsner (1966) calls Temple Square, on the right in Cravengate, 'a pretty Georgian eddy'. A short way north, along Temple Terrace, was the parish workhouse, the site of which is now occupied by Richmond House. Christopher Clarkson (1814) writes that Richmond workhouse was 'a very good substantial building ... where [the poor of the parish] ... are maintained with cloaths and every comfort suitable to their situation.'

Georgian Theatre Royal

The Georgian Theatre Royal is situated on Victoria Road, opposite the friary at the entrance to Friars Wynd, near the site of the former Quaker Meeting House. It was built in 1788 by Samuel Butler who was actor-manager of one of the many theatrical companies touring England at that time. Butler also operated theatres in Beverly, Harrogate, Kendal, Northallerton, Ripon, Thirsk, Ulverston and Whitby, but only traces of them have survived. The Georgian Theatre Royal, writes Christopher Clarkson (1814), was:

> a neat house, well fitted up, and the scenery and other ornaments
> very appropriate ... it is capable of containing near 240. Both the
> Georgian gentry and the townsfolk liked nothing better than a good
> play, and Richmond catered for this need in 1788 when a theatre was
> built ... During the 'season', the great and the good would attend a
> play after a day at the races or an assembly at the Town Hall.

The theatre continued in regular use until 1830, when performances became less frequent; between 1830 and 1848 Edmund and Charles

ROMAN CATHOLIC CHURCH, NEWBIGGIN.

Kean and Ellen Tree appeared there. Like most theatres across the country its fortunes declined in the mid-nineteenth century, and it was closed in 1848. The pit was boarded over, and the building was later used as a corn merchant's store and a furniture store; during the Second World War it was used as a salvage depot. Ella Pontefract (1934) describes its condition before war broke out:

> Few people seem to know of its existence. There is the pay-box at the door, and a tiny dressing-room at the end of a passage. Two doors lead into the pit, down the sides of which there are seats and a barricade … The original galleries remain; it has a box at either end from which stairs led down to the stage.

The Georgian Theatre Royal (Richmond) Trust Ltd was formed in 1960, when an appeal was launched and work began to restore the theatre to its former glory. It re-opened in 1963, and Queen Elizabeth II approved its new name – The Georgian Theatre Royal. The building was further restored and enlarged in 2003, with a sympathetic extension offering a bar, restaurant and mixing space for visitors. The outside of the theatre is plain, solid and assuming, but inside – as Pontefract (1934) points out, even before restoration – it is 'an almost perfect specimen of an eighteenth-century theatre'. Pevsner (1966) agrees, claiming it to be 'One of the oldest and one of the best-preserved Georgian theatres in England. The proscenium especially is nearly perfect. Ground-floor boxes and, on Tuscan columns, upper boxes. Pay-box, stage, dressing rooms, staircases are also original.'

THE GEORGIAN THEATRE ROYAL.

Victoria Road and Reeth Road

Victoria Road – the main road (the A6108) into Richmond from the west – runs west from King Street towards Reeth Road. It is reached from Newbiggin via Rosemary Lane to the east and via Cravengate to the west. William Wise, writing in the 1830s (quoted in Lesley Wenham, 1977), tells us that it was previously known as Back Ends and was renamed in honour of Queen Victoria.

At the eastern end of the road, at the roundabout between King Street and Queens Road, are the Friary Gardens and the Richmond Tourist Information Centre nestled within them. Opposite the gardens and not far west of the bottom end of King Street is The Georgian Theatre Royal.

On the west side of Friars Wynd is the rather striking brick-built Fleece Hotel with its distinctive battlements, which make it look like a baronial Scottish castle with small Disneyesque round turrets on the top. The name commemorates the historic link between Richmond and the hand-knitting woollen industry. Farther along Victoria Road on the same side, opposite the cricket ground, is the former Zetland Cinema which was converted in the 1970s into an independent church, now the Influence Church (Pentecostal).

On the northern side of Victoria Road, adjacent to the Friary Gardens, is Ronaldshay Park – a public park – and Richmond Cricket Ground with its attractive bowl-shaped setting. Over Hurgill Road from the cricket ground is the Nun's Close car park. The site was probably a nunnery in medieval times, but, as T. Bulmer (1890) points out, 'nothing is known of its history; and even the order to which the sisters belonged has passed out of memory'. Bulmer continues: 'The convent [at Nun's Close] is mentioned in the Pipe Roll of the year 1171, but it must have disappeared before the time of Leland's visit in 1538, as the antiquary does not in any way allude to its existence.'

At the western end of Victoria Road, where it meets Quaker Lane, is the site of the former Pinfold Green, where, as Pontefract (1934) notes, 'sheep and cattle on their way to market were penned while the drovers rested'. A short distance to the north, on Hurgill Road, is the site of the former Nags Head Inn on Hurgill Road, which, as William Wise described it in the 1830s (quoted in Lesley Wenham, 1977), 'was the great emporium for lead. Thousands of pigs, as they were called, were piled in the inn yard awaiting transit as back carriage for shipment from Stockton or Yarm to London or Newcastle. Carriers … twice or three times a week brought goods inland from the Tees ports, taking the lead back with them.' Discussions were held in 1833 about the possibility of opening a railway line up Swaledale from the lead depot at the Nags Head Inn, but nothing came of them.

Victoria Road leads west into Reeth Road, the new road built in 1836 between Richmond and Grinton. The section of Reeth Road within the town is today largely residential, but at its western end are the town cemetery (on the northern side) and a residential caravan park on the site of the former Whitcliffe Paper Mill (on the southern side). Halfway along the southern side of the road, overlooking the river Swale, is the site of the former Convent of Our Lady of Peace, now converted into private residences. The convent was built in 1860 for nuns of the order of the Assumption. T. Bulmer (1890) writes that at the end of the nineteenth century there were 25 sisters in the convent 'who devote themselves to the education of [55] young ladies'.

North of Reeth Road is Westfield, the remains of one of the three open fields in medieval Richmond.

Castle Hill and The Green

Castle Hill opens up at the south-west corner of the Market Place. It is linked to Tower Street, the main entrance to the castle, by a narrow backstreet called Castle Wynd, which passes behind the Market Hall and Town Hall. Bogg (1907) considered Castle Wynd 'a picturesque mixty-maxty of crooked roof, out-of-square wall, and old-world interiors and ancient domestic property'.

There are two ways down from Castle Hill to The Green – by foot via the narrow medieval stone gate called The Bar at the top of Cornforth Hill, or down the steep New Road which joins the bottom of Bargate Hill. Castle Hill also gives access to the Castle Walk, past some well-preserved Georgian houses which, as Pevsner (1966) writes, have 'some pretty bow windows of shallow curve, on the ground floors'.

The Castle Walk is a promenade which runs around the base of the castle walls on the top of a very steep hill down to the river Swale, over 100 feet below. Originally called The Terrace, or Castle Terrace, it was created in 1782 as a fashionable Georgian promenade, where the ladies and gentlemen of Richmond could take the air, take in the views and be seen in their finery. Part of its charm was the sense of risk it offered; Christopher Clarkson (1814) writes of how 'presenting to the eye a tremendous precipice [it], makes those who are unaccustomed to the sight of a hilly country not very much at ease, thinking it dangerous to pass'. More positively, *Black's Picturesque Guide to Yorkshire* (1874) notes that it 'affords an agreeable promenade'. The Castle Walk, writes Bogg (1907), is 'not only a duty and a delight, whether taken by sun or moonlight, but gives one a better idea perhaps than any other of the impregnability of this grand old fortress, perched like an osprey's nest on its dizzy cliff, high over brawling water'.

Walking clockwise from Castle Hill, Castle Walk follows the base of the western side of the castle, looking over The Bar and Cornforth Hill to The Green and Culloden Tower. It then passes round the southern side of the castle looking over the river towards Green Bridge, Billy Banks Wood, Sleegill and Earls Orchard. It continues past the south-east corner of the castle, with views over and The Foss, the former gasworks site, The Batts and the old railway station, and then winds uphill along Millgate and past some old houses, back to Tower Street.

The Bar is a narrow lane at the top of Cornforth Hill, which passes through one of the two surviving small postern gates. This was once an important route used by people and horses moving up from Green Bridge to the Market Place.

'The walk to the summit of the hill [at Westfield] will be amply repaid by the romantic and extensive prospects which it presents.' W. R. Robinson (1833)

'This part of the town still retains many antique bits of property, picturesque in crookedness and wrinkles of age.' Edmund Bogg (1907)

Opposite the bottom of Cornforth Hill, where it meets Bargate, is St James Chapel Wynd, which is now housing but was built on the site of a medieval chantry chapel dedicated to St James of Compostella. New Road was opened in 1773 to provide a wider and more accessible (but still unavoidably steep) route between Green Bridge and the Market Place.

The Green, shown on John Speed's 1610 map of Richmond as Bargate Grene, lies west of the castle at the foot of Cravengate, Bargate, New Road and Cornforth Hill. It is a triangular open space which Pevsner (1966) describes as 'like a North Riding village green', and is dominated by a large chestnut tree planted in 1982 to replace one put there in 1897 to commemorate the Diamond Jubilee of Queen Victoria, which had been damaged by a gale. It is one of the most picturesque areas in Richmond, and offers a spectacular view of the west side of the castle and its imposing keep, a view commended by Pontefract (1934): 'The view of the castle from Bargate Green, with the cottages climbing up to its walls … has the mystery and fascination of a foreign scene, a lethargy not typical of England … There are not many days in the summer when an artist does not paint or draw the castle from Bargate Green.'

The Green is now an attractive residential area, but it was previously the town's industrial suburb, located beside the river which provided water and power. In past centuries it consisted of tanneries, corn mills and fulling mills, along with a brewery, nailmaker's and a fish-smoking warehouse; many of the houses were occupied by weavers. In the nineteenth century The Green had little of the charm it has today. It was a hive of activity. For example, on or around The Green in 1834 there were a tanner and fellmonger (who dealt in animal skins for glove leather), a brewery, public house, blacksmith, three shops and a hat-box maker and marine store dealer.

William Wise, quoted in Lesley Wenham (1977), sets the scene a century before Pontefract came along, describing The Green as 'the abode of the worst ne'er-do-wells in Richmond. It was the haunt of every vice and disease. All the houses were tumble-down, rickety and neglected, with small windows, narrow doorways and low ceilings … the general impression was one of decay and neglect.'

Temple Grounds is a large sloping area of parkland at the western side of The Green, a reminder of the prosperous past of this area. A wealthy local family, the Yorkes, bought the land in about 1675 and built a substantial mansion on it called Yorke House. The grounds were landscaped as a park called Temple Gardens. Christopher Clarkson (1814) considers Temple Gardens 'well worthy of the inspection of the traveller, on account of the beauty of the situation, and the great improvements received from art'.

Clarkson (1814) also reports that, to build the house, 'the Old Green Mills were taken down and the Gardens and Stables removed from near the river to their present situation on the Tenter Banks [where cloth was stretched and dried; now Temple Grounds]'. The house was demolished in 1823 because, according to T. Bulmer (1890), it 'occupied an unhealthy situation … [and] the materials were sold for building purposes.' The stables and coach-houses were later converted into cottages known as Yorke Square; these were demolished in 1958 and the area is now a car park. Speight (1897) reports that 'the Temple Lodge was built by John Yorke in 1769, and for some time was used as a menagerie. Subsequently it was . . . [sold and the new owner] considerably enlarged the house and improved the grounds; these are beautifully wooded and fall to the river, and contain some curious grottoes.' Temple Lodge is still there today, towards the top of Cravengate on the western side of the road, opposite the western end of Newbiggin.

John Yorke, who served as Member of Parliament for Richmond, also built Culloden Tower in the grounds of Yorke House, in 1746, to commemorate the Duke of Cumberland's victory over the Scots at Culloden during the Jacobite troubles. William Longstaffe (1852) tells us that it was 'christened "The Cumberland Temple"'. It sits on the site of an old peel tower (fortified house), called Hudswell Peele after its builder William de Hudswell, which had a walled enclosure attached where cattle could be secured if and when Scottish raiding parties

CORNFORTH HILL.

The Green.

194

CULLODEN TOWER IN TEMPLE GROUNDS.

Since its beginnings in Norman times Richmond has relied heavily on the river Swale, which endowed the place with a defensible site for the castle, water power for the mills, and attractive scenery.

Its rocky course has been the subject for many authors. Daniel Defoe wrote in 1724 that the river 'has some unevenness at its bottom, by reason of rocks which intercept its passage, so that it falls like a cataract, but not with so great a force', while William Camden (1590) described the Swale, 'which, with a terrible noise, seems to rush rather than run among the rocks'.

Somewhere along the Swale in the vicinity of Richmond in AD 625, Paulinus (a Christian missionary who became the first Archbishop of York) is said to have baptised more than ten thousand men, women and children. David Brooks (1946) points out that 'Paulinus always baptised his converts in the name of the Holy Trinity, and this has led some writers to assert that Old Trinity in the market-place was originally of his foundation'.

'The river, winding in a serpentine course amidst richly wooded banks, gives to this landscape a delightful charm.' W. R. Robinson (1833)

The current course of the Swale, to the south of the castle and town, is probably a legacy of the last ice age. Pontefract (1934) suggests that the original course flowed farther north, through what is now the Market Place, but was blocked with deposits from the shrinking glaciers while powerful meltwater cut a new channel to the south.

At the western edge of Richmond there is another feature of the river associated with the ice age – Round Howe. The name howe comes from the Old Norse *haugr*, meaning a hill, knoll, or mound. But the word may

swooped on Richmond from the north during the fourteenth and fifteenth centuries. Pevsner wrote in 1966 that the tower was 'high and substantially built … [and] ought to be better known than it is. It is certainly for historical interest and aesthetic pleasure one of the major monuments of Richmond.' Thankfully, Culloden Tower has in recent years been fully restored by the Landmark Trust, which rents it out as a unique holiday cottage.

Rocky bed of the river Swale below Green Bridge, Richmond.

Round Howe.

The Batts viewed from Mercury Bridge.

Sleegill.

THE FOSS. COPYRIGHT *courtesy* OF ALEX HAY.

also refer to a tumulus (man-made barrow), and the origin of the feature has been much debated. Longstaffe (1852) notes that some people thought the Druids had made it, but the general consensus is that it is a natural feature caused either by a landslide, as Christopher Clarkson (1814) suggests, or 'some extraordinary flood', as W. R. Robinson (1833) insists. However it was formed, at the end of the nineteenth century it was 'covered with trees and verdure and had formerly upon it an ornamental summer-house built in the form of a Chinese Temple, by Cuthbert Readshaw, Esq., in 1756', according to Speight (1897). Round Howe, writes William Longstaffe (1852), 'has the outward semblance of a vast tumulus, and rises out of a small but deep amphitheatre of rock and wood'. T. Bulmer (1890) considers it 'a very remarkable natural curiosity, consisting of a conical hill, rising up in the middle of an immense basin of rock'.

Over the river from Round Howe, on the north side, is the site of the former Whitcliffe Paper Mill. Henry Cooke leased the medieval corn mill on the site from Richmond Corporation in 1823 and converted it into a paper mill, which was initially powered by water from the river but later driven by steam. This was the only factory as such in Richmond in the early nineteenth century. Lesley Wenham (1989) notes that the mill flourished for over a century, and 'by 1900 … the factory had three large chimneys and employed over 50 people.' The buildings, weir and water-storage ponds have long since gone, and the site is now a residential caravan park.

Behind Temple Grounds is Billy Banks Wood, which runs along the escarpment south of the river and continues around Round Howe. It is managed by the National Trust, and provides a wonderful backdrop to views looking west from the castle and the Castle Walk. Christopher Clarkson (1814) tells us that Billy Bank was formerly known as Bordel-bank. The word *bordel* is Old French for small house, but it can also refer to a brothel (from the medieval Latin *bordellum*), which raises the question of why the Norman French settlers chose to give the hill the name they did!

The Green Bridge – until 1846 (when Station Bridge was built) the only crossing point over the river Swale in Richmond, and the traditional gateway to the town from the south – crosses the river just south of The Green, to the west of the castle. From the bridge the turnpike road from Richmond to Askrigg and Lancaster climbs up Sleegill to Holly Hill and beyond. The stone bridge, which Pevsner (1966) describes as having 'three beautiful segmental arches and round cutwaters', was built in 1789 to replace an older town bridge which was seriously damaged in severe floods that affected all of north-east England in 1771.

'The first stone bridge had four stone arches, and a sentry-like box at the centre divided Town and Country,' wrote David Brooks in 1946; 'Here, too, the toll was taken on all corn and cattle which passed over the bridge into Richmond.' In *The History of Richmond in the County of York* (1814), Christopher Clarkson describes how the 'new' bridge was of 'a strong, useful fabric, of sufficient height and strength to repel the violent and sudden inundations, which rushing from the surrounding hills, destroy everything that opposes them'.

To the east of the Green Bridge, directly south of the castle and across the river, is Earls Orchard. This patch of relatively flat ground lies on the river's floodplain and flooded regularly in the past. According to tradition, this was where the knights from the castle practised their jousting. Today it houses the Richmond Town Football Club.

Behind Earls Orchard is Sleegill which runs up to Holly Hill and on towards Catterick, Hudswell and Leyburn. The name Sleegill comes from an Old Norse word meaning a narrow valley. Until the beginning of the nineteenth century this was the only way into Richmond from the south. The view from the top of Sleegill:

> … is quite a panoramic view of Richmond, and has been considered strikingly fine by lovers of picturesque scenery … the castle is a prominent object in the centre of the picture. The river, winding in a serpentine course amidst richly wooded banks, gives to this landscape a delightful charm. W. R. Robinson (1833)

Riverside Road, which was opened in the nineteenth century, runs east from the Green Bridge, hugging the north bank of the river round the base of the Castle Walk. It passes the site of the former town gasworks, The Foss waterfall, and joins up with the bottom end of Millgate.

The Foss is located on the river below the south-east corner of the castle. It has long been a popular place for people to sit, play or eat ice-cream. The remains of a brick weir at the site are a reminder of this area's industrial past; this was the site of Castle Mill, a medieval corn mill built to grind corn for the castle and early town, powered by water from the river, and accessed via Millgate. In 1865 the corn mill was converted and extended to become a paper mill, which was destroyed during a great flooding of the river Swale on 29 January 1883.

Richmond is believed to have been one of the first three towns in England to be lit by gas. In 1821 five Richmond tradesmen formed the Richmond Gas Company and built a gasworks at the bottom of Millgate, near The Foss. The Richmond Corporation took over the company in 1849, the buildings were reconstructed in 1877 and extended in 1885, and in 1949 the manufacture of gas was nationalised. Richmond has been supplied by North Sea Gas since 1972, when the gasworks site was cleared and landscaped as amenity land.

For two years there was controversy as to where the station should be – Ryders Wynd, and Clark Green near Clink Bank were among the locations suggested. In the end it was decided to terminate the line on the St Martin's [south] side of the river, because of the engineering difficulties of bringing the railway across the river Swale into the town. Jane Hatcher (2004)

Downstream from the site of the old town gasworks, on the north side of the floodplain, is a flat grassed area called The Batts. Today this is a pleasant open space by the river, but in the past it was an industrial area where water-powered mills ground corn, fulled (hammered) cloth, made paper and sawed wood. Church Mill, the last mill here, was demolished in 1969; its location is now marked by an upright circular grindstone. From The Batts one gets a good view of the former Richmond Grammar School and St Mary's Church, backed by Flint Bank Wood.

Christopher Clarkson (1814) writes that here the river is 'divided by small islands, some having a surface of naked pebbles and others covered with shrubs and verdure'.

At the northern end of The Batts is the bridge over the river Swale at the bottom of Station Road. The four-arched stone bridge was built by the railway company to link the town to Richmond station. It was originally called Station Bridge, but in 1975 was renamed Mercury Bridge, 'in honour of the 8th Military Corps of Signals, one of the four military units which has the Freedom of Richmond', as Jane Hatcher (2006) reports.

In 1846 Richmond was connected to the railway network by a branch line from Darlington which gave a great boost to the local economy, allowing the rapid movement of freight (including lead and cattle) and passengers in and out of the area. Great care was taken with the location of the station, to avoid spoiling the fashionable town centre.

The station was built on the site of St Martin's Mill, in the Gothic style, complete with stone gargoyles and window surrounds. As well as the main station building the complex included a train shed, goods shed, locomotive depot and gasworks, and a turntable near the engine shed. There were also houses for the station manager and the goods manager, and a row of six railway cottages to the south-east of the station, near the ruins of St Martin's Priory. The station development also included the new road bridge, and the former Low Church Wynd was widened and upgraded into Station Road. Jane Hatcher (2004) adds that 'the King's Head ran a horse-drawn omnibus to meet every train arriving in Richmond'.

The railway line was closed in 1968 and the site was acquired by Richmond Rural District Council. The path of the former railway line

Richmond station. Copyright courtesy of National Railway Museum Science & Society Picture Library.

St Martin's Priory, a cell of St Mary's Abbey, York'. The priory was founded in about 1100 as a cell for nine or ten Benedictine monks – known as Black Monks after the colour of their habits – attached to the abbey at York, on land donated by the Earl of Richmond's sewer (chief steward) Whyomar, 'for his own salvation, and that of his heirs', in the words of Christopher Clarkson (1814). After it was dissolved in the sixteenth century much of the stone was robbed for use in other buildings, leaving what Pevsner (1966) could only describe as 'scanty remains', making it difficult to establish the original size, layout and plan of the site. The most prominent remains are the small perpendicular tower and a fine Norman arch with zigzag moulding. The priory had a corn mill on the riverside nearby, underneath where the railway station was built seven centuries later. 'Very little remains of this Priory,' writes Christopher Clarkson (1814), 'except the walls of the Chapel, a Tower, and some other fragments of buildings, which are gradually mouldering away.'

Rimington Avenue, the road that runs past the ruins of St Martin's, was built in 1918 by German prisoners of war to link Station Road with Catterick Camp. The road cuts through a high earth embankment with a trench running parallel to it, known as Scots Dyke, which continues north towards Stanwick. It is thought to have stretched much farther north, extending up to the borders of Scotland, but the remains are most prominent around the outskirts of Richmond. Whilst many theories have been put forward about Scots Dyke's origin and use, there is no firm evidence of its age or purpose. Some think it must be related to the earthworks farther north at Stanwick. A Roman or post-Roman age seems unlikely, and the general view is that it was built as a boundary to separate adjacent tribes – possibly at the eastern edge of the Celtic kingdom of Elmete. Speight (1897) considers Scots Dyke 'one of the most remarkable earthworks in the whole country'.

was converted into a footpath to Easby Abbey, and the station buildings (which by then had Grade II listed building status) were sympathetically converted to leisure uses.

The main station building now includes a cinema, a café/restaurant, an artisan cheese-maker, a micro-brewery, an ice-cream maker, a hand-made confectioner, a honey shop, a specialist bakery, along with a gallery, heritage centre and two office suites. The old engine shed has been converted into a sports centre and an indoor swimming pool has been built on the site.

In 1538 Leland wrote that 'a short distance below Richmond on the nearer bank is

'The humble remains of St Martin's Priory, the oldest religious institution in Richmond … [are] probably the earliest specimen of architecture in the district.'
Ella Pontefract (1934)

Easby Abbey

The tranquil ruins of Easby Abbey are located about a mile below Richmond on the bank of the river Swale. They are easy to reach on foot, either along the path of the old railway line into Richmond or by a scenic riverside footpath on the north side of the river. The walk there, and the site itself, offer wonderful views upstream to Richmond, which Joseph Fletcher (1908) describes: 'there is a view of Richmond which fills lovers of the romantic and the picturesque with impressions and feelings only to be expressed by an eloquent silence.'

Easby is recorded in the *Domesday Book* (1086) as Esebi. The name comes from the Old Norse *byr* or *bœr*, meaning a village or homestead, so Easby means Ese's village.

FOOTPATH FROM RICHMOND TO EASBY ABBEY, ALONG THE ROUTE OF THE OLD RAILWAY LINE.

The abbey was founded there in about 1152 by Roaldus, who was Constable of Richmond Castle. It was dedicated to St Agatha – the abbey's proper name is St Agatha's Abbey – and was home to the so-called White Canons (monks) of the Premonstratensian Order. The order was an open one, like the Franciscans, but it followed a strict rule similar to that of the Cistercians. Their lifestyle was simple and austere. As well as fulfilling their religious duties, the canons went out and about preaching and engaged in teaching and pastoral work in the area.

During the dissolution the abbey was surrendered in 1536 by Robert, the last abbot, and the seventeen remaining canons. The choir stalls were removed to St Mary's Church in Richmond, and it is believed that one of the bells was removed to Muker parish church. Steps were taken quickly to ensure that the buildings were uninhabitable.

> During that summer [1536] the lead was taken off roofs [of Easby Abbey] to be melted down into pigs of lead for transporting to Boroughbridge by land, and then by water to York. To melt the lead, roof timbers were used, and when that supply ran out, 350 trees from the abbey's woods were cut down. Jane Hatcher (2004)

The buildings were abandoned and quickly fell into ruins, no doubt assisted by the robbing of stone for use in other buildings in the area. The ruins are picturesque; Wainwright (1989) calls them 'noble' and Pevsner (1966) writes that Easby Abbey was 'one of the most picturesque monastic ruins in the county richest in monastic ruins'.

The site is now in private ownership but is maintained by English Heritage and entry is free. It includes the remains of the refectory, kitchen, cloister court, chapter house, abbey church, Abbot's House, abbey gateway and abbey granary. The layout of the buildings does not follow the norm for abbeys of this date. Pevsner (1966) explains that 'the Abbey's location in the river valley led to oddities in planning the layout. The monastery was approached from the south-east of the cloister, so that the infirmary buildings which usually occupy this position had to be placed on the north of the site and were entered through the

TOWER OF ST MARTIN'S PRIORY, RICHMOND.

EASBY ABBEY, REMAINS OF THE REFECTORY BUILDING.

'The little church of Easby [is] a gem of rusticity. It realizes all our ideas of the model village temples shown us in pretty story-books.' William Longstaffe (1852)

north transept. For reasons of drainage, the monk's dormitory – conventionally on the upper floor of the east cloister range – was placed on the west side of the cloister.' Site factors also meant that the corners of some buildings are not right-angled and the nave is longer on one side than on the other.

Adjacent to the remains of the abbey is the simple stone building of St Agatha's Church, the parish church more commonly referred to as Easby parish church. The church is older than the abbey; it is believed to have been the parish church before the abbey was built. The site may

'There could be no nobler threshold to so romantic a dale.'
John Leyland (1896)

have been occupied since the eighth century, but the oldest parts of the church date back to the twelfth and thirteenth centuries. Pevsner (1966) describes the church as 'a low, long building with a small bellcote and a slated roof'. Despite undergoing alterations and enlargement in the early fifteenth century and restoration in 1868–69, the church still contains a fine early Norman font and a rare series of medieval frescos (wall paintings) from the mid-thirteenth century. Christopher Clarkson (1814) writes that Easby church 'is remarkable for not standing due East and West, for its rustic simplicity, and a neat, well-ordered, cemetery'.

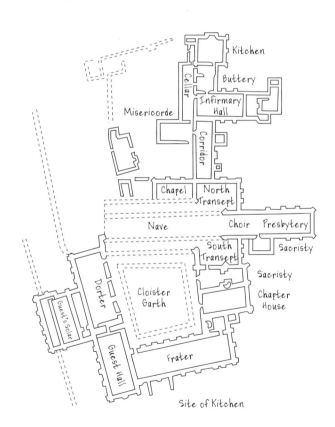

EASBY PARISH CHURCH.

SHEEP ON TRAILER. COPYRIGHT LUCIE HINSON.

Conclusion

This journey through Swaledale has ended, where it began, in Richmond, the town of my birth. Flicking back through the pages, against the course of the Swale and its tributaries, past Reeth, Gunnerside and back to the river's source, I am once again struck by the complex, interwoven layers of wildlife, geology, history and language that make up the valley, threading through it in spite of, or perhaps because of, its remoteness.

I know I'm not alone in feeling the sense of enchantment that I get when I'm physically in Swaledale, or reflecting on memories of being there. The vast number of literary and cultural references relating to the dale over the years illustrates how others, too, have enjoyed its natural charm and beauty, and its rich heritage and tradition.

I hope this book kindles in the reader some sense of the magic of Swaledale that is infused in my being.

Chris Park, 2013.

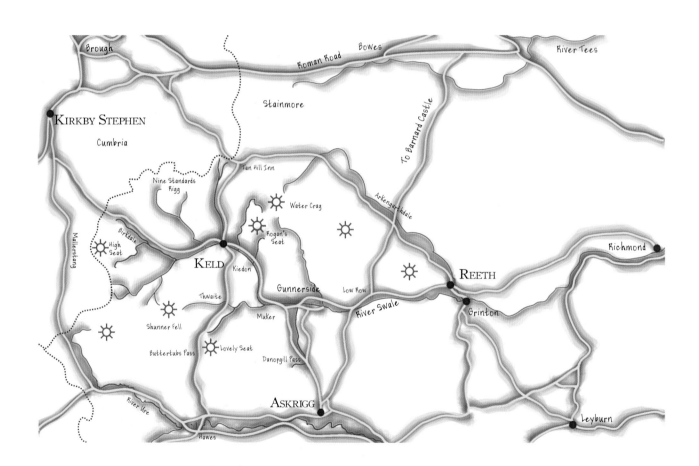

Brough

Roman Road

Bowes

River Tees

Stainmore

To Barnard Castle

KIRKBY STEPHEN

Cumbria

Tan Hill Inn

Nine Standards Rigg

Arkengarthdale

Water Crag

Rogan's Seat

Birkdale

Mallerstang

High Seat

Richmond

KELD

Kisdon

REETH

Gunnerside

Low Row

Thwaite

Grinton

River Swale

Muker

Shunner Fell

Lovely Seat

Buttertubs Pass

Danopgill Pass

ASKRIGG

Leyburn

River Ure

Hawes

BIBLIOGRAPHY

[pages listed are the source of quotations included in the text]

Adamson, D. (1996) *Rides Around Britain by John Byng*. London: The Folio Society. Page 314

Anon (1874) *Black's Picturesque Guide to Yorkshire*. Edinburgh: Adam and Charles Black. Pages 283, 284, 285, 288, 349, 350, 351

Armstrong, T. (1952) *Adam Brunskill*. London: Collins

Bogg, E. (1907) *Regal Richmond and the Land of the Swale*. London: Elliot Stock. Pages 97, 106, 110, 115, 138–139, 140, 143, 150, 184, 188, 191, 196, 205, 214, 219, 239, 240, 241

Bogg, E. (1909) *The Wild Borderlands of Richmondshire: Between Tees and Yore*. London: Elliot Stock. Pages 79, 84, 85, 86, 87, 100, 111–112, 116, 129–130

Bradley, T. (1891) *Yorkshire Rivers. No 4. The Swale*. Leeds: The Yorkshire Post [quotations from 1988 reprint by Old Hall Press, Leeds]. Pages 21, 22, 25, 26, 28, 29, 30, 31

Bray, W. (1778) *Sketch of a Tour Into Derbyshire and Yorkshire*. London: publisher unknown

Brooks, D. (1946) *The Story of Richmond in Yorkshire*. Richmond: Dundas Press. Pages 17, 57, 58, 66–67, 74, 102, 146, 155, 159, 160

Brown, A. (1952) *Fair North Riding*. London: Country Life. Pages 33, 36, 37, 38

Brown, I. (1973) History of the theatre. In *The Georgian Theatre, Richmond, Yorkshire*. Richmond: The Georgian Theatre (Richmond) Trust Ltd

Bulmer, T. (1890) *History, Topography and Directory of North Yorkshire*. Ashton-On-Ribble: T. Bulmer & Co.

Camden, William (1607) *Britain, or, a Chorographicall Description of the most flourishing Kingdomes, England, Scotland, and Ireland*

Charles, Prince (1989) *A Vision of Britain*. London: Doubleday

Clarkson, C. (1814) *The History of Richmond in the County of York, including a Description of the Castle, Friary, Easeby Abbey, and other remains of Antiquity in the Neighbourhood*. London: Richmond: T. Bowman. Pages 25–26, 85, 86, 87, 102–104, 133–134, 146, 147, 192, 193, 195, 230–231, 231–232, 239, 250, 253, 254–255, 255, 260, 261,275, 326–327, 338,

Clifton-Taylor, A. (1978) *Six English Towns*. London: British Broadcasting Corporation. Pages 46, 61

Cooper, E. (1948) *Muker: the story of a Yorkshire parish*. Clapham: Dalesman Books. Pages xiii, xv, 8, 10, 11–12, 28

Cooper, E. (1973) *A history of Swaledale*. Clapham: Dalesman Books. Pages 9, 11, 13, 29, 43, 45, 47, 50–51, 54–55, 58, 71, 77, 80, 81, 88, 89

Defoe, Daniel (1722–24) *A Tour Through the Whole Island of Great Britain. Volume Two*. (1962 edition, edited by G. D. H. Cole and D. C. Browning) London: Dent. Pages 222, 223

Dewhirst, I. (1975) *Yorkshire through the Years*. London: Batsford. Pages 59–60

Feaver, L. F. (1937) *Up Fell, Down Dale*. London: Duckworth. Page 119, 137

Fieldhouse, R. and B. Jennings (1978) *A History of Richmond and Swaledale*. London, Phillimore

Fleming, A. (2010) *Swaledale. Valley of the Wild River*. Oxford: Windgather Press. Pages 1, 25, 161

Fletcher, J. S. (1908) *The Enchanting North*. London: Eveleigh Nash. Pages 37, 38, 44

Gilpin, W. (1792) *Observations Relative Chiefly to Picturesque Beauty, Made in the year 1772, on Several Parts of England, Particularly the Mountains and Lakes of Cumberland & Westmorland*. London: R. Blamire

Goodall, J. (2001) *Richmond Castle and St Agatha's Abbey, Easby*. London: English Heritage. Page 20

Hardy, J. (1998) Swaledale. Portrait of a North Yorkshire Mining Community. Kendal: Frank Peters Publishing

Harland, J. (1873) *Glossary of words used in Swaledale, Yorkshire*. London: Trubner & Co for the English Dialect Society. Pages 225–226, 254

Harland, O. (1951) *Yorkshire North Riding*. London: Robert Hale

Hartley, M. and J. Ingilby (1968) *Life and Tradition in the Yorkshire Dales*. London: Dent

Hartley, M. and J. Ingilby (1978) *The Old Hand-knitters of the Dales*. Clapham: Dalesman Books. Page 21

Hartley, M. and J. Ingilby (1982) *A Dales Heritage*. Clapham: Dalesman Publishing Company

Hartley, M. and J. Ingilby (1986) *Dales Memories*. Clapham: Dalesman Publishing Company

Hatcher, J. (1998) *Richmond Town Trail*. Richmond: Richmondshire District Trust

Hatcher, J. (2004) *The History of Richmond, North Yorkshire. From Earliest Times to the Year 2000*. Pickering: Blackthorn Press. Pages 19, 24, 65–66, 68, 142, 144, 185–186, 190

Hatcher, J. (2006) *Richmond Landscapes*. Richmond: Richmondshire Landscape Trust

Healey, D. (1995) *Denis Healey's Yorkshire Dales*. Skipton: Dalesman Publishing Company. Page 20

Herriot, J. (1979) *James Herriot's Yorkshire*. London: Michael Joseph. Pages 14, 24, 47, 53, 54, 57, 61, 69, 70, 98, 102, 104,

Hill, D. (1984) *In Turner's Footsteps. Through the Hills and Dales of Northern England*. London: John Murray

Hinson, L. and L. Barker (1980) *Swaledale*. Clapham: Dalesman Books

Home, G. (1906) *Yorkshire Dales and Fells*. London: A&C Black. Page 54, 65

Hoskins, W. G. (1970) *The Making of the English Landscape*. Harmondsworth: Penguin. Page 91, 155

Kearton, R. (1922) *At Home with Wild Nature*. London: Cassell. Page 90

Langdale, T. (1822) *A Topographical Dictionary of Yorkshire for the Year 1822*. London: British Library (Historical Print Edition, 2011)

Leather, A. D. (1992) *The Walker's Guide to Swaledale*. Otley: Smith Settle

Leland, John (1535–43) *John Leland's Itinerary: Travels in Tudor England*. Quotations from 1993 edition, edited by J. Chandler. London: Sutton Publishing. Pages 44, 554

Leyland, J. (1896) *Wensleydale and Swaledale Guide*. York: Great North Eastern Railway Company. Pages 5–6, 44

Lofthouse, J. (1950) *Off to the Dales. Walking by the Aire, Wharfe, Ure and Swale*. London: Robert Hale. Pages 7–8, 232, 232–233, 246

Longstaffe, W. H. (1852) *Richmondshire, its Ancient Lords and Edifices: a Concise Guide to the Localities of Interest to the Tourist and Antiquary; with Short Notices of Memorable Men*. London: George Bell. Pages 1, 8, 16, 23, 36, 115, 116–117

Macfarlane, R. (2003) *Mountains of the mind: a history of a fascination*. London: Granta. Page 14

Mitchell, W. R. (1990) *A Dalesman's Diary*. London: Futura. Pages 6–7, 43, 46, 78, 81–82

Morgan, K. (1992) *An American Quaker in the British Isles. The Travel Journals of Jabez Maud Fisher, 1775–1779*. Oxford: Oxford University Press. Page 181

Morris, C. (ed) (1982) *The Illustrated Journeys of Celia Fiennes, 1685–c1712*. London: Macdonald & Co. page 181

Morris, D. (1989). *The Dalesmen of the Mississippi River*. York: Sessions

Morris, D. (1994) *The Swale: a history of the Holy River of St Paulinus*. York: Sessions

Morris, D. (2000) *The Honour of Richmond. A history of the Lords, Earls and Dukes of Richmond*. York: Sessions

Muir, R. (1998) *The Dales of Yorkshire: a Portrait*. Kendal: P. R. Books. Pages 8, 84–85, 85, 88, 168

Muir, R. (2010) *Elegy of the Dales: Nidderdale*. Stroud: The History Press

Norway, A. (1903) *Highways and Byways in Yorkshire*. London: Macmillan & Co. pages 211, 223–224

Peers, Charles (1953) *Richmond Castle, Yorkshire*. London: Her Majesty's Stationery Office

Pevsner, N. (1966) *Buildings of England: Yorkshire – The North Riding*. London: Penguin. Pages 133, 139, 142, 146, 175, 191, 223, 231, 259, 260, 290, 292, 294, 296, 297, 298, 299

Pontefract, E. and Hartley, M. (1934) *Swaledale*. London: J. M. Dent & Sons Ltd. [1988 reprint published by Smith Settle Ltd, Otley] Pages 1, 2, 3, 4, 11, 12–13, 17, 22, 27, 30, 39, 45, 46–47, 48–49, 61, 62, 64, 66–68, 71, 75, 81, 89–90, 90, 91, 95, 99, 109, 111, 112–113, 116, 118, 119, 120–121, 128–129, 131–133, 143, 145, 147, 148, 172, 176–77, 183, 184, 186, 187, 188, 190, 192, 193–194, 195, 196, 197, 199, 201–202,

Prescott, H. F. M. (1952) *The Man on a Donkey*. London: Eyre and Spottiswoode

Radford, G. (1880) *Rambles by Yorkshire Rivers*. Leeds: Richard Jackson. Page 39

Raistrick, A. (1968) *The Pennine Dales*. London: Eyre Methuen. Page 29

Raistrick, A. (1971) *Old Yorkshire Dales*. London: Pan Books. Pages 185, 200

Raistrick, A. (1973) *The Pennine Walls*. Clapham: Dalesman Books

Raistrick, A. and J. L. Illingworth (1967) *The Face of North-West Yorkshire: Geology and Natural Vegetation*. Clapham: Dalesman Publishing Co

Rees, D. M. (2000) *In the Palm of a Dale. A Portrait in Words and Pictures of a Yorkshire Dales Village*. Otley: Smith Settle

Robinson, W. R. (1833) *Robinson's Guide to Richmond*. Richmond: Robinson. Pages 19, 21, 37, 38, 39

Ryder, J. (1979) *A Look at Richmond. A History and Guide*. Richmond: Hinderlagh Press

Sedgwick, A. (1868) *Adam Sedgwick's Dent*. Reprinted in 1984 by RFG Hollett & Son, Sedbergh

Smith, R. and M. Kipling (2008) *Swaledale*. London: Frances Lincoln. Page 8

Speakman, C. (1981) *A Yorkshire Dales anthology*. London: Robert Hale. Pages 25–26

Speight, H. (1897) *Romantic Richmondshire. Being a Complete Account of the History, Antiquities and Scenery of the Picturesque Valleys of the Swale and Yore.* London: Elliot Stock. Pages 41, 60–61, 70, 76,77, 98, 99–100, 102, 205, 207, 211–212, 213, 214, 221, 224, 231, 239, 240, 241, 247, 250–251, 254, 255, 263, 264, 266, 271, 272, 273, 274, 279,

Toulmin Smith, L. (1906–10) *The Itinerary of John Leland in or about the years 1535–43.* 5 vols. London: George Bell & Sons

Tuke, J. (1794) *General View of the Agriculture of the North Riding of Yorkshire: With Observations on the Means of its Improvement.* London: G. Nicol and the Board of Agriculture

Wainwright, A. (1986) *A Pennine Journey.* London: Michael Joseph. Pages 36, 43

Wainwright, A. and D. Drabbs (1989) *Wainwright's Coast to Coast Walk.* London: Mermaid Books. Pages 103, 112, 115, 119, 120, 121, 127, 130, 132, 135, 139, 141, 145,

Waltham, T. (2007) *The Yorkshire Dales Landscape and Geology.* Marlborough: Crowood Press

Watts, V. (1982) The place-name Hindrelac. *Journal of the English Place Name Society* volume 15, pages 3–4

Wenham, L. P. (editor) (1977) *Richmond, Yorkshire, in the 1830s.* Richmond: L. P. Wenham. Pages 5, 7, 8, 20

Wenham, L. P. (1989) *Richmond in Old Photographs.* Gloucester: Alan Sutton. Page 29

Wheeler, M. (1954) *The Stanwick Fortifications, North Riding of Yorkshire.* London: The Society of Antiquities

Whitaker, T. D. (1823) *An History of Richmondshire in the North Riding of the County of York.* 2 volumes. London: Longman. Pages 4, 84, 85, 99, 100–101, 223, 308, 309, 315, 316

White, R. (2002) *The Yorkshire Dales: a Landscape through Time.* Ilkley: Great Northern Books. Pages 31, 32, 76, 77

Whyman, M. (2006) *Richmond at the Start of the 21st Century. An Architectural History.* Richmond; Bargate Publications

Wright, G. (1985) *Roads and Trackways of the Yorkshire Dales.* Ashbourne: Moorland Publishing. Pages 53, 191

Young, A. (1771) *A Six Month Tour through the North of England.V.* London: W. Strahan

INDEX